THE GRANTA BOOK
OF INDIA

The Granta Book of India

Granta Books
London · New York

Granta Publications, 2/3 Hanover Yard, London N1 8BE, United Kingdom

A CIP catalogue record for this book is available
from the British Library.

Typeset by Granta

1 3 5 7 9 10 8 6 4 2

Printed and bound in Great Britain
by Bookmarque Limited, Croydon, Surrey

Contents

Introduction

from *Granta* 57, spring 1997

I first went to India as a reporter. It was late 1976, in the last months of what India knew as 'the Emergency'. In the summer of the previous year, fearing anarchy and more particularly a threat to her own position, Mrs Indira Gandhi, the prime minister, had imposed a form of dictatorship. Troublesome members of the opposition were locked up, the constitution was suspended, the press censored, foreign correspondents withdrawn. I got a visa because I promised to write about subjects which weren't obviously political: the country's great and romantic railways; cataract operations for the poor that were conducted thousands at a time in tented villages called 'eye camps' and of course those relics of the British Empire—summer hill resorts, graveyards, gentlemen's clubs—that survived to touch the colonial heart. Like many people in Britain, I saw myself sentimentally connected to India. My grandmother had been born there, the daughter of an army sergeant. We had Indian mementoes in the house: pictures of soldiers lined up in ranks on sun-baked parade grounds, a small stuffed crocodile, a book in Urdu which had been presented to my great-grandfather for his imperative skill in Hindustani, the mixture of Hindi and Urdu which the British used when they wanted their orders understood and obeyed. Of modern India, of Indian India, I knew almost nothing.

Before I went on that first trip, a newspaper colleague who was Indian gave me some tips. 'Take some Marks & Spencer's nylon shirts,' he said. 'They never go wrong as presents. Indians love them.' I didn't, but in Delhi in that winter spanning 1976 and 1977, I could see that his was not bad advice. India then seemed remote and austere, resolved to cope with its problems and fulfil its aspirations in its own way.

It called itself a 'sovereign socialist secular democratic republic' (it still does, though few people now take the second word seriously) and bought arms and steel mills from the Soviet Union. It was 'non-aligned', the leader of the movement of that name in the Third World, and believed in economic independence. No Coca-Cola then, or foreign cars, and certainly no shirts from M & S. Foreign goods, especially those defined as luxury goods, faced stiff tariff barriers. I remember being invited to a dinner party at Golf Links, the smartest 'colony' (i.e. housing estate) in New Delhi. 'You must come,' said the hostess, 'there will be wine.' Pretty well everything that was sold in India had to be made in India. Jawaharlal Nehru had made that one of the founding principles of the state, remembering how in the previous century cheap imports made by British technology had destroyed native crafts and native employment. Nehru wanted his India to build the 'temples of industry' and initiated a series of Soviet-style five-year plans. Sheltered behind import controls, subsidized and licensed by the government, Indian industry would grow, and out of its taxes, profits and employment would come both the creation and the redistribution of wealth, the abolition of illiteracy, disease and poverty. It was called 'Nehruvian socialism'.

Agriculture had prospered—thanks to irrigation schemes and new strains of wheat, India could feed itself—but the quality of India's manufactured products was often poor. There were scarcities, a thriving black market and corruption. Many things did not work; the middle class was exasperated. But the political rhetoric focused on the poor, for whom a collapsing telephone system was hardly a priority compared to the price of rice and onions. The poor matter in India as they do not in many other developing countries—China, say. They are, of course, a majority. They also have the vote.

This was the kind of India I came to in 1976, though politics

Introduction

had been temporarily suppressed and replaced by Mrs Gandhi's 'twenty-point programme', in which people were exhorted to plant trees, restrict their families to two children, inform on black marketeers and, most of all, to work. There were slogans everywhere—in hotels, on the sides of buses and trains, fluttering above the wide avenues of New Delhi: A SMALL FAMILY IS A HAPPY FAMILY... BE INDIAN, BUY INDIAN... WORK IS WORSHIP. They had an urgent, last-gasp ring to them, as though Mrs Gandhi had woken in a panic and decided to save her country from the five horsemen of its apocalypse—poverty, overpopulation, corruption, disease, bureaucratic sloth—by stamping her feet and shouting a lot (like an empress—there was a saying then, 'Indira is India'). There were mistakes and cruelties, particularly in the family-planning programme, where official zeal about meeting quotas sometimes meant that poor people were sterilized against their will. It was difficult to separate fact from rumour. In a censored state, rumour becomes news.

I travelled for six or seven weeks and met no other foreign correspondent—perhaps only the staff of *Pravda* had been permitted to stay—and few foreigners of any kind. I had never been anywhere so beautiful, so disturbing, so hospitable, so foreign. It never felt physically threatening. One of its attractions was Anglophilia. In railway compartments, I would be asked about my education.

'You must have gone to Oxford.'

'No, actually.'

'Ah, the other place then.'

I had not studied at Cambridge either, but it seemed a shame to disappoint. I invented, for these casual encounters, a career which included punts and creeper-clad Gothic buildings, and also children, though I then had none, because to be childless was to be unblessed. Honesty about this lack would evoke concern and often the blunt query: 'Why?'

Then, in January 1977, Mrs Gandhi announced that she would end the Emergency and hold elections, and my newspaper asked me to stay on to cover them. It became an exciting time. I went to my first village and asked a very poor, skeletal man, an Untouchable, how he would vote. 'Well, sir,' he said with no irony, 'how would you advise me to vote?' India's starkest division, between those with power and those without, could be seen in his deference. Words which in Britain sounded quaint and dead—'the elite... the common man... the masses... feudals... lumpens'—were used in India unselfconsciously; they applied to the living in their white cotton shrouds, to what V. S. Naipaul has called 'the white crowd of India'. But as the election campaign gathered strength and vast outdoor audiences listened to opposition speakers, in what Indian newspapers called 'pin-drop silence', you could also see the force and meaning of political freedom and universal suffrage, with a clarity that is sometimes obscured in the West. Poverty and illiteracy do not equal stupidity. Mrs Gandhi and her Congress party, the party which had ruled India since its independence, were swept to defeat.

For the next thirteen years, India became my second home. I made friends there and married one of them. I acquired in-laws in Calcutta and, for a year or so, a landlord in Delhi. Throughout the 1980s India gave journalists plenty to report. Elections returned Mrs Gandhi to power in 1980, and her son Rajiv in 1985; both were assassinated. A Sikh revolt broke out in the Punjab. India sent troops to Sri Lanka. A leak of poisonous gas from a factory in Bhopal killed thousands; in terms of the dead, it was said to be the largest industrial accident in history. And, the most ominous change, 'communalism' and 'secularism' replaced the phrases of Marxist analysis as the key words in political debate. Perhaps the rich-versus-poor division had been too simple. There had always been in India 'fissiparous tendencies'—an opaque term that stood mainly for regional

Introduction

alienation from the central government—but the politics of religious identity had been more or less held at bay since the creation of India and Pakistan in 1947. That was the success of the Congress party, which drew its support from Muslims and other religious minorities, as well as from the Hindus who comprise more than three-quarters of the population. Now many Hindus began to feel, without much supporting evidence, that the secular state caved in too often to minority pressure. What was India, after all, but a Hindu country? Hindu nationalism moved from the margins to the centre of politics.

These were the broad forces at work, as I understood and tried to convey them, but by then I had moved into a narrower and kinder world. India as a clamouring frieze had been replaced in my sight by a collection of quiet and individual miniatures: the homes and the people that I knew; the names of domestic servants; gardens and rivers lit up the winter sun of Delhi and Calcutta—all the familial privacies of India which are such a vital strength of the Indian novel. When my wife and I separated, in 1991, I did not think that I could easily go back. For six years I stayed away, and missed a great turning-point in Indian history.

Before I went back in November 1996, I telephoned one of my oldest friends in Delhi. Was there anything she would like me to bring? She mentioned a kind of dishcloth that was peculiar to Woolworths. Nothing else? No disposable nappies (in great demand at one time), colour film, wine, replacement parts for food processors? 'No,' she said. 'Everything is available in the market here.'

We met at Delhi airport and drove in her car (Japanese-designed; no longer the old lumberer made from the jigs and tools of post-war England) towards her house in one of Delhi's southern colonies. At the entrance to the colony I noticed that high steel gates had been erected. Guards stood beside them in a sentry box. This was new. 'Every colony has them now—crime,' said my friend.

That night we met her younger brother, Rahul. When I first knew him, Rahul worked in a bank. Sometimes I'd go to see him there, to cash foreign cheques and drink tea among his stacks of cardboard files, each containing sheaves of yellowing stenographer's paper, each tied with a purple ribbon. His was not a particularly convenient branch to get to, but it was better to suffer the inconvenience of the travel rather than the inconvenience of a bank where I knew nobody—to wait, to find another queue, to sign, to wait, to countersign, to find a third queue, to wait, to sign again, to collect the cash, and later to find some notes in the middle of my bundle so worn, torn and stuck together again with tape that even a beggar might hesitate before accepting one.

But now, as well as working in the bank, Rahul was helping to run an export business in rubber toys. He produced some samples from a bag. There was Noddy, there was Big Ears, there was Mr Plod the Policeman. But who was this duller rubber figure in a suit and large spectacles?

'That's Bill, Old Bill, Billy Boy,' Rahul said. He held the doll fondly to his cheek. 'Don't you know Bill Gates?'

Around that time, it was said—one of those uncheckable things—that villagers in the remotest part of India knew who Bill Gates was, would recognize him if he stopped by at the well one day to beg a glass of water. He is famous partly because he has said, or is said to have said, that South Indians are the smartest people in the world after the Chinese. With that remark, India felt that greatness had been conferred upon it from the highest and most modern authority—at long last someone had recognized the truth.

The measurement here was computer programming—

Introduction

Bangalore, in south India, has a burgeoning software industry—but smartness in India is not confined to that particular skill or region. India has smart restaurants, smart clothes, smart cars, smart magazines, three dozen television channels which range through a spectrum of smartness and vulgarity. Expenditure on advertising, a good index of urban prosperity, rose by forty per cent every year in the first half of the 1990s; in 1996, when it rose by only twenty per cent, advertising agencies talked of a slump. Cars, auto-rickshaws, motor scooters, lorries and buses choke the avenues of Delhi, and new hoardings stand high above the flyovers to shine palely in the fumes. The Emergency was only twenty years ago, but seems an unreachable era. The public are not to be instructed, but seduced. WORK IS WORSHIP has long since been replaced by slogans for mobile phones, saris, fans, faxes, airlines. One that I liked read: BEFORE AIR POLLUTION KILLS YOU SLOWLY, CHOOSE 'FOREST AIR' AIR FRESHENER.

Perhaps for the first time, an averagely prosperous western visitor can feel poor here, at least in some parts of Delhi and Mumbai. Certainly, he can no longer think of himself as a herald of popular fashion, an advance party for the changing tastes of the West. These have already reached here from California without stopovers in Europe, directly by the Internet and via the satellites that cross south Asia. America is the model now; slowly, inevitably, the old Indo-Anglian upper class, the anglophone India which had such attractive gentleness, voices courtesy of the BBC, pipes by Dunhill, politics from the Fabian Society, is retreating towards its pyre. An MBA from Harvard is worth three BAs (Oxon).

Nobody really knows how many people this new upper class contains. Figures range between one hundred and two hundred million—between just under ten or twenty per cent of the population—though if a telephone is taken as the index of prosperity, it would seem to be smaller than that. It may also be unwise to overestimate their comfort. In Delhi, which has almost doubled its population (to about ten million) since I first knew it, services which depend on public funding are close to collapse. To get reliable supplies of water and electricity people who have money sink their own tube wells and buy their own generators; the level of groundwater, already dangerously low, sinks further, and generator smoke adds its small quota to the growing population of asthmatics.

And India's poor? The figures for them are even more debatable than for the rich. In 1979 the Indian government set a calorific measurement as the line below which people could be defined as poor—the poverty line. Below it fell the people who could not afford to buy food equivalent to 2,100 calories a day in urban areas and 2,400 calories in rural areas—the rural poor do more physical work. For many years, the figure for this category was about forty per cent of the population. Then in 1996, to jubilation, the government announced that it had fallen to nineteen per cent. Some months later, however, it was revised upwards after further calculation to thirty-eight per cent. Other agencies, which take factors such as stunted growth and the illiteracy of female children into account, estimate it at fifty-two per cent.

More than ever, they and the people just above them seek political action to meet their demands: more subsidized food, more government jobs. They vote for the people who are most like them. In this sense, India has never had such *representative* politicians. Patrician, English-speaking leaders have almost disappeared, though English is the language of the new commercial vitality and many of the people who have benefited from it. The forces of economics and democracy are opposed.

In 1983 I spent a week in Dhanbad, a colliery town in Bihar, and there got to know the man who managed its railways, supervising the movement of the long coal trains which fed power stations all across northern India. I have forgotten almost

Introduction

everything about him, apart from his question. Could I think of any country, at any time in its history, which had achieved these three things simultaneously: one, a dynamic economy; two, a redistribution of wealth and justice; three, a fair and law-abiding democracy?

Sometime in the next forty years, India will overtake China as the world's most populous country. The question remains the greatest conundrum of its future, and ours.

Ian Jack

Blood

Urvashi Butalia

(1997)

The political partition of India caused one of the great human convulsions of history. Never before or since have so many people exchanged their homes and countries so quickly. In the space of a few months, about twelve million people moved between the new, truncated India and the two wings, East and West, of the newly created Pakistan. By far the largest proportion of these refugees—more than ten million of them—crossed the western border which divided the historic state of Punjab, Muslims travelling west to Pakistan, Hindus and Sikhs east to India. Slaughter sometimes prompted and sometimes accompanied their movement; many others died from malnutrition and contagious disease. Estimates of the number of dead vary from 200,000 (the contemporary British figure) to two million (a later Indian speculation), but that somewhere around a million people died is now widely accepted. As always, there was sexual savagery: about 75,000 women are thought to have been abducted and raped by men of religions different from their own. Thousands of families were divided, homes were destroyed, crops left to rot, villages abandoned. Astonishingly, the new governments of India and Pakistan were unprepared for this convulsion. They had not anticipated that the fear and uncertainty created by the drawing of borders based on headcounts of religious identity—so many Hindus and Sikhs versus so many Muslims—would force people to flee to what they considered 'safer' places, where they would be surrounded by their own kind. People travelled in buses, cars and trains, but mostly on foot in great columns, called *kafila*s, which could stretch for dozens of miles. The longest of them, said to comprise 800,000 refugees travelling east to India from western Punjab, took eight days to pass any given spot on its route.

This is the generality of Partition; it exists publicly in books. The particular is harder to discover; it exists privately in the stories told and retold inside so many households in India and Pakistan. I grew up with them. Like many Punjabis in Delhi, I

Blood

am from a family of Partition refugees. My mother and father came from Lahore, a lively city loved and sentimentalized by its inhabitants, which lies only twenty miles inside the Pakistan border. My mother tells of the dangerous journeys that she twice made back there to bring her younger brothers and sister to India. My father remembers fleeing to the sound of guns and crackling fires. I would listen to these stories with my brothers and sister and hardly take them in. We were middle-class Indians who had grown up in a period of relative calm and prosperity, when tolerance and 'secularism' seemed to be winning the argument. The stories—looting, arson, rape, murder—came out of a different time. They meant little to me.

Then, in October 1984, the prime minister, Mrs Gandhi, was assassinated by one of her security guards, a Sikh. For days afterwards Sikhs all over India were attacked in an orgy of violence and revenge. Many homes were destroyed and thousands died. In the outlying suburbs of Delhi more than 3,000 were killed, often by being doused in kerosene and then set alight. Black burn marks on the ground showed where their bodies had lain. The government—headed by Mrs Gandhi's son, Rajiv—remained indifferent, but several citizens' groups came together to provide relief, food and shelter. I was among hundreds of people who worked in these groups. Every day, while we were distributing food and blankets, compiling lists of the dead and missing, and helping with compensation claims, we listened to the stories of the people who had suffered. Often older people, who had come to Delhi as refugees in 1947, would remember that they had been through a similar terror before. 'We didn't think it could happen to us in our own country,' they would say. 'This is like Partition again.'

Here, across the River Jamuna, just a few miles from where I lived, ordinary, peaceable people had driven their neighbours from their homes and murdered them for no other readily apparent reason than that they were of a different religious community. The stories from Partition no longer seemed quite so remote; people from the same country, the same town, the same village could still be divided by the politics of their religious difference, and, once divided, could do terrible things to each other. Two years later, working on a film about Partition for a British television channel, I began to collect stories from its survivors. Many were horrific and of a kind that, when I was younger and heard them second or third hand, I had found hard to believe: women jumping into wells to drown themselves so as to avoid rape or forced religious conversion; fathers beheading their own children so that they would avoid the same dishonourable fate. Now I was hearing them from witnesses whose bitterness, rage and hatred—which, once uncovered, could be frightening—told me that they were speaking the truth.

Their stories affected me deeply. Nothing as cruel and bloody had happened in my own family so far as I knew, but I began to realize that Partition was not, even in my family, a closed chapter of history—that its simple, brutal political geography infused and divided us still. It was then that I decided I would find my uncle Rana—Ranamama as we called him, though he wasn't mentioned often.

Nobody had heard from Ranamama in almost forty years. He was my mother's youngest brother. In 1947 my mother, who was working in the part of the Punjab that became Indian, had gone back to Lahore to bring out her younger brother, Billo, and a sister, Savita. Then she went back a second time to fetch her mother—her father was dead—and Rana. But Rana refused to come and wouldn't let my grandmother go either. Instead he promised to bring her to India later. They never came, but my family heard disturbing news.

Rana had become a Muslim.

Blood

My family didn't think that God had played much part here. They were convinced that both Rana's refusal to leave and his conversion were calculated decisions which would allow him to inherit my grandfather's property—a house, land, orchards—when my grandmother died. Letters were exchanged for a while but they began to draw the attention of the police and intelligence officers. They were opened, and questions were asked. Pakistan and India had so much in common—if not religion then certainly language and ways of life—that the barriers of a nation state became especially important to their governments as proof of difference and nationhood. Travel between the two countries, for the people who lived in them, became nearly impossible. My mother gave up hope of returning to Lahore and soon abandoned correspondence. What was the point of trying to communicate with someone who was so mercenary? And so, though Rana continued to live in my grandfather's house in Lahore, which is fewer than 300 miles from Delhi, forty minutes in a plane, he might just as well have been on another planet. We heard rumours that my grandmother had died, but no one really knew. My mother's grief at losing her home, her mother and brother, gave way to bitterness and resentment, and eventually to indifference. The years passed; Pakistan and India fought two wars; Ranamama's fate remained obscure.

Then, in the summer of 1987, I managed to get a trip to Pakistan, to Lahore. I told my mother I wanted to meet her brother. She was sceptical. Why? What was the good? I felt as though I were betraying her; once in Lahore, it took me three days to pluck up the courage to go to my grandfather's house. I first saw it late one evening—an old and crumbling mansion set in a large bare garden—and found it hard to believe that this was the house we'd heard so much about. Through a window I could see a bare bulb casting its pale light on cracked green walls.

I rang the bell, and three women came to the barred window.

Yes, they said, this was Rana's house, but he wasn't in—he was 'on tour' and expected home later that night. I said I was his sister's daughter, come from Delhi. Door-bolts were drawn, and I was invited in. The women were Rana's wife—my aunt—and her daughters—my cousins. For an hour we made careful conversation and drank Coca-Cola in a luridly furnished living room, and then my friend Firhana came in her car to collect me. I'd met her sister in Delhi and was staying at their house.

At midnight, the phone rang. It was my uncle. He called me *beti*, daughter. 'What are you doing there?' he said, referring to my friend's house. 'This house is your home. You must come home at once and you must stay here. Give me your address, and I'll come and pick you up.'

This was a man I had never seen, who had last seen my mother five years before I was born. We argued. Finally I managed to dissuade him. But the next day I went to his house and stayed there for a week.

Rana looked like a solid citizen of Pakistan. He was six feet tall, strongly built and always dressed in a long cotton shirt and pyjamas—a style Zulfikar Ali Bhutto, the former prime minister who was deposed by the military and executed, had popularized as the *awami*, or people's, suit. He had a deep, enjoyable voice, which I heard a lot that week. I asked questions, he answered them; some facts emerged. My grandmother had died in 1956 (the seven of her eight children who lived in India dated her death variously as 1949, 1952 and 1953), and Rana had married a Muslim.

Why had he not left with his brother and sisters at Partition?

Well, Rana said, like a lot of other people he had never expected Partition to happen in the way it did. 'Many of us thought, yes, there will be change, but why should we have to move?' He hadn't thought political decisions could affect his life and by the time he understood otherwise it was too late. 'I was barely twenty. I'd had little education. What would I have done in India? I had no qualifications, no job, nothing to recommend me.'

I had enough imagination to understand those reasons. In Lahore, Muslims, Hindus and Sikhs had lived alongside each other for centuries. Who could have foreseen that as a Pakistani rather than an Indian city it would become so singularly Muslim, that 'normality' would never return? But his treatment of my grandmother was harder to forgive. She had lived on for nine years after Partition—nine years in which her six daughters heard nothing of her—hidden, alone, isolated. Why had he forced her to stay with him?

'I was worried about your mother having to take on the burden of an old mother, just as I was worried when she offered to take me with her. So I thought I'd do my share and look after her.'

I didn't believe him. What about his decision to become a Muslim?

'In a sense there wasn't really a choice. The only way I could have stayed on was by converting. I married a Muslim girl, changed my religion and took a Muslim name.'

But did he really believe? Was the change born out of conviction or convenience?

He said he had not slept a single night—'no, not one night'— in forty years without regretting his decision. 'You see, my child,' he said, and this became a refrain in the days we spent together, 'somehow a convert is never forgiven. Your past follows you; it hounds you. For me, it's worse because I've continued to live in the same place. Even today when I walk out to the market I often hear people whispering, "Hindu, Hindu". You don't know what it is like.'

That last answer chilled me and softened me. There is a word in Punjabi that is enormously evocative and emotive: *watan*. It's a difficult word to translate: it can mean home, country, land— all and any of them. When Punjabis speak of their *watan*, you know they are expressing a longing for the place they feel they belong. For most Punjabis who were displaced by Partition, their *watan* lay in the home they had left behind. For Rana, the opposite had happened: he continued to live in the family home in Pakistan, but his *watan* had become India, a country he had visited only briefly, once. He watched the television news from India every day; he rooted for the Indian cricket team, especially when they played Pakistan; he followed Indian soap operas.

By the end of my week with him I had a picture of his life. As forty years had gone by, he had retreated into himself. His wife and children, Muslims in a Muslim nation, worried for him; they couldn't understand his longings and silences. But perhaps his wife understood something of his dilemma. She had decided early in their marriage, sensibly I thought, that she would not allow her children to suffer a similar crisis of identity. Her sons and daughters were brought up as good Muslims; the girls remained in purdah and were taught at home by a mullah. One of his younger daughters told me once: 'Apa, you are all right, you're just like us, but we thought, you know, that *they* were really awful.' She meant a couple of distant relatives who had once managed to visit and who had behaved as orthodox Hindus, practising the 'untouchability' that Hindus customarily use in Muslim company. They had insisted on cooking their own food and would not eat anything prepared by Rana's family. They were the only Hindus this daughter had met. Who could blame her for disliking them?

One day, as Rana and I talked intimately into the evening, stopping only for some food or a cup of tea, I began to feel oppressed by him. 'Why are you talking to me like this?' I said. 'You don't even know me. If you'd met me in the marketplace, I would have been just another stranger.' He looked at me for a long time and said, 'My child, this is the first time I have spoken to my own blood.' I was shocked. I protested: 'What about your family? They are your blood, not me.'

Blood

'No,' he said, 'for them I remain a stranger. You understand what I'm talking about. That is why you are here. Even if nothing else ever happens, I know that you have been sent here to lighten my load.' And in some ways, I suppose, this was true.

I went back to India with gifts and messages, including a long letter from Rana to his six sisters (his brother had died by this time). They gathered in our house and sat in the front room in a row, curious but resentful. Then someone picked up the letter and began reading, and soon it was being passed from hand to hand. They cried, and then their mood lightened into laughter as memories were shared and stories recounted. Tell us what the house looks like now, they demanded. Is the guava tree still there? What's happened to the game of *chaukhat*? Who lives at the back these days? Rana's letter was read and reread. Suddenly my mother and my five aunts had acquired a family across the border.

We kept in touch after that. I went to visit Rana several times. Once he wrote to my mother, 'I wish I could lock up Urvashi in a cage and keep her here.' Then, before one of my visits, my mother said to me: 'Ask him if he buried or cremated my mother.'

Muslims bury their dead. Hindus burn them. I looked at her in surprise. Hinduism has never meant much to her—she isn't an atheist but she has little patience with orthodoxy.

'What does it matter to you?' I said.

'Just ask him.'

When I got to Lahore, I asked him.

'How could she have stayed here and kept her original name?' he said. 'I had to make her a convert. She was called Ayesha Bibi. I buried her.'

Late in 1988 I took my mother and her eldest sister back to Lahore. One of Rana's daughters was getting married, and there was a great deal of excitement as we planned the visit. They

25

hadn't seen their brother, their home or Lahore for forty-one years. They had last seen Rana as a twenty-year-old. The man who met them at Lahore airport was in his sixties, balding and greying, and the reunion was tentative and difficult. We made small talk in the car until we reached Rana's house, which had once been home to his sisters but was now occupied by strangers, so they had to treat it politely, like any other house. The politeness and strain between brother and sisters went on for two days, until on the third day I found them together in a room, crying and laughing. Rana took his sisters on a proper tour of the house: they looked around their old rooms, rediscovered their favourite trees, and remembered their family as it had once been.

But as Rana and his sisters grew together, his wife and children grew more distant. Our presence made them anxious—understandably so. A girl was being married. What if her in-laws objected to Hindus in the family? What if the Hindus were there to reclaim their land? What if we did something to embarrass the family at the wedding? Small silences began to build up between the two sides. I was struck by how easy it was to rebuild the borders we thought we'd just crossed.

After that, I managed to go to Pakistan to see Rana again. But it wasn't easy. He began to worry that he was being watched by the police. His letters became fewer and then stopped altogether. For a while my mother continued to send him letters and gifts but eventually she stopped too. I went on sending messages to him via my friends, until one of them returned with a message from him. Try not to keep in touch, he said; it makes things very difficult. The pressure he felt was not just official but came also from inside his family. His sons urged him to break contact with his relations in India. And then the relationship between India and Pakistan, which had grown more relaxed in the 1980s, became stiffer again, and it was more difficult to travel between the two.

It's been many years now since I last saw Ranamama. I no

longer know if he is alive or dead. I think he is alive. I want him to be alive. I keep telling myself, if something happened to him, surely someone in his family would tell us. But I'm not sure I believe that. Years ago, when he told me that he had buried my grandmother, I asked him to take me to her grave. We were standing by his gate in the fading light of the evening. It was, I think, the first time that he'd answered me without looking at me. He scuffed the dust under his feet and said, 'No my child, not yet. I'm not ready yet.'

On the night of 14 August 1996, about a hundred Indians visited the India–Pakistan border at Wagah in the Punjab. They went there to fulfil a long-cherished objective by groups in the two countries: Indians and Pakistanis would stand, in roughly equal numbers, on each side of the border and sing songs for peace. They imagined that the border would be symbolized by a sentry post and that they would be able to see their counterparts on the other side. But they came back disappointed. The border was more complicated than they thought—there is middle ground—and also grander. The Indian side has an arch lit with neon lights and, in large letters, the inscription MERA BHARAT MAHAN—India, my country, is supreme. The Pakistan side has a similar neon-lit arch with the words PAKISTAN ZINDABAD—Long live Pakistan. People bring picnics here and eat and drink and enjoy themselves.

The suffering and grief of Partition are not memorialized at the border, nor, publicly, anywhere else in India, Pakistan and Bangladesh. A million may have died but they have no monuments. Stories are all that people have, stories that rarely breach the frontiers of family and religious community; people talking to their own blood.

My Father's Raj
Mark Tully

(1997)

Iwas born in Calcutta in October 1935 and grew up on the southern outskirts of the city, in one of the areas where the British lived. Our first address was number six, Regent's Park, Tollygunge, but as the family grew—eventually I had five brothers and sisters—we moved to number seven in the same road. This was similar to number six, a two-storey house hidden in its grounds behind high yellow walls, but even larger. The lawn could double as a tennis court. The rear compound was so big that it could house quarters for our dozen and more servants, and those quarters could seem hidden, tucked away.

My father, William Scarth Carlisle Tully, was a businessman, or what Calcuttans knew as a 'box wallah'. In those days, Calcutta was still the commercial capital of the Raj, more important even than Bombay, though by this time the viceroy and the British administration had moved to Lutyens's new capital, New Delhi. My father arrived in Calcutta from London, via a posting in Rangoon, in 1925. He worked for the firm of Gillanders Arbuthnot, which sounds like a character from P. G. Wodehouse but was in fact the oldest of India's major 'managing agencies'. In our house the name had no comic resonance at all. In British India, managing agencies meant power, influence and profit. They existed because, though plenty of companies in Britain wanted to make money in India, they had neither the expertise nor inclination to manage businesses there. Managing agencies did that for them, and behind their names—often with a Scottish inflection: Shaw Wallace, Mackinnon Mackenzie—sheltered wide portfolios of interests. Gillanders, for example, had been founded in the early nineteenth century by the Gladstone family—the same family as the great Victorian prime minister's—to ship textiles to India and indigo back to Britain. By the time my father began to work for them, they managed sixty companies. Gillanders ran tea gardens and the picturesque little railway, the Darjeeling Himalayan, which carried the tea down the mountains. They represented insurance companies and banks. They managed the mining of diamonds, gold, tin, copper and coal.

They were moral and they were mean. They prized their reputation for the former, forbidding their staff to trade privately or play the Calcutta stock exchange, and insisting that they banked their money in the company bank, so that the firm's senior partners could keep an eye on the finances of their young assistants, who might be running up debts or making money on the side. My father approved. He would warn young employees just out from London: 'Gillanders has got a reputation second to none which has taken more than one hundred years to build up, so you have to be on your best behaviour because you could muck the whole thing up in one afternoon.'

He did not approve, however, of the London office, which was dominated by Gladstones and which officially controlled the partners (who made the company's money) in Calcutta. He felt that they were out of touch—understandably so when letters, the main means of communication, took three weeks on their sea voyage between Britain and India—and also incompetent and ridiculously parsimonious. On one important mission to London my father was asked to explain the intricate finances behind the building of the Howrah bridge, the first permanent bridge across the Hooghly river in Calcutta, to the Prudential Assurance company, which Gillanders hoped would provide some of the money. Nobody in the London office was able to do this, and my father was summoned from his home leave in Winchester. Gillanders did not offer to pay his train fare, and when he suggested a taxi might take him between Gillanders and the Prudential, he was told that there was a perfectly good direct bus, a partner adding that he hoped my father had the tuppence for the ticket.

He also remembered, in a similar spirit, events in Rangoon, where his first job had been to 'check steamers', which meant visiting ships riding at anchor which had cargo to be handled by

Gillanders. A small steam launch was the way other agents made these trips, but Gillanders insisted that a sampan was quite good enough for their men. My father and his small boat would toss around like a cork in the wake of launches and tugs. Still, he would say, 'I managed to smoke my Burma cheroot without being sick.'

These were the stories my father told; this was the world he came from.

We did not get on. I sometimes look back on my childhood in Calcutta and wonder how the seeds of our tempestuous relationship came to be sown. My father was a stern man and a moralist, ideal Gillanders material, but he was certainly not brutal. His bright brown eyes could freeze anyone who aroused his anger, which was easy to do. There were sometimes terrifying outbursts of temper. Once he dragged me screaming with fear up to the high diving board of the Tollygunge Club swimming pool, shouting, 'I'll teach you to be a coward,' though that is the only physical clash I can remember. My resentment of him came more, I think, from his constant criticism of me. His life was filled with correctness—the right way to hold a knife and fork, the right way to sit (and stand, and ride a bicycle), the right way to talk to servants—and I managed to get most things wrong. He was particularly keen on the right way to speak and the right way to spell. Any hint of what was known as a 'chi-chi' or Eurasian accent was pounced on; the letters I sent him from my boarding school came back to me with the spelling mistakes underlined in red.

Of course, he accepted without question the convention that the British in India must remain above India and not become part of it. He employed Nanny Oxborrow from England to make sure that we kept our distance to avoid social contamination—to 'go native' was still a meaningful phrase then, and a pejorative one. Nanny did no work herself; there were children's maids and Jaffa, the nursery boy, to do that. Her responsibility was to see that we did not get too close to these Indian servants. When, for example, we went for our morning pony ride, Nanny would come too—walking alongside and slowing our progress—in case we were tempted to talk to the groom, or syce, in his own language. Once I got a sharp slap from her when she found our driver teaching me to count to ten in Hindustani.

We met our parents by regular appointment twice a day. After our pony ride, Nanny would take us to their bedroom to watch them having *chota hazri*, or small breakfast—tea and delicious green bananas. Then in the evening, after Nanny had supervised our baths, she would accompany us to the drawing room, where my parents would be drinking sherry. On Sundays we saw more of our parents—Nanny had the day off and the special privilege of a glass of sherry when she returned from evensong at the Anglican cathedral (I can still remember the sweet smell of it on her breath). It was a formal childhood, but perhaps not quite so formal as it now sounds. We weren't a social family—my father despised cocktail parties and receptions—but we had our share of birthday parties, with roundabouts, conjurors and snake charmers on the lawn and trips to the swimming pools and fancy-dress carnivals of Calcutta's several clubs. Over the past few decades, Calcutta has become a byword for poverty, but in those days the only time poverty impinged on our white lives was (paradoxically) when my mother took us to the fashionable shops near the Maidan, the city's equivalent of Hyde Park or Central Park. There we would see lepers squatting on the pavement begging, fingers reduced to stumps, toes eaten away. I was fascinated. My mother would drag me away.

My fifth birthday should have been the signal to ship me off as a boarder to pre-preparatory school in England—that was the normal practice, so that children could be spared the Indian climate and the risk of disease. But no passenger liners ran during the war, and I was sent instead to a school in the hills at

Darjeeling which had been founded to cater for children like me, cut off from their rightful English education by Hitler. I wept bitterly as I said goodbye to my parents on the station platform at the start of each term, though I now look back fondly on the school itself. It gave us freedom. We were allowed to roam the bazaars, to climb up to the army camp where American troops gave us sweets, and sometimes to visit the cinema. I learned enough Hindustani and Nepali to amuse the rickshaw pullers and porters who carried people and freight up the steep streets and lanes. My father would not have approved if he'd known.

He came to see me at the school only once. Then, early in 1945, before the war with Germany was over, he booked his wife, six children, nanny and father-in-law on a cargo liner, the *Chinese Prince*, which was the first available ship to Britain. I was nine, and relieved to be leaving him behind. He joined us eighteen months later. After that, unshielded by nannies and nurseries, the seeds of our antagonism ripened into wheat and tares.

I often think of him now. Who can explain the dynamics that work between father and son? What made him as he was? I certainly don't think of him as a bigot and a racist. He respected his Bengali clerks, his babus, and made friends of a few Indians he met in the Calcutta Musical Society (he had a magnificent bass voice). He was typical of his time; he had the best as well as the harshest of an older set of values. He was loyal and attracted loyalty. He was absolutely honest. He was generous to relatives who fell on hard times. He wanted (I now see) the best for his children. But he would never have broken the rules that governed the British relationship with India, nor the rules that governed how the British in India behaved among themselves. Indians were a separate and different people, the divide was to be observed and never crossed. As for our fellow Britons, they fell into a hierarchy as rigid as Indian caste. Among the business community, the managing agents were the elite, and retailers were at the bottom of the pile. Barriers could be crossed, but of one upwardly mobile Calcutta friend of our family my father would always observe darkly: 'He has a chip on his shoulder. He can never forget that he came out to Calcutta with Bathgate the chemists.'

My father had a chip on his own. His origins were towards the lower end of the English middle class. His father owned a garage, he'd gone to a minor public school—Weymouth, long since closed. Calcutta society contained much grander people, with more glorious educations and lineages. My father felt they looked down on him. He wanted to be accepted—he was a member of Calcutta's premier club, the Bengal, and was mortified when he was blackballed for the Royal Calcutta Turf—and the fact that my mother's grandfather had been a housemaster at Winchester school, ancient and proud, only made him more prickly and difficult.

He determined that his children would go to 'good schools', and I was sent to Marlborough, where I began my long rebellion against everything my father wanted me to be. When my turn came for National Service, I infuriated my fellow officers by suggesting that the differences between them and their men should be abolished: and by courting the popularity of the men I commanded. My father took work home every evening to his study. I wasted my time at school and university. At the end of every school term he would insist that I submit a receipt for the ten shillings he had sent me for my train fare home. I have never kept any accounts since.

And yet I not only owe my life to him, but also the shape and the satisfaction of it. In my late twenties I got a job in the personnel department of the BBC. A posting in junior management came up—assistant representative of the BBC in Delhi—and I was interviewed for it. I was asked by a member of the appointments board if I could speak Hindi. 'Not well at all,' I replied, 'but I can recite "Humpty Dumpty" and "Little Miss Muffet" in Hindustani.' They were not amused, but I got the job. At the age of thirty, after twenty years, I went back to India.

That was more than thirty years ago. India is where I have lived almost constantly since. My zeal for it began as a reaction to my father's insistence that England was my home, the place I belonged to, the country that made me. For me, it turned out to be India that supplied those feelings, that anchorage.

My father never visited me in Delhi, though we softened to each other in the years before he died, but I owe the one enthusiasm in my life, which became a passion, to him.

Erotic Politicians and Mullahs

Hanif Kureishi

(1985)

The man had heard that I was interested in talking about his country, Pakistan, and that this was my first visit. He kindly kept trying to take me aside to talk. But I was already being talked at.

I was at another Karachi party, in a huge house, with a glass of whisky in one hand and a paper plate in the other. Casually I'd mentioned to a woman friend of the family that I wasn't against marriage. Now this friend was earnestly recommending to me a young woman who wanted to move to Britain with a husband. To my discomfort this go-between was trying to fix a time for the three of us to meet and negotiate.

I went to three parties a week in Karachi. This time I was with landowners, diplomats, businessmen and politicians: powerful people. This pleased me. They were people I wouldn't have been able to get at in England and I wanted to write about them. They were drinking heavily. Every liberal in England knows you can be lashed for drinking in Pakistan. But as far as I could tell, none of this English-speaking international bourgeoisie would be lashed for anything. They all had their trusted bootleggers who negotiated the potholes of Karachi at high speed on disintegrating motorcycles, the hooch stashed on the back. Bad bootleggers passed a hot needle through the neck of your bottle and drew your whisky out. I once walked into a host's bathroom to see the bath full of floating whisky bottles being soaked to remove the labels, a servant sitting on a stool serenely poking at them with a stick.

It was all as tricky and expensive as buying cocaine in London, with the advantage that as the hooch market was so competitive, the 'leggers delivered videotapes at the same time, dashing into the room towards the TV with hot copies of *The Jewel in the Crown*, *The Far Pavilions* and an especially popular programme called *Mind Your Language* which represented Indians and Pakistanis as ludicrous caricatures.

Everyone (except of course the mass of the population) had

videos. And I could see why, since Pakistan TV was so peculiar. On my first day I turned it on and a cricket match was taking place. I settled in my chair. But the English players, who were on tour in Pakistan, were leaving the pitch. In fact Bob Willis and Ian Botham were running towards the dressing rooms surrounded by armed police, and this wasn't because Botham had made derogatory remarks about Pakistan. (He'd said it was a country to which he'd like to send his mother-in-law.) In the background a section of the crowd was being tear-gassed. Then the screen went black.

Stranger still and more significant, was the fact that the news was now being read in Arabic, a language few people in Pakistan understood. Someone explained to me that this was because the Koran was in Arabic, but everyone else said it was because General Zia wanted to kiss the arses of the Arabs.

I was having a little identity crisis. I'd been greeted so warmly in Pakistan, I felt so excited by what I saw and so at home with all my uncles, I wondered if I were not better off here than there. And when I said with a little unnoticed irony, that I was an Englishman, people fell about laughing. Why would anyone with a brown face, Muslim name and large well-known family in Pakistan want to lay claim to that cold decrepit little island off Europe where you always had to spell your name? Strangely, anti-British remarks made me feel patriotic, though I only felt patriotic when I was away from England.

But I couldn't allow myself to feel too Pakistani. I didn't want to give in to that falsity, that sentimentality. As someone said to me, provoked by the fact I was wearing jeans: we are Pakistanis, but you, you will always be a Paki—emphasizing the derogatory name the English used against Pakistanis, and therefore the fact that I couldn't rightfully lay claim to either place.

In England I was a playwright. In Karachi this meant little.

There were no theatres; the arts were discouraged by the state—
music and dancing are un-Islamic—and ignored by practically
everyone else. As I wasn't a doctor, or businessman or military
person, people suspected that this writing business I talked
about was a complicated excuse for idleness, uselessness and
general bumming around. In fact, as I proclaimed an interest in
the entertainment business, and talked loudly about how integral
the arts were to a society, moves were being made to set me up
in the amusement arcade business, in Shepherd's Bush.

Finally the man got me on my own. His name was Rahman.
He was a friend of my intellectual uncle. I had many uncles but
Rahman preferred the intellectual one who understood Rahman's
particular sorrow and like him considered himself to be a
marginal man. In his fifties, a former Air Force officer, Rahman
was liberal, well-travelled and married to an Englishwoman who
now had a Pakistani accent.

He said to me: 'I tell you, this country is being sodomized by
religion. It is even beginning to interfere with the making of
money. And now we are embarked on this dynamic regression
you must know, it is obvious, Pakistan has become a leading
country to go away from. Our patriots are abroad. We despise
and envy them. For the rest of us, our class, your family, we are
in Hobbes's state of nature: insecure, frightened. We cling
together out of necessity.' He became optimistic. 'We could be
like Japan, a tragic oriental country that is now progressive,
industrialized.' He laughed and then said, ambiguously: 'But only
God keeps this country together. You must say this around the
world: we are taking a great leap backwards.'

The bitterest blow for Rahman was the dancing. He liked to
waltz and foxtrot. But now the expression of physical joy, of
sensuality and rhythm, was banned. On TV you could see where
it had been censored. When couples in Western programmes got
up to dance there'd be a jerk in the film, and they'd be sitting

down again. For Rahman it was inexplicable, an unnecessary cruelty that was almost more arbitrary than anything else.

Thus the despair of Rahman and my uncles' 'high and dry' generation. For them the new Islamization was the negation of their lives. It was a lament heard often; this was the story they told: Karachi was a goodish place in the Sixties and Seventies. Until about 1977 it was lively and vigorous. You could drink and dance in the Raj-style clubs (providing you were admitted) and the atmosphere was liberal—as long as you didn't meddle in politics, in which case you'd probably be imprisoned. Politically there was Bhutto: urbane, Oxford-educated, considering himself a poet and revolutionary, a veritable Chairman Mao of the subcontinent. He said he would fight obscurantism and illiteracy, ensure the equality of men and women, and increase access to education and medical care. The desert would bloom.

Later, in an attempt to save himself, appease the mullahs and rouse the dissatisfied masses behind him, he introduced various Koranic injunctions into the constitution and banned alcohol, gambling, horse racing. The Islamization had begun and was fervently continued after his execution.

Islamization built no hospitals, no schools, no houses; it cleaned no water and installed no electricity. But it was direction, identity. The country was to be in the hands of those who elected themselves to interpret the single divine purpose. Under the tyranny of the priesthood, with the cooperation of the army, Pakistan itself would embody Islam. There would now be no distinction between ethical and religious obligation; there would now be no areas in which it was possible to be wrong. The only possible incertitude was interpretation. The theory would be the eternal and universal principles which Allah created and made obligatory for men; the model would be the first three generations of Muslims; and the practice would be Pakistan.

This overemphasis on dogma and punishment strengthened

the repressive, militaristic and rationalistically aggressive state seen all over the world in the authoritarian Eighties. With the added bonus that in Pakistan God was always on the side of the government.

But despite all the strident nationalism, as Rahman said, the patriots were abroad; people were going away: to the West, to Saudi Arabia, anywhere. Young people continually asked me about the possibility of getting into Britain and some thought of taking some smack with them to bankroll their establishment. They had what people called the Gulf Syndrome, a condition I recognized from my time living in the suburbs. It was a dangerous psychological cocktail consisting of ambition, suppressed excitement, bitterness and sexual longing.

Then a disturbing incident occurred which seemed to encapsulate the going-away fever. An eighteen-year-old girl from a village called Chakwal dreamed that the villagers walked across the Arabian Sea to Karbala, where they found work and money. Following this dream, people from the village set off one night for the beach, which happened to be near my uncle's house in fashionable Clifton. Here lived politicians and diplomats in LA-style white bungalows with sprinklers on the lawns, Mercedes in the drives and dogs and watchmen at the gates.

On the beach, the site of barbecues and late-night parties, the men of Chakwal packed their women and children into trunks and pushed them into the sea. Then they followed them into the water in the direction of Karbala. Soon all but twenty of the potential émigrés were drowned. The survivors were arrested and charged with illegal emigration.

It was the talk of Karachi. It caused much amusement but people like Rahman despaired of a society that could be so confused, so advanced in some aspects, so very naive in others.

Erotic Politicians and Mullahs

About twelve people lived permanently in my uncle's house, plus servants who slept in sheds at the back just behind the chickens and dogs. Relatives sometimes came to stay for months, and new bits had to be built on to the house. All day there were visitors, in the evenings crowds of people came over; they were welcomed and they ate and watched videos and talked for hours. People weren't so protective of their privacy.

Strangely, bourgeois-bohemian life in London, in Notting Hill and Islington and Fulham, was far more formal. It was frozen dinner parties and the division of social life into the meeting of couples with other couples to discuss the lives of other coupling couples.

In Pakistan there was the continuity of the various families' knowledge of each other. People were easy to place; your grandparents and theirs were friends. When I went to the bank and showed the teller my passport, it turned out he knew several of my uncles, so I didn't receive the usual perfunctory treatment.

I compared the collective hierarchy of the family and the permanence of my family circle with my feckless, rootless life in London, in what was called the 'inner city'. There I lived alone, and lacked any long connection with anything. I'd hardly known anyone for more than eight years and certainly not their parents. People came and went. There was much false intimacy and forced friendship. People didn't take responsibility for each other. Many of my friends lived alone in London, especially the women. They wanted to be independent and to enter into relationships—as many as they liked, with whom they liked—out of choice. They didn't merely want to reproduce the old patterns of living. The future was to be determined by choice and reason, not by custom. The notions of duty and obligation barely had positive meaning for my friends: they were loaded, Victorian words, redolent of constraint and grandfather clocks, the antithesis of generosity in love, the new hugging, and the transcendence of the family. The ideal of the new relationship was no longer the S and M of the old marriage—it was F and C, freedom plus commitment.

In the large old families of Pakistan where there was nothing but old patterns disturbed only occasionally by new ways, this would have seemed a contrivance, a sort of immaturity, a failure to understand and accept the determinacies that life necessarily involved. So there was much pressure to conform, especially on the women.

'Let these women be warned,' said a mullah to the dissenting women of Rawalpindi. 'We will tear them to pieces. We will give them such terrible punishments that no one in future will dare to raise a voice against Islam.'

I remember a woman saying to me at dinner one night: 'We know at least one thing. God will never dare to show his face in this country—the women will tear him apart!'

In the Sixties of Enoch Powell and graffiti, the Black Muslims and Malcolm X gave needed strength to the descendants of slaves by 'taking the wraps off the white man'; Eldridge Cleaver was yet to be converted to Christianity and Huey P. Newton was toting his Army .45. A boy in a bedroom in a suburb, who had the King's Road constantly on his mind and who changed the pictures on his wall from week to week was unhappy, and separated from the Sixties as by a thick glass wall against which he could only press his face. But bits of the Sixties were still around in Pakistan: the liberation rhetoric, for example, the music, the clothes, the drugs, not as the way of life they were originally intended to be, but as appendages to another, stronger tradition.

As my friends and I went into the Bara Market near Peshawar, close to the border of Afghanistan, in a rattling motorized rickshaw, I became apprehensive. There were large signs by the road telling foreigners that the police couldn't take responsibility for them: beyond this point the police would not go. Apparently the Pathans there, who were mostly refugees from Afghanistan, liked to kidnap foreigners. My friends, who were keen to buy opium which they'd give to the rickshaw driver to carry, told me everything was all right, because I wasn't a foreigner. I kept forgetting that.

The men of the north were tough, martial, insular and proud. They lived in mud houses and tin shacks built like forts for shooting from. Inevitably they were armed, with machine guns slung over their shoulders. In the street you wouldn't believe women existed here, except you knew they took care of the legions of young men in the area who'd fled from Afghanistan to avoid being conscripted by the Russians and sent to Moscow for re-education.

Ankle deep in mud, I went round the market. Pistols, knives, Russian-made rifles, hand grenades and large lumps of dope and opium were laid out on stalls like tomatoes and oranges. Everyone was selling heroin.

The Americans, who had much money invested in Pakistan, this compliant right-wing buffer zone between Afghanistan and India, were furious that their children were being destroyed by an illegal industry in a country they financed. But the Americans sent to Pakistan could do little about it. The heroin trade went right through Pakistani society: the police, judiciary, the army, landlords, customs officials were all involved. After all, there was nothing in the Koran about heroin. I was even told that its export made ideological sense. Heroin was anti-Western; addiction in Western children was what those godless societies with their moral vertigo deserved. It was a kind of colonial revenge. Reverse imperialism, the Karachi wits called it, inviting nemesis. The reverse imperialism was itself being reversed.

In a flat high above Karachi, an eighteen-year-old kid strung out on heroin danced cheerfully around the room in front of me pointing to his erection, which he referred to as his Imran Khan, the name of the handsome Pakistan cricket captain. More and more of the so-called multinational kids were taking heroin now. My friends who owned the flat, journalists on a weekly paper, were embarrassed.

But they always had dope to offer their friends. These laid-back people were mostly professionals: lawyers, an inspector in the police who smoked what he confiscated, a newspaper magnate and various other journalists. Heaven it was to smoke at midnight on the beach, as local fishermen, squatting respectfully behind you, fixed fat joints; the 'erotic politicians' themselves, The Doors, played from a portable stereo while the Arabian Sea rolled on to the beach. Oddly, heroin and dope were both indigenous to the country, but it took the West to make them popular in the East.

The colonized inevitably aspire to be like their colonizers—you wouldn't catch anyone of my uncle's generation with a joint in their mouth. It was infra dig, for peasants. They shadowed the British, they drank whisky and read *The Times*; they praised others by calling them 'gentlemen'; and their eyes filled with tears at old Vera Lynn records.

But the kids discussed yoga, you'd catch them standing on their heads. They even meditated. Though one boy who worked at the airport said it was too much of a Hindu thing for Muslims to be doing; if his parents caught him chanting a mantra he'd get a backhander across the chops. Mostly the kids listened to the Stones, Van Morrison and Bowie as they flew over ruined roads to the beach in bright red and yellow Japanese cars with quadrophonic speakers, past camels and acres of wasteland.

I often walked from my uncle's house several miles down a road towards the beach. Here, all along a railway track, the poor and diseased and hungry lived in shacks and huts; the filthy poor gathered around rusty standpipes to fetch water; or ingeniously they resurrected wrecked cars, usually Morris Minors; and here they slept in huge sewer pipes among buffalo, chickens and wild dogs. Here I met a policeman who I thought was on duty. But he lived here, and hanging on the wall of his falling-down shed was his spare white police uniform, which he'd had to buy himself.

A stout lawyer in his early thirties of immense charm—for him it was definitely the Eighties, not the Sixties. His father was a judge. He was intelligent, articulate and fiercely representative of the other 'new spirit' of Pakistan. He didn't drink, smoke or fuck. Out of choice. He prayed five times a day. He worked all the time. He was determined to be a good Muslim, since that was the whole point of the country existing at all. He wasn't indulgent, except religiously, and he lived in accordance with what he believed. I took to him immediately.

We had dinner in an expensive restaurant. It could have been in London or New York. The food was excellent, I said. The lawyer disagreed, with his mouth full, shaking his great head. It was definitely no good, it was definitely meretricious rubbish. But for ideological reasons only, since he ate with relish. He was only in the restaurant because of me, he said. There was better food in the villages. The masses had virtue, they knew how to eat, how to live. Those desiccated others, the marginal men I associated with and liked so much, were a plague class with no values. Perhaps, he suggested, this was why I liked them, being English. Their education, their intellectual snobbery, made them un-Islamic. They didn't understand the masses and they spoke in English to cut themselves off from the people. Didn't the best jobs go to those with a foreign education? He was tired of these Westernized elders denigrating their country and its religious nature.

The lawyer and I went out into the street. It was busy. There were dancing camels and a Pakistan trade exhibition. The exhibition was full of Pakistani imitations of Western goods: bathrooms in chocolate and strawberry, TVs with stereos attached; fans, air conditioners, heaters; and an arcade full of Space Invaders. The lawyer got agitated.

These were Western things, of no use to the masses. The masses wanted Islam, not strawberry bathrooms or...or elections. Are elections a Western thing? I asked. Don't they have them in India too? No—they're a Western thing, the lawyer said. How could they be required under Islam? There need be only one party—the party of the righteous.

This energetic lawyer would have pleased and then disappointed Third World intellectuals and revolutionaries from an earlier era, people like Fanon and Guevara. This talk of liberation—at last the acknowledgement of the virtue of the toiling masses, the struggle against neocolonialism, its bourgeois stooges, and American interference—the entire recognizable rhetoric of freedom and struggle ends in the lawyer's mind with the country on its knees, at prayer. Having started to look for itself it finds itself...in the eighth century.

I strode into a room in my uncle's house. Half-hidden by a curtain, on a veranda, was an aged woman servant wearing my cousin's old clothes, praying. I stopped and watched her. In the morning, as I lay in bed, she swept the floor of my room with some twigs bound together. She was at least sixty. Now, on the shabby prayer mat, she was tiny and around her the universe was endless, immense, but God was above her. I felt she was acknowledging that which was larger than she, knowing and feeling her own insignificance. It was not empty ritual. I wished I could do it.

I went with the lawyer to the mosque in Lahore, the largest in the world. I took off my shoes, padded across the immense courtyard with the other man—women were not allowed—and got on my knees. I banged my forehead on the marble floor. Beside me a man in a similar posture gave a world-consuming yawn. I waited but could not lose myself in prayer. I could only travesty the woman's prayer, to whom it had a world of meaning.

Did she want a society in which her particular moral and religious beliefs were mirrored, and no others, instead of some plural, liberal melange? A society in which her own cast of mind, her customs, way of life and obedience to God constituted authority? It wasn't as if anyone had asked her.

In Pakistan, England just wouldn't go away. Relics of the Raj were everywhere: buildings, monuments, Oxford accents, libraries full of English books, and newspapers. Many Pakistanis had relatives in England; thousands of Pakistani families depended on money sent from England. While visiting a village, a man told me that when his three grandchildren visited from Bradford, he had to hire an interpreter to speak to them. It was happening all the time—the closeness of the two societies, and the distance.

Although Pakistanis still wanted to escape to England, the old men in their clubs and the young eating their hamburgers took great pleasure in England's decline and decay. The great master was fallen. It was seen as strike-bound, drug-ridden, riot-torn, inefficient, disunited, a society which had moved too suddenly from puritanism to hedonism and now loathed itself. And the Karachi wits liked to ask me when I thought the Americans would decide the British were ready for self-government.

Yet people like Rahman still clung to what they called British ideals, maintaining that it is a society's ideals, its conception of human progress, that define the level of its civilization. They regretted, under the Islamization, the repudiation of the values which they said were the only positive aspect of Britain's legacy to the subcontinent. These were: the idea of secular institutions based on reason, not revelation or scripture; the idea that there were no final solutions to human problems; and the idea that the health and vigour of a society was bound up with its ability to tolerate and express a plurality of views on all issues, and that these views would be welcomed.

The English misunderstood the Pakistanis because they saw only the poor people, those from the villages, the illiterates, the peasants, the Pakistanis who didn't know how to use toilets, how to eat with knives and forks because they were poor. If the British could only see them, the rich, the educated, the sophisticated, they wouldn't be so hostile. They'd know what civilized people the Pakistanis really were. And then they'd like them.

White Lies

Amit Chaudhuri

(2001)

He rang the doorbell once, and waited for the door to open. It was an ornate door, with a rather heavy, ornamental padlock. When the old, smiling maidservant opened it, there was a narrow corridor behind her which revealed a large hall and further rooms inside, like shadows contained in a prism.

It was a particularly beautiful flat. He sat on the sofa, as the maidservant went inside and said, 'Memsaab, guruji aaye hai.' He glanced at the Arabian Sea and the Marine Drive outside; and then looked at the brass figure of Saraswati, from whose veena all music is said to emanate, on one end of a shelf. When ten minutes had passed, he briefly consulted his watch, its hands stuck stubbornly to their places, and then desultorily opened a copy of *Stardust*. Now and again, he hummed the tune of a devotional.

After another five minutes, a lady emerged, her hair not yet quite dry. 'Sorry, masterji,' she said, but, glancing quickly over her shoulder, was clearly more concerned about the 'fall' of her sari.

The 'guruji' shifted uncomfortably. Although he was, indeed, her guru (and without the guru, as the saying goes, there is no knowledge), he had also the mildly discomfited air of a schoolboy in her presence and in this flat: this had to do not only with the fact that she was older, but with the power people like her exercised over people like him.

'That's all right, behanji,' he said; from the first day, she had been his 'respected sister'. 'We'll have less time for the lesson today, that's all,' he said, chuckling, but also asserting himself subtly. Then, to placate her, he said quickly, 'Maybe I arrived a little early.'

This morning was quiet, except for the activity in the kitchen that indicated that the essentials were being attended to. In the bedroom, next to the huge double bed, the harmonium had already been placed on the carpet by the bearer, John. The air inside had that early morning coolness where an air conditioner has not long ago been switched off.

White Lies

'A glass of thhanda paani,' he said after sitting down.

This request materialized a couple of minutes later, the glass of cold water held aloft on a plate by John, while Mrs Chatterjee turned the pages of her songbook unhurriedly, glancing at bhajan after bhajan written in her own handwriting. They were too high up—on the fourteenth floor—to hear the car horns or any of the other sounds below clearly; the sea was visible from the windows, but too distant to be audible. Sometimes her husband, Mr Chatterjee, would be present—and he'd shake his head from time to time, while sitting on the bed, listening to the guru and his wife going over a particular phrase, or a line. Sometimes he was content doing this even while taking off his tie and waiting for tea, his office-creased jacket recently discarded on the bed, beside him.

Indeed, he had married her twenty-two years ago for this very reason; that he might hear her sing continually. Not everyone might agree about the enormity of her talent; but something had touched him that day when he'd met her in the afternoon in his still-to-be in-laws' place in one of the more distant reaches of a small town, and heard her sing, not the usual Tagore song, but a Hindi devotional by Meerabai. He was the 'catch', then—a medium-sized fish that had the potential to be a big one.

Fifteen years they'd lived together in Bombay now, and for ten years in this flat that gave the illusion from certain angles that sea approached very near it. And for fifteen years, almost, he had wanted his wife's voice to be heard more widely than it was—what he thought of as 'widely' was a hazy audience comprising mainly colleagues from his company, and from the many other companies he had to infrequently, but repeatedly, come into contact with—though it wasn't as if he'd mind terribly if the audience extended beyond this group of semi-familiar faces into the unclear territory of human beings outside.

She had a weak voice, admittedly. It managed one and a half octaves with some difficulty; it was more at ease in the lower register, but quavered when it reached the upper sa and re, something the guru had grown used to. When she sang 'Meera ke prabhu' now, towards the end of the song, there was, again, that quaver. It was something she met reasonably bravely, head on, or ignored altogether, as did the guru. Neither could continue their respective pursuits, she, of being a singer, he, of being her teacher, if they took the quaver and its signal too seriously; they knew that one or two of these limitations were irremediable, but without much significance in relation to the other dimensions of their partnership.

'How was that?' she asked after she'd finished. She needed to know, in a perfunctory but genuine way, his opinion.

'It was all right today,' he said. He was never quite ingratiating in his response, but never harshly critical either. They had reached a silent mandate that this was how it should be. He went over a phrase as the servant brought in a tray with teacups, and a small plate of biscuits.

It was always a pleasure to hear him, even when he was humming, as he was now. And he was always humming. There was no denying his gift; but he probably still didn't quite know what to do with it. He was almost careless with it. He sipped the tea slowly, and carefully selected a biscuit. Sometimes they might give him a gulab jamun, towards which he'd show no lack of intent and no hesitation, or a jalebi.

He was certainly not the first teacher she'd had. He was the latest in a line that went back these fifteen years; he'd arrived to take his place at the head of the line, and to succeed his predecessors, roughly sixteen or seventeen months ago. She had interviewed him, of course, or conducted a little audition in the sitting room, during which she'd asked him, respectfully, to 'sing something'. He had descended on the carpet self-consciously, between the glass table and the sofas, and enchanted her, humbly but melodiously, with a bhajan she couldn't remember having heard before. She shook her head slowly from side to side to denote her acknowledgement of his prowess, and his ability to touch her, and because she hadn't heard anyone sing quite so well in a long time; and yet it *was* an interview, at the end of which there was a silence; and then she said: 'Wah! Very good!'

At first, she'd called him 'Masterji' (which she still did at times), as she had all her former teachers. There was no formal, ceremonial seal on the relationship, as there is between guru and shishya; he was there to do his job, to be a teacher, and she to learn. Nevertheless, the relationship had its own definition. They'd grown dependant on each other; he, for the modicum of respect he received here (fit enough for a guru, even though he might be a mere purveyor of knowledge rather than a repository of it), and the by-no-means negligible amount he got paid; there were also the little ways in which Mr Chatterjee helped him out, with his official contacts. As for Mrs Chatterjee, she liked the tunes he set the bhajans to, and could also recognize the presence of accomplishment; and she was too tired to look for another teacher. She used to change teachers every three or four years, when they began to dominate her too much; or when they became irregular. But he was much younger than her, and she'd grown fond of him—he was very mild and had none of the offensive manners that gurus sometimes have; she'd come to call him 'Masterji' less and less, and addressed him, increasingly, as 'Mohanji' or 'Mohan bhai'.

Mr Chatterjee came home at a quarter to seven, and called out to his wife, 'Ruma!'

Later, they had tea together in the balcony, facing Marine Drive, and watching the sun set at seven-thirty, because it was late summer. Everywhere, the glow of electricity became more apparent as the swathe of pink light permeating the clouds above the sea slowly disappeared; now darkness, and with it a different, artificial, nocturnal light, was coming to this part of Bombay.

'Sometimes I feel we have so much, Ruma,' Mr Chatterjee sighed.

She didn't know what he meant; she didn't even know if it was a complaint or an uncharacteristic confession of gratitude. Of course it wasn't true; that was obvious—they didn't have children. Towards the beginning, they'd tried out various kinds of treatment; and then they'd given up trying without entirely giving up hope. Now, as you slowly cease to miss a person who's no longer present, they no longer missed the child they didn't have. They gave themselves to their lives together.

'We should go to the party by nine at least,' he said. In spite of the tone of alacrity he used with his wife, the idea of having to go to a party exhausted him tonight. To change the subject, and also to allow the communion they'd had with the evening to survive a little, he asked: 'What did he teach you today? A new bhajan?'

Today was Thursday, the day the 'he' in the enquiry came to the house. She thought briefly, half her mind already busying itself with the social activity ahead, with the new sari to be worn, and said: 'No, the one he gave me last week. It still needs polishing. The one about the Rana—"My Ranaji, I will sing the praises of Govind." It's a beautiful tune.'

'Well, you must sing it for me,' he said, sighing as he got up from the sofa, resigned to the evening ahead. She looked at his back with a sort of indulgence.

The song, which she'd once sung to a different tune, and which she'd been practising assiduously for the last ten days or so, was about how Meera had given herself from childhood to her one lord, the Lord Krishna, and couldn't bring herself to live with her husband, the Rana, the king. The Rana, said the song, sent her a cup of poison, which became nectar when she touched it to her lips; if the Rana was angry, she sang, she could flee his province, but where would she go if her lord turned against her? Mrs Chatterjee rather liked the song; in her mind, of course, there was no confusion about who her Rana and who her lord was. Krishna's flute was second fiddle for her, although it, too, had its allure. But its place in her life was secondary, if constant.

In another age, Mr Chatterjee, with his professional abilities and head for figures and statutes, his commitment to see a project through, might have been a munshi in a court, or an adviser to a small feudal aristocracy. Now, it was he who, in a sense, ruled; he ran a company; he was the patron as far as people like Mohanji were concerned. It didn't matter that, when he sang before him, Mr Chatterjee didn't understand the talas, that he simply smiled quizzically and shook his head from side to side in hesitant appreciation. That hesitant appreciation, to Mohanji, meant much.

Coming back home from a party, Mrs Chatterjee would be so tired that sometimes she fell asleep with make-up still on her face. At such times, she almost felt glad she didn't have children, because she'd have lacked the energy to look in on them. All the same, she couldn't sleep for very long, and was awake, although she looked as if she needed more rest, when the cleaner came in for the keys to wash their two cars. She stood near the balcony with a teacup in her hand, as the day began, not really seeing the sea, its water resplendent with sunlight. Then, she might remember the guru was to come that day, and begin to think of the last song she'd learned from him.

On these days, she'd sometimes be a bit listless during the lesson, and the guru would say, 'Behanji, you seem a bit tired today.'

'It's this life, Mohanji,' she'd say, preoccupied, but not entirely truthful in the impression she sought to give of being someone who was passively borne by it. 'Sometimes it moves too quickly.' And she'd recall the exchanges of the previous night, now gradually growing indistinguishable from each other. Mohanji would regard her with incomprehension and indulgence; he was used to these bursts of anxiety and lassitude; the way an evening of lights, drinks, and strangers, when she was transformed into something more than herself, should change back into this sluggish morning, when she was unreceptive to the lesson and to him.

In this building itself, there were other amateur singers. On the seventh floor, Mrs Prem Raheja sang devotionals. Her husband was a dealer in diamonds, and occasionally flew to Brussels. For her, singing was less an aesthetic pastime (as it was for Mrs Chatterjee) than a religious one; she was devoutly religious. Then there was Neha Kapur on the eleventh floor, who liked to sing ghazals. No one really knew what her husband did; some said he was in 'import–export'. These people were really traders made good, many times richer, in reality, than Mr Chatterjee, though they lacked his power and influence, and inhabited a somewhat different world from his.

The guru had increased his clientele, if his students could be described by that word, in visiting this building and this area. Mrs Raheja was now one among his students, as was Mrs Kapur; and there were others in the neighbouring buildings. When he came to this area, he usually visited two or three flats in a day. The 'students' were mainly well-to-do or even rich housewives, with varying degrees of talent and needs for assurance, their lives made up of various kinds of spiritual and material requirements. What spiritual want he met was not clear, though it was certain he met some need; and his own life had become more and more dependent, materially, on fulfilling it.

Mohanji's life was a round of middle-aged women, mainly in

White Lies

Colaba and Cuffe Parade, and a few in Malabar Hill; in his way, he was proud of them, and thought of them as Mr So-and-So's wife, or, where the surname denoted a business family, Mrs So-and-So. He moved about between Cuffe Parade and Malabar Hill and the areas in between using buses and taxis, glimpsing, from outside and within, the tall buildings, in which he ascended in lifts to arrive at his appointed tuition. This was a daily itinerary, before this part of the city disappeared, too temporarily for it to be disturbing to him, when he took the fast train to Dadar at night.

Mr Chatterjee's company (although he didn't own the company, it was known among his friends as 'Amiya's company' and among others as 'Mr Chatterjee's company') manufactured, besides other things, detergent, which was its most successful product; and, since the company had substantial foreign shareholdings—the word 'multinational', like a term describing some odd but coveted hybrid, was being heard more and more these days—he, with his wife, made occasional trips to Europe (he to study the way detergent was marketed there), every one and a half to two years.

Returning, the vistas and weather of London and Zurich would stay with them for about a week as they resumed their life in Bombay. They'd distribute the gifts they'd brought between friends and business associates; deodorants, eau de toilette, ties; for Mohanji, a cake of perfumed soap, polished like an egg, serrated like a shell. He, in his gentle, qualified way, would pretend to be more grateful than he was, but nevertheless wonder at this object that had travelled such a huge distance.

There were so many projects inside Mr Chatterjee's head; he had only a year to bring them to fruition. Yet, though he was to retire, he was inwardly confident he'd get an extension.

In other ways, he felt that he was entering the twilight of his life in the company; though there was nothing more substantial than an intuition to suggest this. He suppressed this feeling before it could become a concrete thought. Among the more minor and personal, but persistent and cherished, projects he had in mind was to present his wife, Ruma, before an audience of friends and peers, with the repertoire of new songs she'd learned from the guru. With this in mind, he'd ask her sometimes, with a degree of impatience: 'Isn't he teaching you anything new? I've been hearing the same two songs for the last three weeks!' This might be said in the midst of talking about three or four other things, after he'd returned, yet again, late from the office.

He asked the teacher the same question in the course of the week, when he happened to come back earlier than usual, and find the lesson midway, in progress. He'd had a distracting day at the office; and he was about to go out again. He said, looming in his navy-blue suit over the teacher sitting on the carpet with the harmonium before him: 'Do give her another one, guruji! I've been hearing the same one—the one about "Giridhar Gopal"— for about two weeks now.' He called him 'guruji' at times, not as a student or acolyte might, but to indicate a qualified respect for a walk of life he didn't quite understand. He used the term as one might use a foreign word that one was slightly uncomfortable with, but which one took recourse to increasingly and inadvertently.

The guru looked a little bemused, and embarrassed on Mr Chatterjee's behalf. He picked up a printed songbook.

'I did give behanji a new bhajan, Chatterjee saab,' he said, weakly, but not without some humour and his characteristic courtesy. 'Maybe you haven't heard it. It's a lovely tune,' he said, with a kind of innocent and immodest delight in his own composing abilities.

'Really?' said Mr Chatterjee, lowering himself upon the edge of the bed and apparently forgetting the appointment he had to keep. 'Do sing it for me, guruji.' He could spare five minutes. 'Your behanji doesn't tell me anything!'

The guru began to sing almost immediately, first clearing his throat with excessive violence; then an unexpectedly melodious voice issued from him; he looked up, smiling, twice at Mr Chatterjee while singing.

'Wah!' said Mr Chatterjee with unusual candour after the guru finished, the song fading in less than three minutes. He turned to his wife and asked, 'Have you picked it up?' She waved him away with an admonitory gesture of the hand. 'See? She doesn't listen to anything I say.' The guru was greatly amused at this untruth. On his way out, he looked into the room and said, 'It's a particularly lovely bhajan.'

The guru smiled, almost as if he were a child who'd entered forbidden territory; as if, through the bhajan, he'd entered a space, and a mind, generally reserved for official appointments and more weighty transactions than these; how else could he obtrude upon such a space?

Two months later, they had a party in the flat; it came in the wake, ostensibly, of a new diversification for the company, but it had, actually, little to do with that. There were parties every two weeks, sometimes for no good reason, except to satisfy the addiction to the same set of faces; though these events were justified as being necessary for off-duty chatter among colleagues and associates, and, more importantly, because there was a persuasive myth that it was an extension of business activity. Usually, however, the party turned out to be none of these, but an occasion for bad jokes, bickering, and mild drunkenness and indigestion.

This party was a little different, though; Mrs Chatterjee was to sing tonight. Of course, she could be found standing by the door, a small smile on her face, responding to the exclamations of 'Ruma!' and 'Mrs Chatterjee!' and 'Where's Amiya?' as guests walked in with little nods and smiles, half her mind on the kitchen. They didn't know yet that she was to be a prima donna that evening; going in, however, they noticed a harmonium and tables kept on one of the carpets, and continued to circulate loudly among themselves, exploding noisily at moments of hilarity.

No one was surprised, or took more than a cursory note of the instruments; 'musical evenings' were less and less uncommon these days, and were seen to be a pleasant diversion or a necessary hazard in polite society. Meanwhile, people cupped potato wafers and peanuts like small change in their hands; and a platter of shami kababs passed from person to person. The guru had come earlier, and was sitting with members of his family— his wife, his mother, his cousin, a shy and thin man who'd play the tabla today, and his son—cloistered in the air-conditioned guest room, semi-oblivious of the noise outside; they were having their own party, chattering in their own language, holding glasses of Limca or Fanta in their hands, unmindful of the party outside.

Mrs Chatterjee had hardly time to think now of the songs she'd rehearsed; she went frequently to the kitchen, her face pale, to see how the pulao was coming along, and to leave a regulatory word or two with the servants, whom she could never trust entirely. As she checked to see if the right cutlery was out, and the correct arrangement of crockery, a ghost of a tune hovered in the back of her head. She wasn't really missed; one was missed at other people's parties, but not at one's own; one was not so much the centre of attention at one's own as a behind-the-scenes worker. Other people became centres of attention, like the advertising man, Baig, who was holding forth now about the travails of advertising in a 'third world country'. Yet, forty-five minutes later, leaving the kitchen on autopilot, she had to suffer herself to be, briefly, the cynosure of all eyes.

The cook measured out the koftas, while, in the hall, Mrs Chatterjee lowered herself awkwardly on the carpet, the guru sitting down not far away from her, unobtrusively, before the harmonium. He looked small and intent next to her, in his white kurta and pyjamas, part accompanist and part—what? At first, it wasn't the guests who listened to them, but they who listened, almost attentively, to the sound the guests made, until whispers travelled from one part of the room to another, the hubbub subsided, and the notes of the harmonium became, for the first time, audible. Mohanji could hear the murmurs, in English, of senior executives who worked in twenty-storey buildings nearby, and knew more about takeovers than music; it must be a puzzling, but oddly thrilling, experience to sing for them. It was odd, too, to sit next to Mrs Chatterjee, not as if he were her guru (which he wasn't, not even in name), waiting for her to begin, indispensable but unnoticed. The guests were looking at her.

She began tentatively; she couldn't quite get hold of the first song, but no one noticed. Certainly, Mr Chatterjee looked relaxed and contented. The only doubt was on Mrs Chatterjee's own face; the second one, however, went off better than the first. 'You're a lucky guy,' said Motwane, a director in a pharmaceuticals company, prodding Mr Chatterjee in the shoulder from behind. 'I didn't know she had so many talents.' Mr Chatterjee smiled, and waved at another friend across the room. Now, in the third song, her voice faltered in the upper register, but no one seemed to hear it, or, if they did, to be disturbed. Once her performance was over, the shami kababs were circulated again; a faint taste of 'culture' in their mouths, people went to the bar to replenish their glasses.

That night, as they were getting into bed, Mr Chatterjee said, 'That went quite well.' It wasn't clear to what he was referring at first, but it was likely he meant the party itself. Mrs Chatterjee was removing her earrings. 'And the songs?' she asked pointedly, making it sound like a challenge, but only half serious.

'Those were nice,' he said. To her surprise, he began to hum a tune himself, not very melodiously—she couldn't tell if it was one of the songs she'd sung earlier—something he did rarely before others, although she'd heard him singing in the bathroom, his voice coming from behind the shower. He seemed unaware that anyone else was listening. Seeing him happy in this way— it couldn't be anything else—she felt sorry for him, and smiled inwardly, because no one, as he was so successful, ever felt sorry for him, or thought of his happiness.

'We must have one of these "musical evenings" again,' he said simply, following an unfinished train of thought, as if he were a child who spoke impulsively, trusting to intuition. Yet, if he were a child, he was one that had the power to move destinies. Not in a godlike way perhaps, but in the short term, materially. But she loved his childlike side, its wild plans, although it tired her at times. She said nothing.

In his childlike way, he could be quite hard. Not with her; but no investment justified itself to him except through its returns. That was because he couldn't run a company on charity or emotions; or his own head would roll. Nor did he believe that the country could be run on charity or emotion.

She, in the long hours that he was away, leaned more and more on the guru. It wasn't that she felt lonely; but no one leading her kind of life in that flat, her husband in the office, could help but feel, from time to time, alone. The best she could think of someone like the guru, given his background, was as a kind of younger brother, 'kind of' being the operative words— not as a friend; certainly not as the guru he was supposed to be. There was one guru in her life, and that was her husband. But she needed Mohanji. She might spend a morning shopping at Sahakari Bhandar, but needed also to learn new songs. And yet her mind was focused on a hundred other things as well. When her focus returned to her singing, it was sometimes calming, and sometimes not.

One day she said to him, mournfully: 'I wish I could sing like you, Mohanji. There are too many parties these days. I can't practise properly.'

Mohanji was always surprised by the desires that the rich had, a desire for what couldn't be theirs. It also amused him, partly, that it wasn't enough for Mrs Chatterjee that she, in one sense, possessed him; she must possess his gift as well. Perhaps in another life, he thought, not in this one. The guru was a believer in karma phal, that what you did in one life determined who and where you were in the next; he was convinced, for instance, that his gift, whatever he might have done to perfect it in this life, had been given to him because of some sadhana, some process of faith and perseverance, he had performed in an earlier one. Of course, there were advantages to the position he was in now; in another time, he'd have had to submit to the whims of a raja, with the not inconsiderable compensation that the raja loved music. That empathy for music was still not good enough, though, to make you forget the frustrations of living under a tyrant. Now, in this age, all he had to do was attend to the humours of executives and businessmen and their wives who thought they had a taste, a passing curiosity, for music; it was relatively painless.

'Why do you say such things, behanji,' he said, unruffled. He scratched the back of his hand moodily. 'There's been a lot of improvement.' His eyes lit up slightly. 'All those bada sahibs and their wives came up and congratulated you the other day after you sang, didn't they, behanji,' he said, recalling the scene, 'saying, "Bahut acche, Rumaji," and "Very nice".' He shook his head. 'If you'd come to me ten years ago, I could have...' He sometimes said this with a genuine inkling of accomplishment at what he might have achieved.

'They may be bada sahibs,' said Mrs Chatterjee, vaguely dissatisfied that this appellation should be given to someone else's husband. 'But Mr Chatterjee is a bigger bada sahib than all of them.'

The guru did not dispute this.

'Bilkul!' he said. 'Even to look at he is so different.' He said this because he meant it; Mr Chatterjee, for him, had some of the dimensions of greatness, without necessarily possessing any of its qualities. There were so many facets to his existence; so little, relatively, one could know about him.

But the guru wasn't always well. A mysterious stomach ulcer—it was an undiagnosed ailment, but he preferred to call it an 'ulcer'—troubled him. It could remain inactive for days, and then come back in a sharp spasm that would leave him listless for two days. To this end, he'd gone with his mother and wife to a famous religious guru, called, simply, Baba, and sat among a crowd of people to receive his benediction. When his turn came, he was only asked to touch the Baba's feet, and, as he did so, the Baba whispered a few words into his ear, words that he didn't understand. But, after this, Mohanji felt better, and the pain, though he hadn't expected it would, seemed to go away.

When his 'behanji' heard about this one day, she was properly contemptuous. 'I don't believe in baba-vaaba,' she said. The guru smiled, and looked uncomfortable and guilty; not because he'd been caught doing something silly, but because Mrs Chatterjee could be so naively sacrilegious. It was as if she didn't feel the need to believe in anything, and affluent though she might be, the guru was not certain of the wisdom of this. 'If you have a problem, it should be looked at by a real doctor,' she went on. The guru nodded mournfully, seeing no reason to argue.

Of course, the problem was partly Mohanji's own fault. As he went from flat to flat, he was frequently served 'snacks' during the lesson, the junk food that people stored in their homes and dispensed with on such occasions. Sometimes the food could be quite heavy. Mohanji could never resist these, eating them while thinking, abstractedly, of some worry that beset him at home. This irregular consumption would leave him occasionally dyspeptic.

He suffered from tension as well, a tension from constantly having to lie to the ladies he taught—white lies, flattery—and from his not having a choice in the matter. He had raised his fee recently, of course; he now charged a hundred rupees for lessons all around, pleading that a lot of the money went towards the taxi fare. In this matter, his 'students' found him quietly inflexible. 'I can't teach for less,' he said simply. And because he was such an expert singer, his 'students' couldn't refuse him, although a hundred rupees a 'sitting' was a lot for a guru; making him one of the highest-paid teachers doing the rounds. But they'd begun to wonder, now and again, what they were getting out of it themselves, and why their singing hadn't improved noticeably, or why they—housewives—couldn't also become singers with something of a reputation: it would be a bonus in the variegated mosaic of their lives.

'But you must practise,' he'd say; and when a particular murki or embellishment wouldn't come to them, he'd perform a palta or a vocal exercise, saying, 'Practise this: it's for that particular murki,' as if he were a mountebank distributing charms or amulets for certain ailments.

Mr Chatterjee's office had a huge rosewood table; now, on the third anniversary of his being made Chief Executive of this company, a basket of roses arrived; after a couple of files were cleared away, it was placed on a table before him, and a photograph taken by a professional photographer arranged by Patwardhan, the Personnel Manager. 'Okay, that's enough; back to work,' he said brusquely, after the camera's shutter had clicked a few times. Once the photograph was developed and laminated, its black and white colours emphasized, rather than diminished, the roses.

The guru loved this photograph. 'Chatterjee saheb looks wonderful in it—just as he should,' he said, admiring it. 'He must have a wonderful office.' He ruminated for a little while, and said, 'Brite detergent—he owns it, doesn't he, behanji?'

'He doesn't own it,' said Mrs Chatterjee, tolerant but short. 'He runs it.' The guru nodded, not entirely convinced of the distinction.

He continued to give her new songs, by the blind poet Surdas, and by Meera, who would accept no other Lord but Krishna. During these lessons, he came to know, between songs, in snatches of conversation, that Mr Chatterjee had got his two-year extension at the helm of the company. He took this news home with him, and related it proudly to his wife.

Two days later, he brought a box of ladoos with him. 'These aren't from a shop—' he pointed out importunately. 'My wife made them!'

Mrs Chatterjee looked at them as if they'd fallen from outer space. There they sat, eight orbs inside a box, the wife's handiwork.

'Is there a festival?' asked Mrs Chatterjee. In the background, John, the old servant, dusted, as he did at this time of the day, the curios in the drawing room.

'No, no,' said the guru, smiling at her naivety and shaking his head. 'She made them for you—just eat them and see.'

She wasn't sure if she wanted to touch them; they looked quite rich.

'I'll have one in the evening,' she consoled him. 'When Chatterjee saheb comes. He'll like them with his tea.'

But, in the evening, Mr Chatterjee demurred.

'This'll give me indigestion,' he said; but he was distracted as well. No sooner had he been given his extension than a bickering had started among a section of the directors about it; not in his presence, of course, but he was aware of it. At such times, he couldn't quite focus on his wife's music lessons, or on the guru; the guru was like a figure who'd just obtruded upon Mr Chatterjee's line of vision, but whom he just missed seeing. 'You know sweets like these don't agree with me.' The sweets were an irrelevance; if the two directors—one of whom, indeed, he'd appointed himself—succeeded in fanning a trivial resentment, it would be a nuisance, his position might even be in slight danger; he must be clear about that. You worked hard, with care and foresight, but a little lack of foresight—which was what appointing Sengupta to the board had turned out to be—could go against you. Sometimes, he knew from experience and from observing others, what you did to cement your position was precisely what led to undoing it.

Mrs Chatterjee felt a twinge of pity for Mohanji. As if in recompense, she ate half a ladoo herself. Then, unable to have any more, she asked John to distribute them among the cook, the maidservant, and himself. 'They're very good,' she told them. She could see her husband was preoccupied, and whispered her instructions.

Sensing a tension for the next couple of weeks, which was unexpected since it came at the time of the extension being granted, a time, surely, for personal celebration, she herself grew unmindful, and withdrew into conversations with a couple of friends she felt she could trust. Once or twice, the guru asked her, full of enthusiasm, what she'd thought of the ladoos, but never got a proper answer. 'Oh, those were nice,' she said absently, leaving him hungry for praise. A slight doubt had been cast upon the extension, although it was trivial and this was most probably an ephemeral crisis; still, she felt a little cheated that it should happen now. It also made her occasionally maudlin with the guru, less interested in the lesson than in putting unanswerable questions to him.

'Mohan bhai, what's the good of my singing and doing all this hard work? Who will listen?'

How quickly their moods change, he thought. There you are, he thought, with your ready-made audience of colleagues and colleagues' wives; what more do you want? The questions she'd asked chafed him, but he skirted round them, like a person avoiding something unpleasant in his path. One day, however, he was feeling quite tired (because of a bad night he'd had) and lacked his usual patience; he said: 'One mustn't try to be what one can't, behanji. You have everything. You should be happy you can sing a little, and keep your husband and your friends happy. You can't be a professional singer, behanji, and you shouldn't try to be one.'

Mrs Chatterjee was silenced briefly by his audacity, and wondered what had made him say it. For the first time in days, she saw him through the haze of her personal anxieties; for a few moments she said nothing. Then she said: 'Perhaps you're right.' Her eyes, though, had tears in them.

When Mr Chatterjee heard of this exchange, however, he was very angry. In spite of all they had, he'd never felt he'd given his wife enough. And because she sang, and sometimes sang before him, it was as if she gave him back something extra in their life together, and always had. It wasn't as if she had the presence or the personality or the charm that some of the wives in her position had; it wasn't as if she were an asset to the society they moved about in. Her singing was her weakness, and it was that weakness that made him love her more than he otherwise would have.

'How dare he say such a thing?' he said, genuinely outraged. He was angry enough to forget, temporarily, the little factions that had come into being in the company. 'I will speak to him.

White Lies

As if he can get away just like that, disclaiming all responsibility.' Without really meaning it, he added, 'You can always get another teacher, you know.'

Two days later, he delayed setting out for his office, and deliberately waited for the guru to arrive. Barely had the music lesson begun, and the recognizable sounds of voice and harmonium emerged from the room, than he looked in, fully suited, and ready to go. The guru, seeing him, this vision of executive energy, bowed his head quickly in mid-song, privileged that the Managing Director should have stopped to listen to him for a few moments. Mr Chatterjee was impatient today, and wasn't taking in the Surdas bhajan; he had a meeting with the Board.

'Ji saab,' said the guru, stopping.

'Guruji,' said Mr Chatterjee, 'please don't say things that will upset my wife. That is not your job. You are here to give her songs and improve her singing. If you can't do that properly...'

'What did I say, Chatterjee saab?' asked the guru, interrupting him, and noticeably concerned. 'Saab, she has ten new songs now...'

'Don't evade the issue,' snapped Mr Chatterjee. 'You told her, didn't you, that she could never be a real singer. What is your responsibility, then? Do you take a hundred rupees a turn just to sit here and listen to her?'

The guru's hands had grown clammy. 'I won't listen to such nonsense again,' said Mr Chatterjee, shutting the door behind him. 'Please switch off the air conditioner, behanji,' the guru said after Mr Chatterjee had gone. 'I'm feeling cold.'

It wasn't as if the guru began to dislike Mr Chatterjee after this. He took his words, in part, as a childish outburst, and they couldn't quite hurt him. One thing he understood anew was how little Mr Chatterjee knew about music, about the kind of ardour and talent it required. But why should he? Mr Chatterjee's lack of knowledge of music seemed apposite to his position. If he'd been a musician, he wouldn't be Mr Chatterjee.

The guru knew that if he wasn't careful, the Chatterjees might discard him; Mrs Chatterjee might find herself someone else. He'd also begun to feel a little sorry for her, because of what he'd said; he could have replied, perhaps, that, given the right training from early childhood, she might have been a better-known singer, or, if she'd been in the right place at the right time, she might have become one; there had been no need to quite expose her like that.

For the following two days, Mrs Chatterjee, going around in her chauffeur-driven car from the club to the shops in the mornings, couldn't bring herself to hum or sing even once; the driver noted her silence. She'd suddenly realized that her need to sing had been a minor delusion, that both she and her husband and the world could get by without it—she hadn't been honest with herself; and no one had been honest with her. She remained polite with the guru when he came—they'd started to watch each other warily now, in secret—but went through the new bhajans with him without any real involvement, glancing again and again at her watch until the hour was up. Then, after a few more days, she realized she was taking herself too seriously, the force of the guru's words diminished, and she began to, once more, look forward to the lesson.

In the meanwhile, Mr Chatterjee had dealt with the problem at his end, after making, first of all, several late-night telephone calls to some of the foreign shareholders and directors. He had to shout to make himself heard, sometimes keeping his wife from sleep. 'Are you sure, Humphrey?' he asked, putting the onus of responsibility on the Englishman. And, then, 'Yes, I can see there's no other way...'

White Lies

Two days later, he met Sengupta, the man he'd employed four years ago, and appointed to the Board last year, face to face across the large rosewood table. 'R. C.,' he said, referring to him by his initials (he himself was 'A. K.'—Amiya Kumar—to his colleagues) 'you know why we're here. If there was any dissatisfaction or disagreement, we could have thrashed it out between ourselves. But that was not to be.' As if digressing philosophically, he observed, 'Brite has had a grand history, it has a present, and a future. No person is more important than that future.' Interrupting himself, he sighed. 'Anyway, I've spoken to Dick and Humphrey, and they agree that even the project that was your undertaking is going to fold up. It shows no signs of promise. It was a mistake.'

Sengupta had said nothing so far, not because he felt he was in the wrong, but because he thought his position, because of what he'd done and the way he'd done it, was a weak one; changes were necessary, but he could see now that he should have gone about looking for them in a more knowing way.

'One thing I want to say before I resign, A. K.,' interjected Sengupta, looking at the bright space outside the large glass windows, 'is that I've had a wonderful few years at Brite, and I regret it couldn't be for longer. However, I don't always agree with the company's style of functioning—it's not democratic.'

'Companies aren't democracies, R. C.,' said Mr Chatterjee, with the exaggerated patience of a man who was getting his way. 'You weren't elected to the Board, I appointed you to it. The election was a formality. Anyway, if you wanted to effect some changes, you should have waited a couple of years. You were certainly in the running.'

Sengupta shook his head and smiled. 'I don't know about that. Some of us make it, some of us don't—it's both a bit of luck and a bit of merit, and a bit of something else.' He looked at his hands. 'I know my opportunity won't come again; that's all right. But—

another thing—I don't think our personal world should encroach upon our business world, should it? I'm a great admirer of Ruma, a simple soul, a very pure person, but do you think that those costly parties with all that music and singing are necessary?'

'Social gatherings and parties have always been part of company policy; they raise its profile and perform all kinds of functions, you know that. The music came at no extra cost,' Mr Chatterjee observed firmly.

R. C. Sengupta waved a hand. 'You're right, you're right, of course! But the teacher, excellent singer, what's his name, I heard you were going to sponsor some show or performance to showcase him. Of course, I don't know if what I've heard…'

Mr Chatterjee bristled. 'Who told you that? That's absolute rubbish. He teaches my wife—I think it's unfair to draw either of them into this.' He paused and reflected. 'An idea may have been floated at one time, as such things are, but it was revoked.' He straightened some papers on the table. 'I personally thought it was a good idea. More and more companies are doing it, you know. Music is a great but neglected thing, a great part of our tradition. We should extend patronage where it's due. It can do Brite no harm.' He looked at his watch. 'We're late for lunch,' he said.

The guru collapsed on the street, not far from his house, one afternoon, when he was on his way home. One moment he was squinting at the sun, and trying to avoid someone's shoulder brushing past him, and the next moment, almost inadvertently, without quite realizing it, he'd crumpled—bent and fallen over. A few passers-by and loiterers ran towards him; he was familiar to them as the one who taught music, and from the window of whose ground-floor chawl they could sometimes hear singing. He wasn't unconscious, but had had a temporary blackout; he kept saying, 'Theek hai bhai, koi baat nahi, it's all right, it's fine,' as they helped him up, and one of the people, a sixteen-year-old boy who knew the way to his home, insisted on accompanying him, holding him by the arm during the slow progress homeward.

'Dadiji,' said the boy to Mohanji's mother, who'd been unprepared for what greeted her, 'Panditji fell down. He should rest for a while.' He sounded conciliatory, as if he didn't want to alarm her.

'Haan, haan, rest; I've been telling him to rest,' said the mother, as Mohanji, saying, 'Theek hai, beta,' to his companion, lay down on the divan and put one arm across his eyes.

His wife was not at home, nor were his two children; they'd gone to visit his wife's father in another part of the city. This chawl was where he'd grown up, and where he'd also got married. His father, who was a teacher and singer himself (he'd died eleven years ago) had moved here thirty years ago, and they'd had no intention, or opportunity, of moving out since. Gradually the house had come to be known in the chawl as 'Panditji's house'. It was here, when he was nine or ten years old, that his father had taught him kheyal and tappa and other forms of classical music.

'Mohanji,' said Mrs Chatterjee, 'what happened to you?' It wasn't as if she'd been worried; it was just that she abhorred practising alone—she preferred him there when she sang.

'I don't know what happened, behanji,' said the guru with a look of ingenuous puzzlement. 'I fell ill.'

'I heard,' said Mrs Chatterjee, nodding slightly. 'Mrs Raheja told me...she told me you fell down.'

The guru looked discomfited, as if he'd been caught doing something inappropriate. At the same time, he looked somewhat triumphant.

'It might be low blood pressure.'

She took him to her doctor—Dr Dastur, a middle-aged physician. He saw his patients in a room on the second storey of a building in Marine Lines. Mrs Chatterjee sat with Mohanji in a waiting room with three other patients, waiting to be called in. Half an hour later, when they went inside, Dr Dastur greeted her with: 'Arrey, Mrs Chatterjee, how are you? How is your husband—his name is everywhere these days?'

'Dr Dastur,' she said, 'this is my music teacher. He sings beautifully.'

Dr Dastur couldn't remember having seen a music teacher at close quarters before. Not that he was uninterested in music— his daughter now played Chopin and Bach's simpler compositions on the piano; but he himself was inordinately proud of the Indian classical tradition about which he knew as little as most of his contemporaries.

'Masterji,' he said, bequeathing this title upon Mohanji in an impromptu way, 'it's a pleasure meeting you.'

Dr Dastur prescribed him medication, but Mohanji didn't take the pills with any regularity. Indeed, he had an antipathy towards pills, as if they were alive. Instead, he kept a photograph of his spiritual guru—the 'Baba'—close to him.

He kept his blackout from his other students. The ghazal was in boom: everyone wanted to sing songs about some imminent but unrealizable beloved. Mohanji, in keeping with this, taught Neha Kapur on the eleventh floor songs by Ghalib and more recent poets; almost every week, he, sitting at his harmonium, hummed under his breath and composed a tune.

Bhajans, too, had become big business of late; women wore their best saris and diamonds and went to the concert halls to listen to the new singers. And, somehow, everyone felt that they too could sing, and be singers, and be famous. Even Mrs Kapur had a dream that her voice be heard. And it took so little to achieve it—a bit of money could buy one an auditorium for a night, and a 'show' could be held. Even the guru had come to believe in the simplicity of this rather uncomplicated faith.

White Lies

Although he was keeping indifferent health, he'd begun to sing more and more at businessmen's mehfils, and wedding parties; someone, moved by his singing, might come up to him in the middle of a song and shyly but passionately press a hundred-rupee note to his hand. Unaccounted-for money circulated in these gatherings; they were different from the parties in the corporate world, but, in a way, these people, always ostentatious with both money and emotion, seemed to care more for the music, and, moved by the pathos of some memory, shook their heads from side to side as he sang his ghazals.

These mehfils lasted late into the night, and sometimes Mohanji and the members of his family who'd accompanied him would return home in a taxi at two or half past two in the morning. Late night, and the heat of the day would have gone, and they'd be sleepy and exhausted but still know they were a thousand rupees richer. By this time, the housewives who'd heard him sing too would be setting aside their large gold necklaces and yawning and going to bed.

This year, when the ghazal was in boom, had been a better year than most for the guru. He'd gone round from home to home, patiently teaching new songs to housewives about the wave of long hair and sudden gestures and sidelong glances, singing at small baithaks, or even bhajans at temples before Sindhi businessmen if they so demanded it. This would leave him tired and moody, though, when he visited Mrs Chatterjee. She couldn't decide whether he was unhappy for some personal reason, or because he still hadn't made a name as some other singers had.

As the guru's health worsened, he began to sleep for more and more of the time. Sometimes the phone might ring in his small room, and he might speak for a few moments to a student who was enquiring after where he was. When he made the effort of going into the city, he slept on the train, carried along by its rhythm; and sometimes Mrs Chatterjee, finding him tired, would feel sorry for him and let him fall asleep after a lesson on one of the wicker sofas on the balcony, overlooking the Arabian Sea and the office buildings on Nariman Point. As he rested, she might be getting ready, to go out, once her husband returned, for dinner. Now and again, she'd go to the veranda to check how the guru was, put her hand on his forehead, and shake her head well-meaningly and say, 'No fever.' She would glance towards the traffic on Marine Drive, because it was from that direction that her husband would be approaching.

At such times, the guru was like a pet, or a child, left to himself and intermittently tended to. As Mrs Chatterjee and her husband prepared to go out they would talk about him as if he were a child they were leaving behind. Occasionally, if he heard her humming a song he'd taught her as she went out, he'd open his eyes, smile slightly, and close them again.

Mumbai
Suketu Mehta

(1997)

Bombay (now officially Mumbai) is a city with an identity crisis; a city experiencing both a boom and a civic emergency. It's the biggest, fastest, richest city in India. It held twelve million people at the last count—more than Greece—and thirty-eight per cent of the nation's taxes are paid by its citizens. Yet half the population is homeless. In the Bayview Bar of the Oberoi Hotel you can order Dom Perignon champagne for 20,250 rupees, more than one-and-a-half times the average annual income; this in a city where forty per cent of the houses are without safe drinking water. In a country where a number of people still die of starvation, Bombay boasts 150 diet clinics. *Urbs prima in Indis*, says the plaque outside the Gateway of India. By the year 2020, it is predicted, Bombay will be the largest city in the world.

Four years ago this divided metropolis went to war with itself. On December 6, 1992 the Babri Masjid, a mosque in Ayodhya, was destroyed by a fanatical Hindu mob. Ayodhya is many hundreds of miles away in Uttar Pradesh, but the rubble from its mosque swiftly provided the foundations for the walls that shot up between Hindus and Muslims in Bombay. A series of riots left 1,400 people dead. Four years later, at the end of 1996, I was back in Bombay and was planning a trip with a group of slum women. When I suggested the following Friday, December 6, there was a silence. The women laughed uneasily, looked at each other. Finally, one said: 'No one will leave the house on that date.'

The riots were a tragedy in three acts. First, there was a spontaneous upheaval involving the police and Muslims. This was followed, in January, by a second wave of more serious rioting, instigated by the Hindu political movement Shiv Sena, in which Muslims were systematically identified and massacred, their houses and shops burnt and looted. The third stage was the revenge of the Muslims: on March 12, ten powerful bombs went off all over the city. One exploded in the Stock Exchange, another in the Air India building. There were bombs in cars and scooters.

Mumbai

Three hundred and seventeen people died, many of them Muslims.

Yet many Muslims cheered the perpetrators. It was the old story: the powerful wish of minorities all over the world to be the oppressor rather than the oppressed. Almost every Muslim I spoke to in Bombay agreed that the riots had devastated their sense of self-worth; they were forced to stand by helplessly as they watched their sons slaughtered, their possessions burnt before their eyes. There are 1.6 million Muslims in Bombay: more than ten per cent of the city's total population. When they rode the commuter trains, they stood with their heads bent down. How could they meet the eyes of the victorious Hindus? Then the bombs went off, and the Hindus were reminded that the Muslims weren't helpless. On the trains, they could hold their heads high again.

Last December I was taken on a tour of the battlegrounds by a group of Shiv Sena men and Raghav, a private taxi operator, a short, stocky man wearing jeans labelled 'Saviour'. He was not officially a member of Shiv Sena, but he was called upon by the leader of the local branch whenever there was party work to be done. He led me through Jogeshwari, the slum where, on January 8, 1993, the second wave of trouble began. A Hindu family of mill workers had been sleeping in a room in Radhabai Chawl, in the Muslim area. Someone locked their door from the outside and threw a petrol bomb in through the window. The family died screaming, clawing at the door. One of them was a handicapped teenage girl.

Raghav and a couple of the others took me into the slums through passages so narrow that two people cannot walk abreast. They were cautious, at first. But as we passed a mosque, Raghav laughed. 'This is where we shat in the Masjid,' he said. One of his companions shot him a warning look. Only later did I learn what he meant. The Sena zealots had burnt down this mosque; it was one of the high points of the war for them, and they recalled it with glee. One man had taken a cylinder of cooking gas, opened the valve, lit a match and rolled it inside. He then joined the police force, where he remains to this day.

We were discussing all this not in some back room, in whispers, but in the middle of the street, in the morning, with hundreds of people coming and going. Raghav was completely open, neither bragging nor playing down what he had done; just telling it as it happened. The Sena men—the *sainiks*—were comfortable; this was their turf. They pointed out the sole remaining shop owned by a Muslim: a textile shop that used to be called Ghafoor's. During the riots some of the boys wanted to kill him, but others who had grown up with him protected him, and he got away with merely having his stock burnt. Now it has reopened, under the name Maharashtra Mattress. Raghav pointed to the store next to it. 'I looted that battery shop,' he said.

He led me to an open patch of ground by the train sheds. There was a vast garbage dump on one side, with groups of people hacking at the ground with picks, a crowd of boys playing cricket, sewers running at our feet, train tracks in sheds in the middle distance, and a series of concrete tower blocks beyond. A week ago I had been standing on the far side with a Muslim man, who pointed towards where I now stood, saying, 'That is where the Hindus came from.'

Raghav remembered. This was where he and his friends had caught two Muslims. 'We burnt them,' he said. 'We poured kerosene over them and set them on fire.'

'Did they scream?'

'No, because we beat them a lot before burning them. Their bodies lay here in the ditch, rotting, for ten days. Crows were eating them. Dogs were eating them. The police wouldn't take the bodies away because the Jogeshwari police said it was in the Goregaon police's jurisdiction, and the Goregaon police said it was the railway police's jurisdiction.'

Raghav also recalled an old Muslim man who was throwing

hot water on the Sena boys. They broke down his door, dragged him out, took a neighbour's blanket, wrapped him in it and set him alight. 'It was like a movie,' he said. 'Silent, empty, someone burning somewhere, and us hiding, and the army. Sometimes I couldn't sleep, thinking that just as I had burnt someone, so somebody could burn me.'

I asked him, as we looked over the waste land, if the Muslims they burnt had begged for their lives. 'Yes. They would say, "Have mercy on us!" But we were filled with such hate, and we had Radhabai Chawl on our minds. And even if there was one of us who said, let him go, there would be ten others saying no, kill him. And so we had to kill him.'

'But what if he was innocent?'

Raghav looked at me. 'He was Muslim,' he said.

A few days later I met Sunil, deputy leader of the *Jogeshwari shakha*, or branch, of the Shiv Sena. He came with two other Sena boys to drink with me in my friend's apartment. They all looked around appreciatively. We were on the sixth floor, on a hill, and the highway throbbed with traffic below us. Sunil looked out of the window. 'It's a good place to shoot people from,' he said, making the rat-tat-tat motion of firing a sub-machine gun. I had not thought of the apartment this way.

Sunil was one of the favourites to be *pramukh*, the leader, of the entire *shakha* one day. He first joined the Shiv Sena when he needed a blood transfusion, and the Sena boys gave their blood, an act which touched him deeply—his political comrades were, literally, his blood brothers. He was in his twenties now, helpful, generous and likeable. He has a wide range of contacts with Muslims, from taking his daughter to a Muslim holy man to be exorcised, to buying chickens in Mohammedali Road during the riots, for resale to Hindus at a good profit. But what preyed on his mind now was the conviction that the handicapped girl who died in the fire in Radhabai Chawl had been raped by her Muslim assailants. There was no evidence for this; the police report did not mention it. But that didn't matter. It was a powerful, catalytic image: a disabled girl on the ground with a line of leering Muslim men waiting their turn to abuse her, while her parents matched her screams with their own as their bodies caught the flames.

Sunil insisted on referring to the riots as a 'war'. Certainly, at the J. J. Hospital, he had witnessed scenes typical of wartime: corpses identifiable only by numbered tags. And at Cooper Hospital, where Hindus and Muslims were placed next to each other in the same ward, fights would break out; wounded men would rip saline drips out of their arms and hurl them at their enemies. During the riots, the government sent tankers of milk to the Muslim areas. Sunil, with three of his fellow *sainiks* dressed as Muslims, put a deadly insecticide in one of the containers: the Muslims smelt it and refused all the milk. Sunil's men also shut off the water supply to the Muslim quarter. After six days, he said, the Muslims were forced to come out to the big *chowk* in the centre of the quarter. 'That's when we got them,' he recalled.

I asked him: 'What does a man look like when he's on fire'

The other Shiv Sena men looked at each other. They didn't trust me yet. 'We weren't there,' they said. 'The Sena didn't have anything to do with the rioting.'

But Sunil would have none of this. 'I'll tell you. I was there,' he said. He looked directly at me. 'A man on fire gets up, falls, runs for his life, falls, gets up, runs. It is horror. Oil drips from his body, his eyes become huge, huge, the white shows, white, white, you touch his arm like this'—he flicked his arm—'the white shows, it shows especially on the nose.' He rubbed his nose with two fingers, as if scraping off the skin. 'Oil drips from him, water drips from him, white, white all over.

'Those were not days for thought,' he continued. 'We five people burnt one Mussulman. At four in the morning, after we heard about the Radhabai Chawl massacre, a mob assembled, the like of which I'd never seen. Ladies, gents. They picked up any weapon they could. Then we marched to the Muslim side. We met a *pau* wallah [bread-seller] on the highway, on a bicycle. I knew him, he used to sell me bread every day. I set him on fire. We poured petrol over him and set light to him. All I thought was that he was a Muslim. He was shaking. He was crying, "I have children, I have children." I said: "When your Muslims were killing the Radhabai Chawl people, did you think of your children?" That day we showed them what Hindu dharma is.'

Island dwellers

'We used to roller skate down Teen Batti,' an architect said to me. He used the past imperfect tense; he meant that he *used to be able* to roller skate down Teen Batti. Teen Batti is at the top of the road that winds up from the sea; the Ridge Road leads from there up Malabar Hill. The area is now a shabby high-rise ghetto where the cars leave no room for the juvenile traffic of roller skates and bicycles. What he said stuck with me because I used to roller skate down Teen Batti and cycle around there too. I cannot imagine a twelve-year-old boy doing so now.

The sounds, colours and moods of the sea lent heft and weight to my childhood. From my uncle's apartment I can still see the rocks where the boys from our building would catch little fish trapped in the hollows when the tide went out. We sat down there and watched the whole progress of the sunset, from light to dark, and planned our lives—who would become the police inspector, who the astronaut. Gradually, a colony of hutments took over those rocks, and when we walked on them we would sometimes slip and fall on shit. The rocks are now a public latrine, full of strange smells. There are two million people in Bombay who have to defecate in any space they can find. The sea air sometimes wafts the stench over the skyscrapers of the rich, nudging them, reminding them.

We lived in Bombay and never had much to do with Mumbai. Mumbai was what Maharashtrans called the city; and Bombay was the capital of Maharashtra. But so far as we Gujaratis— migrants, like so many in Bombay—were concerned, Mumbai meant the people who came to wash our clothes or look at our electricity meters. We had a term for them—*ghatis*: people from the ghats—meaning someone coarse, poor. There were whole worlds in the city which were as foreign to me as the ice fields of the Arctic or the deserts of Arabia. I was eight years old when Marathi, the language of Maharashtra, became compulsory in our school. How we groaned. It was a servants' language, we said.

I moved to New York when I was fourteen. When I went back I found that the city had grown in wild and strange ways. In front of my uncle's building, for instance, was a monstrous skyscraper, its skeleton completed more than a decade before, lying vacant. Several such buildings dot the city. The flats have been bought for huge sums but are empty because they violate municipal height limits. The builders knew they would not get planning consent but went ahead anyway. The first priority was to put up the concrete reality; they could deal with the extraneous issues—municipal clearances, legal papers, bribes—later. But the city corporation put its foot down, and the fate of the buildings entered the courts. While the most expensive, most desirable real estate in Bombay lies vacant, half the population sleeps on the pavement.

Land is to Bombay what politics is to Delhi: the reigning obsession, the fetish, the *raison d'être* and the topic around which conversations, business, newspapers and dreams revolve. Property is the mania of island dwellers all over the world, and Bombay is washed by water on three sides. It regards the rest of India much as Manhattan looks on the rest of America: as a place distant, unfamiliar and inferior. The lament I kept hearing—from both Hindus and Muslims—was that the riots were an ungentle reminder that Bombay was part of India.

Mumbai

In 1994 a survey revealed that real-estate prices in Bombay were the highest in the world. There was general jubilation in the city. It confirmed something that Bombayites had long felt: that this was where the action was, not New York or London. Here, if you wanted a flat in a new building shooting up from the narrow strip of land behind the National Centre for the Performing Arts in Nariman Point, you would need three million dollars.

My uncle

My father's brother is a diamond merchant. He came to Bombay in 1966, against the will of my grandfather, who saw no reason why anyone should leave the family jewellery business in Calcutta. But my uncle was a young man, and the economic twilight of Calcutta had begun. In Bombay he built up a diamond-exporting business and is now rich. He owns a large four-bedroom flat on Nepean Sea Road with a fine view of the ocean. He travels to New York and Antwerp as often as if he were going to Ahmedabad or Delhi.

I am very fond of him. When I was a child he bought me everything, from airline tickets to meetings with influential people.

During the riots he sheltered two small Muslim boys in his flat. They were friends of his son who were scared of the Hindu wrath in their own neighbourhood. They had to be smuggled into my uncle's building because the neighbours would have objected if they had known he was sheltering Muslims; it might even have attracted the attention of the rampaging mobs outside. My family remembers the boys, then seven and twelve years old, as being very quiet, not fully understanding what was going on, but aware that their family was in great danger.

My uncle also cooked food in a Jain temple and went, at great risk, to the Muslim areas, to distribute it to people trapped by the curfew: 5,000 packets of rice, bread and potatoes a day.

The man who did these things could also say: 'The riots taught the Muslims a lesson. Even educated people like me think that with such *junooni* [wild] people we need the Shiv Sena to give them *takkar* [counterforce]. The Shiv Sena are fanatics, but we need fanatics to fight fanatics.'

He looked past me, out of the window, and told me a story.

He had a good Muslim friend in Calcutta, a friend who was at school with him in the tenth standard; they would have been about fifteen. He went with this friend to see a movie, and before the main show a newsreel came on. There was a scene with many Muslims bowing in prayer, doing their *namaaz*. Without thinking, my uncle said out loud in the darkened theatre, perhaps to his friend, perhaps to himself, 'One bomb would take care of them.'

Then he realized what he had said, and that the friend beside him was Muslim. But the friend said nothing, pretending he had not heard. 'But I know he heard,' said my uncle, the pain still evident on his face, sitting in this flat in Bombay thirty-five years later. 'I was so ashamed,' he said. 'I have been ashamed of that all my life. I began to think, how did I have this hatred in me? And I realized I had been taught this since childhood. Maybe it was Partition, maybe it was their food habits—they kill animals—but our parents taught us that we couldn't trust them. The events of Partition washed away the teachings of Gandhiji. Dadaji [my grandfather] and Bapuji [his brother] were staunch Gandhians except when it came to Muslims. I could never bring a Muslim friend home and I couldn't go to their home.'

The next day my uncle sat in the room with the little temple, doing his morning puja. 'Don't write what I told you,' he said.

I asked him why.

'I've never told anyone that before.'

I have written it anyway. He had something to explain to himself and he's not through sorting it out in his mind—he's a long way away from it, as most of us are—but he's begun.

In the Bombay I grew up in, being Muslim or Hindu or Catholic was merely a personal eccentricity, like a hairstyle. We had a boy in our class—Arif—who, I realize now, must have been Muslim. He was an expert in scatology and taught us an obscene version of a patriotic song in which the heroic exploits of the country's leaders were replaced by the sexual escapades of Bombay's movie stars. He didn't do this because he was Muslim, but because he was a twelve-year-old boy.

In Bombay, back then, it didn't matter. In Mumbai, now, it matters very much.

Powertoni

Sunil, the deputy leader of the Shiv Sena's Jogeshwari branch, could afford to be relaxed. 'The ministers are ours,' he said. 'The police are in our hands. They cooperated during the riots. If anything happens to me, the minister calls.' He nods. 'We have *powertoni*.'

He repeated the word a few times before I realized what it meant. It was a contraction of 'power of attorney', the ability to act on someone else's behalf, or to have others do your bidding, sign documents, release criminals, cure illnesses, get people killed. In Mumbai, the Shiv Sena is the one organization that has *powertoni*. So far, the only people punished for their involvement in the riots have been fourteen Muslims. And the man with the greatest *powertoni* is the leader of Sena, Balasaheb Thackeray—the Saheb.

Sunil and the Sena boys described him to me. He did not actually hold any office of state, but it was impossible to talk directly to him, they said; even the most eloquent, fearless man like their branch leader became tongue-tied, and the Saheb would berate him, 'Stand up! What's the matter, why are you dumb?' It was impossible to meet his eyes. Nevertheless, he liked people to be direct. 'You should have the daring to ask direct questions. He doesn't like a man who says, er...er...'

They told me what to say if I met the Saheb. 'Tell him: "Even today, in Jogeshwari, we are ready to die for you." But ask him: "Those people who fought for you in the riots, for Hindutva, what do you think of them? What can your Shiv Sena do for them? Those who laid their lives down on a word from you? What should their mothers do? What can the old parents of the Pednekar brothers, who have no other children, do?"

I felt like a go-between carrying messages from the lover to the loved one: 'Tell her I am ready to die for her!' But there was also a hint of reproach in their questions, as if they felt that their Saheb had been neglecting them, these people who had died for his love; and that somehow the blood sacrifice their comrades had made had gone unacknowledged.

Bal Thackeray's monstrous ego was nurtured from birth. His mother had five daughters and no sons. She prayed ardently for a boy and was blessed with Bal, whom she believed was a *navasputra,* a gift from God.

He worked for most of his life as a cartoonist. Then, in 1966, he formed a new political party of the people we called *ghatis*. He named it the Shiv Sena, Shivaji's Army, after the seventeenth-century Maharashtran warrior-king, who organized a ragtag band of guerrillas into a fighting force that defeated the Mogul emperor Aurangzeb and held sway over most of central India.

The Shiv Sena branch in Jogeshwari is a long hall filled with pictures of Thackeray and his late wife, a bust of Shivaji and Raghunath Kadam, the branch leader, sits behind a table and listens to a line of supplicants. A handicapped man is looking for work as a typist. Another wants electricity in his slum. Warring couples come to him for mediation. An ambulance is parked outside, part of a network of ambulances all around Bombay that the Sena operates at nominal charges. In a city where municipal services are in a state of crisis, going through the Sena ensures access to such services. The Sena also acts as a parallel government, like the party machines in American cities that helped immigrants find jobs and fixed street lights.

Thackeray, now seventy, is a cross between Louis Farrakhan and Vladimir Zhirinovsky. He appears in Salman Rushdie's *The Moor's Last Sigh* as Raman Fielding, leader of a thuggish political movement called Mumbai Axis. Thackeray has the cartoonist's art of being outrageous and loves to bait foreign journalists with his professed admiration for Adolf Hitler. In an interview with *Time* magazine at the height of the riots, he was asked if Indian Muslims were beginning to feel like Jews in Nazi Germany. 'Have they behaved like the Jews in Nazi Germany? If so, there is nothing wrong if they are treated as Jews were in Nazi Germany,' he said.

His party has an uncomplicated way of dealing with its opponents. Its newspaper, *Saamna* (the word means confrontation), has waged a fierce campaign against M. F. Hussain, India's best-known painter, for painting a nude portrait of the goddess Saraswati, twenty years ago. *Saamna* suggested that by painting the Hindu goddess naked, Hussain had 'displayed his innate Muslim fanaticism'. Hussain had for a long time had an inkling that he would be targeted eventually. In October 1996 he went to London and dared not return. In his absence, the police filed multiple criminal cases against him for insulting religious beliefs and inciting communal disharmony.

Saamna's editor, Sanjay Nirupam (a Member of Parliament), put the case clearly: 'Hindus,' he wrote, 'do not forget Hussain's crime! He is not to be forgiven at any cost. When he returns to Mumbai he must be taken to Hutatma Chowk and be publicly flogged until he himself becomes a piece of modern art. The same fingers that have painted our Mother naked will have to be cut off.'

What's striking about the writer's notions of punishment is that they seem to be derived straight from the sharia.

'Thackeray is more Muslim than I am,' said Shabana Sheikh, a woman in the Jogeshwari slums. He is a man obsessed by Muslims: 'He watches us: how we eat, how we pray. If his paper doesn't have the word Muslims in its headline, it won't sell a single copy.'

In March 1995 the Shiv Sena, as the majority partner in a coalition government, came to power in Maharashtra state (the city government had already belonged to them for a decade). It examined the awesome urban problems plaguing the city, the infestation of corruption at all levels of the bureaucracy, the abysmal slate of Hindu-Muslim relations, and took decisive action. It changed the name of the capital city to Mumbai; the station, Victoria Terminus, became Chhatrapati Shivaji Terminus. Ironically, Thackeray himself has an English name: his father anglicized the spelling to chime with the novelist he most admired.

I was never able to carry the Sena boys' message to the Saheb. He had grown wary of journalists. over by the Srikrishna Commission, an official inquiry into the riots. Instead, I went to meet the man who will lead the Sena after Thackeray's death: his nephew, Raj.

I was nervous as I entered the *Saamna* office. It has a reputation. Ramesh Kini, for instance, was a supervisor in an eyeliner factory, a middle-class Maharashtran resident of Matunga, such as form the core of Sena support. He was also the victim of a campaign of harassment by his landlord, who was trying to get his family evicted from his rent-controlled flat. His landlord also had connections in the Sena. One morning Kini came here to this office; by midnight he was dead. The police found his body in a theatre in Pune, several hours away, and registered a case of suicide. Then his widow went public and named Raj Thackeray, the man I was about to meet, the Saheb's twenty-eight-year-old nephew, as one of the murderers.

Mumbai

Before entering his office, I was asked to take off my shoes. When I went in, I found out why. Behind where the short, slim, intense man sits is a shrine decorated with images of gods; there is also the usual photograph of the Saheb. The whole office looked rather like a film set, so replete was it with iconography, and after a while I realized that Raj's mannerisms—the way he held his hand to his mouth, his glare, were also taken directly from the movies. There was an air of unconvincing menace about him. A policeman with an automatic rifle follows him everywhere; when he visits the bathroom, the policeman stands outside.

I asked him about the city. He glared at me. 'You're calling it Bombay.' I realized my transgression and referred to it as Mumbai for the rest of our meeting.

Raj has been groomed to fill the older Thackeray's place to the extent of following in his career path—he is also a cartoonist; prominent on his desk is a calligraphy set and a book, *WWII in Cartoons*. I asked him about his favourite cartoonists. 'Balasaheb Thackeray,' he said without thinking.

'All Balasaheb is saying,' he said, with the air of a man advancing a perfectly reasonable proposition, some civic improvement scheme, perhaps, 'is that whoever is against this nation should be shot and killed.' He paused. 'And if the Muslims are more this way, then we are not guilty.'

He told me about the Shiv Sena's answer to Bombay's problems. 'There should be a permit system to enter Mumbai, just like a visa. This would be checked at the railway stations, airports, highways. The constitution should be changed, if you want to save the city. Those people who have work should come and do it and go away. Outsiders should be stopped from immigrating. Who are they? They are not Maharashtrans.'

Almost as we spoke, a group of Sena members, including a former mayor of the city, was visiting the offices of a Marathi newspaper that had dared to print a speech critical of the Saheb.

A former deputy municipal commissioner in Bombay, G. R. Khairnar, who has a reputation for fighting corrupt politicians, had lashed out at Thackeray in a hysterical speech, calling him, among other things, the Devil. The Sena duly broke the windows in Khairnar's house and beat up journalists, blackening one editor's face with coal tar. The police filed a case against the newspaper, 'for wantonly creating provocation with intent to spread discontent and cause riot'.

Thackeray loves big business, and big business loves him. The Sena cut its teeth fighting communists in the factories, so the Sena-controlled unions are much more dependable than the Left-controlled ones. The party's money comes not from the rank and file but from the city's leading businessmen. The main opposition comes from rural areas and from Marathi writers.

The Sena also shows a distinct bias towards kitsch. Last November, for instance, Thackeray allowed Michael Jackson to perform in India for the first time. This may or may not have had to do with the fact that the singer had promised to donate the profits from his concert (more than a million dollars) to a Sena-run youth-employment project. The planned concert offended a number of people in the city, including Thackeray's own brother, who asked: 'Who is Michael Jackson, and how on earth is he linked to Hindu culture which the Shiv Sena and its boss Thackeray talk about so proudly?'

But the Shiv Sena supremo (as he sometimes signs his letters), responded, 'Jackson is a great artist, and we must accept him as an artist. His movements are terrific. Not many people can move that way. You will end up breaking your bones.' Then he got to the heart of the matter. 'And well, what is culture? Jackson represents certain values in America which India should not have any qualms in accepting.' The pop star acknowledged Thackeray's praise by stopping off at the leader's residence on the way to his hotel from the airport and pissing in his toilet, a fact which Thackeray brought with pride to the attention of the city's media.

Sunil and his friends talked with equal pride about the time every year on the Saheb's birthday when they go to his bungalow, and watch a long line of the city's richest, most eminent people line up to pay homage to their Saheb. 'We watch all the big people bow and touch his feet.' Another *sainik* added: 'Michael Jackson only meets presidents of countries; he came to meet Saheb.' The movie industry, especially, is in thrall to the Saheb, seeking his favour in everything from exempting a movie from entertainment tax, to getting an errant actor released from jail. In August 1996 the prime minister himself, Deve Gowda, flew to Bombay to meet the Saheb at a dinner organized at the residence of the movie star and entertainment magnate Amitabh Bachhan. Every time one of the corporate or screen gods, or a foreigner, or the prime minister, kowtows before him, the foot soldiers of the Sena get a thrill of pride, and their image of the Saheb as a powerful man, a man with *powertoni*, is reinforced.

A lover's embrace

The manager of Bombay's suburban railway system was recently asked when the system would improve to a point where it could carry its five million daily passengers in comfort. 'Not in my lifetime,' he answered. Certainly, if you commute into Bombay, you are made aware of the precise temperature of the human body as it curls around you on all sides, adjusting itself to every curve of your own. A lover's embrace was never so close.

One morning I took the rush hour train to Jogeshwari. There was a crush of passengers, and I could only get halfway into the carriage. As the train gathered speed, I hung on to the top of the open door. I feared I would be pushed out, but someone reassured me: 'Don't worry, if they push you out they also pull you in.'

Asad Bin Saif is a scholar of the slums, moving tirelessly among the sewers, cataloguing numberless communal flare-ups and riots, seeing first-hand the slow destruction of the social fabric of the city. He is from Bhagalpur, in Bihar, site not only of some of the worst rioting in the nation, but also of a famous incident in 1980, in which the police blinded a group of criminals with knitting needles and acid. Asad, of all people, has seen humanity at its worst. I asked him if he felt pessimistic about the human race.

'Not at all,' he replied. 'Look at the hands from the trains.'

If you are late for work in Bombay, and reach the station just as the train is leaving the platform, you can run up to the packed compartments and you will find many hands stretching out to grab you on board, unfolding outward from the train like petals. As you run alongside you will be picked up, and some tiny space will be made for your feet on the edge of the open doorway. The rest is up to you; you will probably have to hang on to the door frame with your fingertips, being careful not to lean out too far lest you get decapitated by a pole placed close to the tracks. But consider what has happened: your fellow passengers, already packed tighter than cattle are legally allowed to be, their shirts drenched with sweat in the badly ventilated compartment, having stood like this for hours, retain an empathy for you, know that your boss might yell at you or cut your pay if you miss this train and will make space where none exists to take one more person with them. And at the moment of contact, they do not know if the hand that is reaching for theirs belongs to a Hindu or Muslim or Christian or Brahmin or untouchable or whether you were born in this city or arrived only this morning or whether you live in Malabar Hill or Jogeshwari; whether you're from Bombay or Mumbai or New York. All they know is that you're trying to get to the city of gold, and that's enough. Come on board, they say.

6 March, 1989

Salman Rushdie

(1989)

6 March, 1989

Boy, yaar, they sure called me some good names of late:
e.g. opportunist (dangerous). E.g. full-of-hate,
self-aggrandizing, Satan, self-loathing and shrill,
the type it would clean up the planet to kill.
I justjust remember my own goodname still.

Damn, brother. You saw what they did to my face?
Poked out my eyes. Knocked teeth out of place,
stuck a dog's body under, hung same from a hook,
wrote what-all on my forehead! Wrote 'bastard'! Wrote 'crook'!
I justjust recall how my face used to look.

Now, misters and sisters, they've come for my voice.
If the Cat got my tongue, look who-who would rejoice—
muftis, politicos, 'my own people', hacks.
Still, nameless-and-faceless or not, here's my choice:
not to shut up. To sing on, in spite of attacks,
to sing (while my dreams are being murdered by facts)
praises of butterflies broken on racks.

Salman Rushdie

Kabir Street

R. K. Narayan

(1997)

Nagaraj had begun to have doubts about his standing in his ancestral home, 14 Kabir Street. He was the titular head of the family, his wife, Sita, being the real ruler of the empire extending from the street to the lichen-covered backyard wall with a door opening on to the sands of the River Sarayu.

The river had provided water for their domestic needs, till a well was dug, when the traffic towards the river ceased, and the back door, through disuse, got welded to the frame with ancient rust and dust. Otherwise the backyard remained unchanged with its tin-roofed bathroom and toilet beside the well. Four tall coconut trees loomed challengingly, in addition to guava, jackfruit, pomelo and a spreading tamarind, shedding leaves which remained unswept amid a jungle of wild vegetation.

Nagaraj's nephew Tim commented on the wild state of the backyard whenever he saw it. 'Too bad! Uncle, you must get a couple of men to clear the jungle.'

'Yes, yes,' Nagaraj would say. 'I have asked them to come,' inwardly wondering who 'they' were.

Sita was more emphatic. 'If they can't get anyone, tell me plainly, I will do something. Cobras may be living under the fallen leaves. What a lot of trouble your father used to take to keep the place clean! You are indifferent.'

'Naturally, not being my father,' he retorted silently, but aloud, 'Sita, leave it to me.'

'Cobras,' she began again, but he cut her short. 'Nonsense! Cobras have better business than counting dead leaves.'

'Not only your father, but your mother was cleaning and clearing.'

'She was a busybody—all the time sweeping and dusting...'

'That was why everything was so tidy.'

'Why don't you follow her example?'

This could only be a brief exchange while he passed from the puja room into the kitchen.

Kabir Street

After lunch Nagaraj dressed in a silk jibba, white dhoti and an upper cloth dyed in ochre (as ordered by a swami he had met in the park long ago), surveyed himself in their ancient oval mirror and set off with a brief, 'I'm off. Shut the door.'

Sita moved into the kitchen, muttering. 'No use talking to him. He doesn't care. Must find someone to clear the jungle.'

Nagaraj went down Kabir Street, paused for a second at the archway to the market to greet his friend Jayaraj the photo-framer, who was hunched over some coloured prints of gods and nailing gilt frames around them. His next stop was the corner stall, where he held out his palm while his friend Kanni placed on it a couple of betel leaves and a pinch of scented areca nut, which he popped into his mouth and chewed contentedly, saying, 'Put it on my account.'

'No need to say it,' muttered Kanni as a routine formula.

Crossing Market Road, Nagaraj reached Margosa Avenue and then Coomar's Boeing Sari Emporium. Coomar had not come yet. A couple of attendants were stacking up saris in showcases. Nagaraj settled in his usual corner, took out the ledgers and scanned the columns.

He asked loudly, addressing nobody in particular, 'Where is the proprietor?'

'Sent word he will be late.'

'Thank God,' Nagaraj said to himself, feeling relieved. He glanced through the columns on a page or two and put away the ledger, got up on an impulse and while passing the manager murmured, 'I'll be back,' whispering under his breath, 'no need to count Coomar's profits today.'

He stepped out and went down the street without any plan. He paused at the junction. If he went straight ahead, his steps would lead him home. 'I don't need to go home and face Sita's endless questioning. I want to be a free man at least for a couple of hours. Home is not the best place at the moment.' Tim and his wife Saroja had moved in permanently. Saroja was always playing her harmonium, and Tim had taken up amateur dramatics. Now he and his gang would be there—as usual—rehearsing *Harischandra*. If the moral of the famous story affected the unwashed, unshaven ruffians even slightly, things would not be so bad. But they were an untidy lot whose touch would contaminate. How dare they usurp his seat on the *pyol*.

Sita should be advised to scrub the place and wash it with phenol. But it was unlikely she would take it in the right spirit, since she constituted herself champion of Tim in every misdeed. She was a good wife but a muddle-headed aunt. Last evening the lounging fellows ignored him as he stood there glaring at them to convey his distaste for the whole lot.

They were chattering away while another set was singing to the accompaniment of Saroja's harmonium. He wondered for a while, 'Why not push them off the *pyol* on to the street?' but retreated to Sita's room with the intention of shouting at her. She was lying on the bare, cool cement floor reading a magazine.

He felt tongue-tied in her presence. Plucking up courage, he said, 'I can hardly hear my own voice in this house.' She lowered the magazine, looked at him over the frame of her spectacles and asked, 'What is it that you want to say?'

Nagaraj muttered within himself, 'She looks owlish with the spectacles over her nose,' but said aloud, 'Nothing really... I don't even know where I can sit.'

She pulled off her spectacles, obviously getting ready for a duel, and said: 'With so many rooms built by your worthy forefathers! You don't even know who built this house!'

'I could tell you a lot when we have a little silence.

'You always have a grudge against Tim and his friends. After all, you were the one to pamper him, separating him from his parents.'

This angered Nagaraj, but he could only say, 'Well, if you are going on that line... I don't know... I don't know how to live in this house!'

'As we have always done. What is special now?'

'I have no place to sit quietly and watch...'

'Watch what? The street? To watch mongrels fighting in the dust or the drunken engineer tottering homeward? You lose nothing by not watching. You speak as if you were missing a royal procession.'

'I don't know where to sit.'

She laughed at his complaint. 'Second time you are complaining. Could it be that you have suddenly assumed giant proportions, like the Vamana avatar of Vishnu who appeared like a pygmy at first?'

'I know the story; you don't have to repeat it.'

She was adamant and continued her narrative. 'He appeared as a pygmy and asked Bali, the demon king who had to be destroyed, for three paces of the Earth as a gift. King Bali, who never refused an appeal, readily granted it. Vamana assumed a giant stature...'

'I know the story,' repeated Nagaraj weakly.

'Vamana's first stride spanned the whole Earth, the second spanned all Heaven. "Where is the space for my third?" asked Vamana, and the King bowed down and offered his head, and the God placed one foot on it and pressed him down to extinction.'

'Why?' asked Nagaraj.

'You said you knew the story. Why don't you conclude it?' teased Sita. 'Why don't you throw away all those notebooks in which you have scribbled notes about Narada and sit down to write the story of Vamana?'

'Excellent advice,' Nagaraj cried in joy, and hugged her after making sure no one was watching.

After this she said, 'Follow me,' and led him to the veranda *pyol* where the rehearsal group had fallen asleep, leaning on each other. She clapped her hands, and when they woke up, she ordered them out. 'You may all go. Tim won't be back.' They scrambled to their feet and made their exit.

She turned to Nagaraj and said, 'There, I have found space for your first step…for your second and third we will also find space.'

At this point Saroja's harmonium ceased. She appeared at the door to declare with some heat, 'Tim said they should wait for him.'

'At the street corner, I believe,' Nagaraj said with a chuckle. Saroja retreated to her room grumbling.

Nagaraj sat on the *pyol* watching the street. The vendor of sweets with a tray-load on his head passed down the street, crying sonorously, 'Bombay *mittai*, Delhi Durbar *mittai*.' He made his appearance at the same hour in the evening to reach the school gate at closing time.

Nagaraj reflected on the sweet vendor, who probably made the sweets in one of those huts in a slum at the end of Kabir Street on what was once open ground. Where was the need for slums in Malgudi? He was not able to find an answer. He must ask Zachariah (the only creature on earth apart from the zebra using a 'Z', an otherwise neglected and useless letter of the alphabet) who taught at St Joseph's and who read many newspapers and was well informed.

Why go so far? There was the Talkative Man living in the first house in their row. He saw him emerge from his home pushing out his bicycle. Nagaraj was about to hail him but changed his mind. If T. M. was asked one question he would invent ten other questions and grab his attention for hours.

Nagaraj looked away from T. M. and tried to resume his reflections on the sweet vendor but lost the thread of his thoughts. Sita brought him a tumbler of coffee.

'Oh, I'd have come in myself,' he said.

'The boys are rehearsing, and I thought…' she said.

Kabir Street

He paused to listen to the players. A gruff voice was saying, 'Summon the executioner.'

'No, Your Majesty...the woman must be spared...'

At this a female voice pleaded, 'I am a helpless woman...'

Nagaraj drank his coffee in one gulp and, wiping his lips with the towel on his shoulder, cried, 'A female voice! Is it mimicry or a eunuch in their midst?'

'They must have a real girl—Saroja's friend. Tim brought her in two days ago for a role. She is talented and will go far.'

Nagaraj returned the brass tumbler. He felt disturbed. A girl in the midst of this riff-raff! He must tell Tim bluntly to put an end to this nonsense. He rehearsed his speech: 'Tim, kick out your friends. I did not bring you here for this sort of thing. When I am provoked, you will find me a different man and tremble. Take care! Don't push me too far. I don't want to speak bitter words which I may regret later...'

If Tim should turn round and ask, 'What is wrong with us?' he must have a ready answer. Burning words that would prove a turning point in his career. It was, however, difficult to corner Tim who was always going out or coming in with his gang. But if he was available, Sita must be out of earshot. She was a contradicting type. Hence he must compose his talk suitably.

Probably the best course for him would be to say, 'Sita, don't you think Tim is developing marvellously? He reminds me of Shakespeare, who brought home actors and displeased his father. I've heard all about it from Zachariah who has visited Shakespeare's birthplace.'

This sentence ought to draw out a contradiction. She should say, 'I don't know. Only thing I want is that Tim should be handled properly. He must do useful things or go back to his father with Saroja and her harmonium. I won't have him here.'

'What about the girl who has come with the group?'

'She must be thrown out along with the rest.'

107

This imaginary conversation ended abruptly when Sita moved in softly and asked, 'Are you talking to yourself?'

Nagaraj simpered and explained, 'I was repeating, "*Om Namasivaya*," as I always do when alone.'

'Excellent habit. But I did not notice it all these days.'

'How could you? I repeat the mantra mentally and meditate.'

'It will do you good,' she said and left him.

He continued his meditation on the subject of Tim. 'It is better I put it all down in writing. Talk to him and also hand him a document, that'll work.'

He got up, went in to pick up pen and paper, and resumed his seat on the *pyol* with a notebook on his lap. 'Hey Tim,' he wrote. 'This won't do. I didn't bring you down here to make our home a retreat for loafers and now a girl in addition! What sort of girl is she? You are a married man with a wife and her harmonium, which I have tolerated long enough. Now this is too much. If you don't kick out that girl and the gang immediately, I'll talk to your father.'

At this point he paused to speculate on what his brother, Tim's father, would say. Was he likely to respond with: 'I'm happy you have brought it to my notice. Thrash him and throw him out. I'll also give him the same treatment when he comes here. God bless you for your forethought'?

Sita came out, threw a brief glance at him and his notebook and went down the steps. The girl's voice rang out again, 'I'm a woman. Have mercy.' And another voice over it, 'Say "I am a woman" louder. Don't swallow the last words.'

Nagaraj resumed his letter to Tim: 'If I see your friends again, I'll call the police. I'll tell Coomar, who is chummy with the police chief, who will send policemen with batons to beat up your gang and lock them in a cell...and if they include you, I won't come to your rescue. Poor Saroja. Her father must come down and take her away.'

Kabir Street

The last proved prophetic. The following week a letter arrived from Trichy. Saroja's father had written, 'Is it true? Saroja is complaining that her fingers ache playing the harmonium to a set of rowdies Tim brings home. He has become indifferent to her welfare and is paying attention to some adventuress. What are you doing about it? You must check him. Otherwise I am preparing to bring Saroja home, which is better than tolerating a vagabond of a son-in-law. What are you going to do about it? I must know immediately. I am sending a copy of this letter to Tim's father, Gopu. As a father, he must show some responsibility...'

Luckily, Sita had gone out to meet her friend as usual. She was not the sort to stay at home in the afternoon. Nagaraj felt thankful for this habit of hers. He was home when the letter came and he would hide it from her. Why? No. Better that she understood Tim, her great favourite. But the prospect of Saroja going away saddened him. He liked her to be around, but without her harmonium. It was a good sign that she was complaining of aching fingers. She probably needed some outlet for her artistic aspirations, but why not take to painting or writing poetry, activities performed in dead silence and never a nuisance to others?

Saroja's father would expect a reply. He dare not write one without discussing the subject with Sita. But she need not be told. He quietly carried the letter to the backyard, tore it to bits and dropped them into the well, then walked to the post office at the market gate and sent off a telegram to the gentleman in Trichy. It was more expensive than a postcard, but then you didn't have to go through the pains of composition. 'Am watchful. Pray let's not force the pace.' He had come across the phrase in a news-sheet the Talkative Man had shown him a couple of days earlier. He had no idea what it meant, but it sounded profound, and also sounded like 'forceps'—he was reminded of a cousin in Kumbam who was known as 'Forceps Kuppu' since he was a forceps-delivery case. But that family was out of touch. He felt sad for a moment over how one's kith and kin could become scattered and vanish like a spray of water.

While Nagaraj was going to his seat on the *pyol*, Tim arrived with four of his mob, all talking loudly. Their dress was offensive—coloured pants, flowery shorts, lungis, long hair, shaven pates, beards, quite an assortment.

Tim himself was unshaven, crowned with an untended, wild crop. He came in like an invader, and his mob rushed in and blocked the kitchen doorway, chattering away simultaneously:

'The story of *Harischandra* is popular…'

'We must start with a popular subject…'

'What about costumes?'

'I know a fellow who will give us costumes on hire…'

At this moment, Tim shouted, 'Auntie, can you give us coffee?'

Before she could answer, another demanded, 'Tea for me.'

'Lemonade for me,' said a third.

Sita explained over the babble, 'Tim has started a theatre group.'

Nagaraj ignored her information, shut his eyes and ruminated, 'Am I or am I not the head of this family? Nobody cares for me.' He felt an aversion to this crowd and self-pity for being isolated.

His wife tolerated and admired the scamp with his harmonium-playing wife and drama crowd. Sita's smugness angered Nagaraj. It seemed as if he had no place in the scheme of things. Best thing for him would be to get away—like the Buddha, without a word to anyone, carrying nothing except his soul.

The next day he went through his daily routine quietly. Ate and dressed in his usual manner, took leave of Sita while she was still in the kitchen, 'I am off; bolt the door.' He went through the daily exercises with precision, but only up to a point—till he reached Market Road. There, instead of going straight on to Margosa Avenue to his seat at Coomar's to write accounts, he turned to his right and found himself in the Town Hall park, where he sought a bench away from the habitual loungers to brood in peace over his life.

Looking round he found a hermit-like figure under a banyan tree, with beads around his neck, clad in ochre and vermilion with sacred ash splashed across his forehead. Wondering if it could be the same swami he had met long ago, Nagaraj got up and paced up and down, throwing quick side glances at the swami to make out whether he was the old one or another.

Difficult job distinguishing one swami from another—they looked alike, like soldiers in an army. 'A swami lost in meditation will not notice me,' he said to himself.

But on his tenth trip, the swami called out, 'Hey, what makes you perambulate in this manner? Have you no better business?'

Nagaraj felt overwhelmed and suppressed the question, 'Are you the old swamiji or a different one?' but he halted his steps and made a deep obeisance.

The ascetic commanded, 'Be bold, come here and sit down.' Nagaraj sat down immediately facing the swami. The swami roared out a second command, 'Move to the side! Have you not noticed the worshippers line up on two sides? Never stand plumb straight in front of God. Do you know why?'

Nagaraj remained dumb, reflecting, 'It is my fate to blink like a schoolboy wherever I go,' as he hurried out of the straight line. He wanted to have his say in the matter, 'The rule applies only to the God in a shrine. You are only a swami,' but left it unsaid, debating within himself whether he should not get up and run away.

The swami explained, 'If you sit in the direct vision of God, you will get scorched.' Then he said, 'Ask any question that may be troubling your mind.'

While Nagaraj was considering this offer, the swami suddenly asked, 'Do you know who you are?' While Nagaraj was trying to frame a proper answer, wondering if his name and address would be sufficient and regretting that he had been postponing the printing of a visiting card, the swami said, 'Don't answer now. Brush aside all other thoughts and concentrate on, "Who am I?" and see me again in fifteen days with whatever answer you get. Now go.'

'Will your holiness still be here?'

'No.'

Nagaraj felt bewildered but relieved, prostrated hurriedly, scrambled to his feet and left in a state of confusion.

Unsteady People
Ian Jack

(1989)

On August 6 last year a launch overturned in the River Ganges near Manihari Ghat, a remote ferry station in the Indian state of Bihar. Many people drowned, though precisely how many will never be known. The district magistrate estimated the number of dead at around 400, the launch-owner at fourteen. The first estimate was reached by subtraction: 529 tickets had been sold and only a hundred passengers had swum ashore. The second estimate came from the number of bodies the launch-owner said he had counted stretched out on the bank. But then the river was in flood; hundreds of bodies could have been swept far downstream; scores may still be entangled in the wreckage or buried in the silt. The launch-owner had good reason to lie.

It was, in its causes and consequences, an accident which typified the hazards of navigating the River Ganges. Monsoon rains had swollen the river and changed its hydrography, cutting new channels and raising new shoals. The launch was overcrowded. Licensed to carry 160, it seems to have set out with at least three times that number, nearly all of whom were fervent Hindu pilgrims travelling from their villages in north Bihar to a shrine which lies south of the river. Devotees of Lord Shiva, the destroyer, they wore saffron robes and carried pots of sacred Ganges water on their shoulders. Eyewitnesses said the launch left the north bank to the chanting of Shiva's name, the chorus '*bol bam*' rising from the massed saffron on the upper deck; until, hardly a hundred metres from the shore, the chants turned into screams.

According to a survivor quoted in the Calcutta newspapers, what happened was this. As the launch moved off, its stern got stuck in the shallows near the bank. The skipper decided to redistribute his vessel's weight, to lighten the stern by weighing down the bow. He asked his passengers to move forward; the stern bobbed up and the launch surged forward, head down and listing badly, to run a few hundred feet into a submerged sandbank and capsize.

In Bihar a revengeful clamour arose which sought to identify the guilty and exact punishment. The Bihar government and its the police. According to Ajit Kumar Sarkar, a Marxist member of the Bihar Legislative Assembly, the launch took six hours to sink, and many victims could have been saved had not the police beaten back agitated crowds of would-be rescuers on the shore. According to the police, corruption had made their job impossible; almost every Ganges ferry flouted safety legislation because the ferry-owners organized 'gangs to protect their interest'. Bihar had a 'steamer mafia' whose profits had perverted the political administration. Chief among this mafia was Mr Bachcha Singh, the 'steamer tycoon of Bihar' and owner of the launch that had gone down at Manihari Ghat.

Some days after the accident another of Mr Singh's vessels approached the wreck, ostensibly with the task of dragging it off the sandbank and on to the shore. Watchers on the bank, however, saw something different. They saw the second vessel pressing down on the wreckage of the first. It seemed to them that the other ship had come to bury the launch and not to raise it, thus destroying the evidence and, in the words of the *Calcutta Telegraph*, 'obscuring the gravity of the tragedy'. In the face of public protest the second ship backed off.

Where, meanwhile, was the steamer tycoon, Mr Bachcha Singh? Nobody could say. The Chief Minister of Bihar promised 'stern action', charges of murder and negligence were registered in the courts and some of Mr Singh's property was seized. But the police said they could not find Singh himself. He was, in the English of official India, 'absconding' and so the courts declared him an 'absconder'.

Thereafter public interest evaporated with the monsoon rains. Manihari Ghat became just another Ganges launch disaster. The people who had died were poor. None had relatives influential enough to secure the lasting attention of the press or the government, both of which in any case were soon preoccupied with other problems.

What was the precise truth of the affair? Nobody could say. Truth in its least elevated and most humble sense, truth as detail, truth as times and numbers, truth arrived at by observation and deduction—this kind of truth left the scene early. Like Mr Singh, it absconded. Unlike Mr Singh, it did not reappear.

Six months later I met the steamer tycoon at his house in Patna, the state capital. To European eyes, the house looked like something a Nazi cineaste might have built. It had the smooth curves of a pre-war suburban Odeon and a large tower with two large swastikas etched high up in the concrete; they were visible from my cycle rickshaw long before the mansion itself swung into view. Mr Singh had called it 'Swastika House'—the name was on the gate—but only because he was a devout Hindu and the swastika is an ancient Hindu symbol of good fortune.

Fortune had been good to Mr Singh. It was manifest in his living arrangements, the dozens of domestic servants, his house's fifty bedrooms and thirty bathrooms, the superior quality of his tipped cigarettes. All of this (and a good deal else—apartments in Calcutta, real estate in the USA) derived from Mr Singh's role as the Ganges' principal ferryman. But his person as opposed to his surroundings seemed untouched by wealth. He was a small old man with heart trouble who wore loose Indian clothes and tapped ash from his Gold Flake King Size into an old spittoon.

We sat on his terrace and drank tea from mugs. I wondered about the murder charge. What had happened to it?

Nothing, said Singh, the case would never come to court. Did I understand the caste system? In Bihar caste was the key to everything. The murder charge had been instigated by the then Chief Minister, who was a Brahmin. Singh belonged to the Rajput caste, and Rajputs were the Brahmins' greatest political rivals. The charge had been politically inspired.

And now?

'Now the Chief Minister is a Rajput. He is known to me. Case finish.'

He apologized for his English and called for his son, who, he said, would be more intelligible to me. This proved to be only partly true. The younger Singh was reading Business Administration at Princeton University, ferry profits having dispatched him to the United States when he was an infant, and his English crackled with the abrasive nouns of the new capitalism. 'Cash-burn...acquisition and diversification...buy-out.' It was strange to hear these words in Bihar, still governed by ancestry and feudal law, but they completely matched the younger Singh's appearance. In T-shirt, shorts and sneakers, he might have stepped out of a college tennis game. The sight of son next to father, crouched beside his spittoon, was a testament to the transforming power of money.

The father had recalled his son to Patna soon after what both referred to, opaquely, as 'the tragedy'. The son looked at his new surroundings with cold eyes. Corruption, poverty, ignorance, tradition—they ruled life here. It was sickening. Outside the family, nobody could be trusted. Did I know, for example, that after the tragedy peasants from adjacent villages had brought newly-dead relatives to the river, so that their bodies could be discreetly inserted among the launch's victims and compensation claimed?

I hadn't heard that, but maybe it was true; Bihar can sometimes be a desperate place. But what did he think had caused the accident?

'Panic and stupidity,' said the younger Singh. He thought for a moment. 'Basically these people weren't willing to make the smart move and analyse the situation.'

Of course these were ludicrous words; passengers packed on a tilting motor launch cannot be expected to plan their next five minutes like Wall Street commodity brokers. But the longer I travelled through Bihar, squashed on trains and river boats, the more I recognized the younger Singh's detachment as an indigenous sentiment rather than an American import.

Certain facts about Bihar were undeniable. The launch-owners were greedy and their craft decrepit and dangerous; the police were corrupt and tended to enforce the law of the highest bidder—the younger Singh said himself that his family had put off police inquiries with a few thousand rupees; and covert supplies of money moved through the system at every level—an honest police-officer could have his orders countermanded by a corrupt district administrator, an honest district administrator could be transferred or demoted by a corrupt politician. To behave dutifully and honestly in this amoral environment involved great courage and sacrifice. It was no surprise that the safety of the travelling public, especially a public so lacking in clout, did not figure highly in the minds of their appointed guardians.

My fellow-travellers would talk quite frankly about all this—humbug is not a Bihari vice—but then they also echoed the younger Singh: people in Bihar, they would say, did not know how to behave. They were 'uneducated' and 'ignorant' and, most of all, 'backward'. The populations of western democracies hesitate—still—to describe their fellow-citizens so bluntly, at least in public. But Biharis have no such inhibitions. The ancient social pyramid of caste enables those at the top to look down at those below with a dispassionate prejudice, at an inferior form of human life.

'I'm afraid we are not a *steady* people,' an old man said to me one day, and I could see exactly what he meant. Often the unsteadiness was frightening. The resources of transportation are scarce all over India; there is a continual press and scramble for tickets and seats wherever you go. But young Biharis travel on the roofs of trains even when the compartments below are empty and rush listing ferries like a piratical horde. Even the old and lame press forward as though fleeing some imminent disaster.

Unsteady People

Towards the end of my journey in Bihar I met another Singh, a relative of the steamer tycoon, who operated a couple of old steamboats just upriver from Manihari Ghat. In an interval between crossings he took me up on to the bridge of his ferry, which was berthed at the foot of a steep bank, glistening and slippery with unseasonal rain. At the top of the slope men with staves, Singh's employees, were restraining a crowd of waiting passengers. Then the steamer's whistle gave two hoots; the men with staves relented; and the crowd, with its bicycles and milk-churns, came rushing down the bank towards us, slithering and whooping.

Singh looked down at his customers as they milled across the gangplank and then laughed like a man in a zoo. 'Crazy people. What can you do with them?'

On 15 April this year ninety-five people were crushed to death on the terraces of a football stadium in Sheffield, northern England. Most of the dead came from Liverpool, and all of them were supporters of Liverpool football club, who that day were to play Nottingham Forest in the semi-final of English football's premier knock-out competition, the Football Association Cup. The deaths came six minutes after the kick-off. The match was then abandoned.

I read about the disaster in Delhi on my way back to London. Newspaper reports speculated on the possible causes and recalled that the behaviour of Liverpool fans had prompted the crush which killed thirty-nine people at the European Cup Final in Brussels in 1985, all of them Italian supporters of the other finalists, Juventus of Turin. It seemed something similar had happened in Sheffield. Liverpool fans had swept into the ground and pressed their fellow-supporters forward until they were squashed against the barriers and fences which had been erected some years before to prevent unruly spectators rushing on to the pitch and interfering with the game.

119

All that winter in India I'd heard about death in Britain. Planes fell to earth and trains left the rails, and Mrs Thatcher's face appeared on Indian television talking of her sympathy and concern. There were shots of disintegrated fuselages, body bags, shattered railway coaches. Indian friends tutted at the carnage, and I recognized in their reaction the momentary interest—the shake of the head, the small ripple of fascination—that passes through a British living-room when news of some distant tragedy flits before it; say, of the last typhoon to strike Bengal.

Meanwhile, the India I saw reported every day on the news—orderly, calm, soporific—looked more and more like the country I came from—or at least as I had once thought of it. Accidents such as Manihari Ghat were certainly reported, but rarely filmed. We watched the prime minister greeting foreign delegations at the airport, men in good suits addressing seminars and shaking hands, women cutting tapes and accepting bouquets. Indian news, or what India's government-controlled television judged to be news, took place indoors in an atmosphere notably free of dust, flies and mess. There was a lot of cricket. The mess—grief and ripped metal under arc lights—came from abroad, imported by satellite and shiny film-cans—they were like luxury items, a new spice trade going the other way—which the makers of Indian bulletins slotted in between the hand-shaking and the seminars as if to prove that disaster could overtake the foreign rich as well as the native poor, and that it was not confined to terrorism in the Punjab or the chemical catastrophe at Bhopal.

There were two train crashes in the southern suburbs of London (forty dead); a Pan Am Jumbo which exploded over Lockerbie (270 dead); a Boeing forced to crash-land on a motorway (forty-seven dead). All of them had specific and identifiable causes—a bomb, signal failure, faulty engines—though the roots (what caused the cause?) led to a vaguer territory: under-investment in public utilities, 'international terrorism', the collapse of civic feeling under a political leader who has said she cannot grasp the idea of community. This kind of worry—the cause of the cause—had bobbed to the surface of British life like old wreckage ever since the Channel ferry *Herald of Free Enterprise* turned over at Zeebrugge in 1987, the first in a series of large accidents which has marked Britain out as a literally disastrous country. But from the distance of India, Sheffield looked different. It seemed to turn on the behaviour of a fervent crowd; there was, in that sense, something very Indian about it.

When my landlord in Delhi said he thought football in England must have assumed 'a religious dimension', it was difficult to resist the parallel: saffron pilgrims struggling to board their launch at Manihari Ghat, the mass of Liverpudlian red and white which surged into the stadium at Sheffield. And the parallels did not end there. In fact the nearer I got to home the closer they became.

Changing planes in Paris, I bought a newspaper and read about M. Jacques Georges, the French president of the European Football Association. An interviewer on French radio had asked M. Georges if he thought Liverpool was peculiar in some way, given its football club's recent history of violent disaster. Well, said Georges, Liverpool certainly seemed to have 'a particularly aggressive mentality'. The crowd that had stormed into the ground at Sheffield had scorned all human feeling. 'I have the impression—I am distressed to use the expression—but it was like beasts who wanted to charge into an arena.'

The English are not a steady people. Today all Europe knows that. None the less M. Georges's words had scandalized England. At Heathrow the papers were full of him, even though he had said little more than the Sheffield police. According to Mr Paul Middup, chairman of the South Yorkshire Police Federation, there was 'mass drunkenness' among the 3,000 Liverpool supporters, who turned up at the turnstiles shortly before the kick-off: 'some of them were uncontrollable. A great number of them had obviously been drinking heavily.' According to Mr Irvine Patrick, a Sheffield MP, the police had been 'hampered, harassed, punched, kicked and urinated on.'

But then the police themselves had behaved ineptly. Seeking to relieve the crush outside the stadium, they had opened a gate and sent an excited crowd—drunks, beasts or otherwise—into a section of the terracing which was already filled to capacity. And then, for some minutes at least, they had watched the crowd's desperate attempt to escape over the fences and mistaken it for hooliganism. They had hardly made a smart move and analysed the situation.

It would have all been familiar to any citizen of Bihar. An underclass which, in the view of the overclass, did not know how to behave. 'Drunks…beasts…uneducated…ignorant.' An antique and ill-designed public facility. A police force which made serious mistakes. Clamorous cross-currents of blame.

At home, I watched television. The disaster excited the medium. For several days it replayed the scene at Sheffield and then moved on to Liverpool, where the football ground was carpeted with wreaths. Funeral services were recorded, football players vowed that they might never play again and political leaders in Liverpool demanded the presence in their city of royalty—a prince, a duke— so that the scale of the 'national tragedy' might be acknowledged. When members of Liverpool's rival team turned up at a burial, the commentator spoke reverently of how the disaster had 'united football', as though the French and Germans in Flanders had stopped bombardment for a day to bury their dead. One football official said he hoped that ninety-five people had not 'died in vain'. Another said that they had 'died for football'.

Nobody in Bihar would have suggested that the dead of Manihari Ghat had made such a noble sacrifice. Nobody would have said: 'They died to expunge corruption, caste and poverty.' Whatever their other faults, Biharis are not a self-deluding people.

What Bengali Widows Cannot Eat

Chitrita Banerji

(1995)

My father died at the beginning of a particularly radiant and colourful spring. Spring in Bengal is teasing and elusive, secret yet palpable, waiting to be discovered. The crimson and scarlet of *palash* and *shimul* flowers post the season's banners on high trees. Compared to the scented flowers of the summer and monsoon—jasmine, *beli*, *chameli*, *kamini*, gardenias, all of which are white—these scentless spring flowers are utterly assertive with the one asset they have: colour. My father, who was a retiring, unassuming man, took great pleasure in their flaunting, shameless reds. When I arrived in Calcutta for his funeral, I was comforted by the sight of flowers in full bloom along the road from the airport.

That first evening back home, my mother and I sat out on our roof, talking. As darkness obscured all colours, the breeze became gusty, laden with unsettling scents from out-of-season potted flowers on neighbouring roofs.

My mother had always been dynamic, forceful, efficient: the family's principal breadwinner for nearly thirty years, she had risen above personal anxiety and ignored social disapproval to allow me, alone, young and unmarried, to pursue my studies in the United States. Yet overnight, she had been transformed into the archetypal Bengali widow—meek, faltering, hollow-cheeked, sunken-eyed, the woman in white from whose life all colour and pleasure must evaporate.

During the thirteen days of mourning that precede the Hindu rituals of *shraddha* (last rites) and the subsequent *niyambhanga* (literally, the breaking of rules), all members of the bereaved family live ascetically on one main meal a day of rice and vegetables cooked together in an earthen pot with no spices except sea salt, and no oil, only a touch of ghee. The sanction against oil embraces its cosmetic use too, and for me, the roughness of my mother's parched skin and hair made her colourless appearance excruciating. But what disturbed me most was the eagerness with which she seemed to be embracing the trappings of bereavement. Under the curious, observant and critical eyes of female relatives, neighbours and visitors, she appeared to be mortifying her flesh almost joyfully, as if those thirteen days were a preparation for the future. As if it is utterly logical for a woman to lose her self and plunge into a life of ritual suffering once her husband is dead.

Hindu tradition in Bengal holds that the widow must strive for purity through deprivation. In contrast with the bride, who is dressed in red and, if her family's means permit, decked out in gold jewellery, the widow, regardless of her wealth and status, is drained of colour. Immediately after her husband's death, other women wash the *sindur*, a vermilion powder announcing married status, from the parting in the widow's hair. All jewellery is removed, and she exchanges her coloured or patterned sari for the permanent, unvarying uniform of the *thaan*, borderless yards of blank white cotton. Thus transformed, she remains, for the rest of her life, the pallid symbol of misfortune, the ghostly twin of the western bride, dressed in virginal white, drifting down the aisle towards happiness.

As recently as fifty years ago, widows were also forced to shave their heads as part of a socially prescribed move towards androgyny. Both of my grandfather's sisters were widowed in their twenties: my childhood memories of them are of two nearly identical creatures wrapped in shroud-like white who emerged from their village a couple of times a year and came to visit us in the city. Whenever the *thaan* covering their heads slipped, I would be overcome with an urge to rub my hands over their prickly scalps that resembled the spherical, yellow, white-bristled flowers of the *kadam* tree in our garden.

Until the Hindu Widow Remarriage Act was passed in 1856, widows were forbidden to marry for a second time. But for more than a hundred years after the act became law, it did not translate into any kind of widespread social reality (unlike the 1829 edict abolishing the burning of widows on the same pyre as their dead husbands—the infamous practice of suttee). Rural Bengali households were full of widows who were no more than children, because barely pubescent girls often found themselves married to men old enough to be their fathers.

It was not until the morning before the actual *shraddha* ceremony that I was forced to confront the cruellest of the rules imposed on the widow by the Sanskrit *shastra*s, the body of rules and rituals of Hindu life to which have been added innumerable folk beliefs. One of my aunts took me aside and asked if my mother had made up her mind to give up eating fish and meat— *amish*, non-vegetarian food, forbidden for widows. With a sinking heart, I realized that the image of the widow had taken such a hold of my mother that she was only too likely to embrace a vegetarian diet—all the more so because she had always loved fish and had been renowned for the way she cooked it. If I said nothing, she would never again touch those wonders of the Bengali kitchen—*shorshe-ilish, maacher jhol, galda chingrir malaikari, lau-chingri, doi-maach, maacher kalia*. It was an unbearable thought.

The vegetarian stricture is not considered a hardship in most regions of India where the majority, particularly the Brahmins and some of the upper castes, have always been vegetarians. But Bengal is blessed with innumerable rivers criss-crossing a fertile delta, and it is famed for its rice and its fish. Even Brahmins have lapsed in Bengal by giving in to the regional taste for fish, which plays a central part in both the diet and the culinary imagination of the country. Fish, in its ubiquity, symbolism and variety, becomes, for the Bengali widow, the finest instrument of torture.

Several other items are forbidden to widows simply because

What Bengali Widows Cannot Eat

of their associations with *amish*. *Puishak*, for instance, a spinach-like leafy green often cooked with small shrimps or the fried head of a *hilsa* fish, is disallowed. So are onion and garlic, which were eschewed by most Hindus until the last century because of their association with meat-loving Muslims. They are further supposed to have lust-inducing properties, making them doubly unsuitable for widows. Lentils, a good source of protein in the absence of meat, are also taboo—a stricture which might stem from the widespread practice of spicing them with chopped onion.

Social historians have speculated that these dietary restrictions served a more sinister and worldly function than simply that of moving a widow towards a state of purity: they would also lead to malnutrition, thus reducing her lifespan. A widow often has property, and her death would inevitably benefit *someone*—her sons, her siblings, her husband's family. And in the case of a young widow, the sooner she could be dispatched to the next world, the less the risk of any moral transgression and ensuing scandal.

My grandmother lived the last twenty-seven of her eighty-two years as a widow, obeying every stricture imposed by rules and custom. The memory of her bleak, pinched, white-robed widowhood intensified my determination to prevent my mother from embracing a similar fate. I particularly remember a scene from my early teens. I was the only child living with an extended family of parents, uncles and aunts—and my grandmother. It had been a punishingly hot and dry summer. During the day, the asphalt on the streets would melt, holding on to my sandals as I walked. Night brought sweat-drenched sleeplessness and the absorbing itchiness of prickly heat. Relief would come only with the eagerly awaited monsoon.

The rains came early one morning—dark, violent, lightning-streaked, fragrant and beautiful. The cook rushed to the market and came back with a big *hilsa* fish which was cut up and fried, the crispy, flavourful pieces served at lunchtime with *khichuri*, rice and dhal cooked together. This is the traditional way to celebrate the arrival of the monsoon. Though I knew my grandmother did not eat fish, I was amazed on this occasion to see that she did not touch either the *khichuri* or the battered slices of aubergine or the fried potatoes. These were vegetarian items, and I had seen her eat them before on other wet and chilly days. This time, she ate, in her usual solitary spot, *luchis*, a kind of fried bread, that looked stale, along with some equally unappetizing cold cooked vegetables.

Why? I asked in outrage. And my mother explained that this was because of a rare coincidence: the rains had arrived on the month of Asharh that, according to the almanac, marks the beginning of the rainy season. The ancients visualized this as the period of the earth's receptive fertility, when the summer sun vanishes, the skies open and mingle with the parched land to produce a red or brown fluid flow of earth and water, nature's manifestation of menstruating femininity. How right then for widows to suffer more than usual at such a time. They were not allowed to cook during the three-day period, and, although they were allowed to eat some foods that had been prepared in advance, boiled rice was absolutely forbidden. Since nature rarely conforms to the calculations of the almanac, I had never noticed these Ambubachi strictures being observed on the long-awaited rainy day.

The almanac was an absolute necessity for conforming to the standards of ritual purity, and my grandmother consulted it assiduously. On the day before Ambubachi started, she would prepare enough *luchis* and vegetables for three midday meals. Sweet yogurt and fruit, mixed with *chira*—dried, flattened rice— were also permissible. That first night of monsoon, newly aware of the sanctions of Ambubachi, I went to look for my

What Bengali Widows Cannot Eat

grandmother around dinner time. All she ate was a small portion of *kheer*, milk that had been boiled down to nearly solid proportions, and some pieces of mango. I had hoped she would at least be permitted one of her favourite evening meals—warm milk mixed with crushed mango pulp. But no. Milk cannot be heated, for the widow's food must not receive the touch of fire during Ambubachi. The *kheer*, a traditional way of preserving milk, had been prepared for her the day before.

It is true that despite deprivations, household drudgery and the imposition of many fasts, widows sometimes live to a great age, and the gifted cooks among them have contributed greatly to the range, originality and subtlety of Hindu vegetarian cooking in Bengal. A nineteenth-century food writer once said that it was impossible to taste the full glory of vegetarian food unless your own wife became a widow. And Bengali literature is full of references to elderly widows whose magic touch can transform subtlety with spices cannot be reproduced by other hands.

But however glorious these concoctions, no married woman envies the widow's fate. And, until recently, most widows remained imprisoned within the austere bounds of their imposed diets. Even if they were consumed with temptation or resentment, fear of discovery and public censure were enough to inhibit them.

I knew the power of public opinion as I watched my mother during the day of the *shraddha*. My aunt, who had been widowed when fairly young, had been bold enough, with the encouragement of her three daughters, to continue eating fish. But I knew that my mother and many of her cronies would find it far less acceptable for a woman in her seventies not to give up *amish* in her widowhood. As one who lived abroad, in America, I also knew that my opinion was unlikely to carry much weight. But I was determined that she should not be deprived of fish, and with the support of my aunt and cousins I prepared to fight.

The crucial day of the *niyambhanga*, the third day after the *shraddha*, came. On this day, members of the bereaved family invite all their relatives to lunch, and an elaborate meal is served, representing the transition between the austerity of mourning and normal life—for everyone except the widow. Since we wanted to invite many people who were not relatives, we arranged to have two catered meals, lunch and dinner, the latter for friends and neighbours. My mother seemed to recover some of her former energy that day, supervising everything with efficiency, attending to all the guests. But she hardly touched any food. After the last guest had left, and the caterers had packed up their equipment, leaving enough food to last us for two or three days, I asked her to sit down and eat dinner with me. For the first time since my father's death, the two of us were absolutely alone in the house. I told her I would serve the food; I would be the grown-up now.

She smiled and sat down at the table. I helped her to rice and dhal, then to two of the vegetable dishes. She held up her hand then. No more. I was not to go on to the fish. Silently, we ate. She asked for a little more rice and vegetables. I complied, then lifted a piece of *rui* fish and held it over her plate. Utter panic filled her eyes, and she shot anxious glances around the room. She told me, vehemently, to eat the fish myself.

It was that panic-stricken look around her own house, where she was alone with me, her daughter, that filled me with rage. I was determined to vanquish the oppressive force of ancient belief, reinforced by whatever model of virtue she had inherited from my grandmother. We argued for what seemed like hours, my voice rising, she asking me to be quiet for fear of the neighbours, until finally I declared that I would never touch any *amish* myself as long as she refused to eat fish. The mother who could not bear the thought of her child's deprivation eventually prevailed, though the woman still quaked with fear of sin and retribution.

What Bengali Widows Cannot Eat

I have won a small victory, but I have lost the bigger battle. My mother's enjoyment of food, particularly of fish, as well as her joyful exuberance in the kitchen where her labours produced such memorable creations, have vanished. Sometimes, as I sit and look at her, I see a procession of silent women in white going back through the centuries. They live as household drudges, slaves in the kitchen and the field; they are ostracized even in their own homes during weddings or other happy ceremonies—their very presence considered an invitation to misfortune.

In the dim corners they inhabit, they try to contain their hunger. Several times a year, they fast and pray and prepare spreads for priests and Brahmins, all in the hope of escaping widowhood in the next life. On the eleventh day of each moon, they deny themselves food and water and shed tears over their blameful fate, while women with husbands make a joyous ritual out of eating rice and fish. Their anguish and anger secreted in the resinous chamber of fear, these white-clad women make their wasteful progress towards death.

Jihadis
Pankaj Mishra

(2002)

Peshawar is a mess. And last winter—the winter before September 11 became a significant date, before the word 'Taliban' became part of the ordinary American vocabulary, when Osama Bin Laden, once resident in the city, was still merely infamous—it seemed at its worst. The smog above the city trapped the acrid smoke from the burning tyres that the Afghan refugees huddled around for warmth; Pakistani traffic policemen wearing new-looking gas masks flailed helplessly in the slow swirl of donkey carts, trucks, auto rickshaws and cars; and even the brighter carpets in the old bazaar blended into the greyness. I began to wonder, somewhat resentfully, if the romance of Peshawar, last renewed during the anti-communist jihad a decade before, had been an invention of jaded adventurers from the West, the predecessors of the eager white men and women I occasionally saw walking in the narrow alleys of the old quarters: visitors in the first flush of their enchantment with the Orient, for whom even the heroin addicts slumped on broken pavements could blend easily into the general quaintness of the East.

I felt oppressed by the city. Its shapeless squalor as well as its new aspirations to respectability reminded me too much of the small-town India of my childhood. Relief, along with proportion and order, seemed to lie only in the British-created cantonment, the military quarter: in the low red-tiled bungalows and whitewashed trees and brick-lined flower beds and the lone guard standing stiff before smoothly gravelled driveways. It was where I often found myself during the long evenings—browsing through the boldly pirated American and British paperbacks at Saeed Book Bank and visiting newspaper offices in Saddar Bazaar.

I was always nervous while visiting the cantonment. My visa for Pakistan said, NOT VALID FOR CANTT AREAS. I wasn't sure what this meant since Cantt areas in the cities of the subcontinent are impossible to avoid. I was expected to stay away from 'sensitive military installations', but since I didn't know what these were I had to play it safe. I never turned my head sideways when my rickshaw passed the grander-looking buildings, never made it apparent that I was curious about anything except the dreary progression of the well-paved road, and the proud replicas of new Pakistani missiles mounted on traffic islands—the missiles named provocatively after the Muslim conquerors of India.

This timidity was partly created by the three men in a beat-up Toyota who followed me every time I left my hotel. They would have been representatives of one or all of the three major intelligence agencies in Pakistan. Their interest in me seemed exaggerated: a reflex from the days of the spy-infested jihad. It would have mortified the very amiable Pakistani diplomats in New Delhi who arranged for my visa and gave me, an Indian writer, what I learned later was an unprecedented liberty of travel within Pakistan. But then to be an Indian in Pakistan—or, for that matter, a Pakistani in India—is to be trapped by the prickly nationalisms of the two neighbouring countries; it is to be automatically suspect.

Not that the spies did anything, or even looked, particularly ominous. The most visible among them, a plump, rosy-cheeked man in a pink salwar kurta, could have been one of the shopkeepers idle behind the open sackfuls of dry fruits in the narrow dark rooms of the old bazaar.

Still, if you are not used to being followed and watched, it can get stifling. The world seems full of a vague menace, the friendly, rather camp bellboy with slicked-down hair that you think you have tipped generously turns into an ungrateful informer, and the most variegated and lively street scene begins to look like an elaborate preparation for an arrest.

Paranoia was what the spies embodied and conveyed to me. But there was a deeper unease I felt throughout the first three weeks I spent in Pakistan, waiting to go to Afghanistan. It was an unease about Islam and Muslims I had so far attributed to others: something I sensed, while living in London, in the reports and outraged editorials (a few, even then) in the British and American press about the Taliban and Osama Bin Laden and other Islamic extremists, and to which I thought I could only be immune after my experience of Kashmir.

About 50,000 people—militants, soldiers and civilians—have been killed in the uprising that the Muslims of the Kashmir valley began against Indian rule in 1990. The Indian press prefers to describe the situation in the valley as a spillover from the jihad in Afghanistan, the timid Kashmiris having been overwhelmed by Pakistani and Afghan terrorists looking to wage fresh holy wars. This broad picture, which depicted Pakistan and Islamic fundamentalists as the major villains, blurred and then dissolved altogether during the several weeks I spent in Kashmir last year. Most Kashmiris still follow an unorthodox Sufi version of Islam. The brutalities of the 400,000 Indian soldiers in the valley was, in my view, what had pushed a small number of young Kashmiri Muslims into the kind of jihadi extremism promoted by religious groups in Pakistan and created popular support for the increasingly large number of Pakistan-backed militants fighting the Indian army in Kashmir.

The articles I published subsequently in an American magazine described the stages through which India, a Hindu-majority, if officially secular, nation, had become, despite many good intentions, a repressive colonial power for the four million Muslims of the Kashmir valley. Soon after the articles came out, officials from the Indian IB (Intelligence Bureau) visited my retired parents in India and interrogated them at some length about my 'pro-Pakistan' proclivities (which would have been confirmed for them when the Pakistani High Commissioner in New Delhi praised my articles in print and then, not long afterwards, arranged my exceptionally generous visa for Pakistan). Indian

Jihadis

newspaper columnists denounced me as unpatriotic and, while wondering what would lead an apparently well-to-do upper-caste Hindu to betray his country in an American magazine, concluded that I was pandering to white pro-Muslim audiences in the West.

This was optimistic. You wouldn't have thought that such audiences existed, going by the little attention paid to Kashmir, or Chechnya—another place where Muslims led a popular but hopeless uprising against a powerful pro-West nation-state—in the British or American newspapers. Even the more detailed reports about Muslim terrorists turning up in the Philippines, Canada and Yemen barely mentioned, if at all, how the United States, during the Cold War, had helped establish the global network of Islamic militants that men like Osama Bin Laden now evidently controlled. Bereft of any recognizable context, the international news pages often seemed a kind of brisk atrocity-mongering. Islam in all its diversity appeared in them as little more than the West's 'other', in the same way communism had once been: the aggressive ideology of an unfree and dangerously deluded people.

I didn't expect that I would share this view of Islam and Muslims when I first thought, soon after returning from Kashmir, of travelling to Pakistan and Afghanistan. I wanted to find out more about the CIA-led jihad in the 1980s and the rise of the Taliban. I was curious about the much discussed, if always vaguely defined, conflict between Islam and the West. One evening in Srinagar, Kashmir, an old Muslim politician, routinely described as 'fundamentalist' in the Indian papers, had spoken to me of how the West feared Islam even more after the demise of communism because the religion, which a quarter of humanity followed, alone offered an alternative to the modern civilization of the West. It was hard for me then to work through such large generalizations. Later, when I began to read more Islamic history, it became clearer to me how quickly—in the past two hundred years, after several European centuries of cultural and technological backwardness—the West had caught up with the Islamic world, and then begun to subjugate it.

The India I had grown up in had also been radically and often traumatically reshaped by the great imperial power of the West, so I had some understanding of how people in demoralized societies could grow inflexible while trying to protect their older way of living. But in the case of Pakistan this understanding came from the books I read in London, before I had spent any time in a Muslim-majority country. In my first few days in Pakistan, I couldn't avoid feeling an almost atavistic fear of Islam and Muslims; and when, not long after I arrived there from London, Jamal in Peshawar said, 'They are all such fanatics here,' I immediately warmed towards him. For I had found myself silently nurturing this commonplace prejudice, although I wouldn't have wanted to articulate it myself. The sympathetic books I had read in London faded temporarily from my memory, and I forgot my high-minded suspicion of reporting in the Western press.

Jamal worked as a subeditor for *The Frontier Post*, one of Peshawar's English-language dailies. I got into the habit of dropping in to see him at his paper's offices, which were guarded at the reception desk by an old Pathan in a military coat, a Kalashnikov leaning against his wicker chair. Upstairs, low doors led to rooms lit by the dim screens of grimy computers. Delicate plumes of cigarette smoke hung in the air.

It was a difficult time for the newspaper. Its owner, a local Pathan businessman called Rahmat Shah Afridi, had been arrested in 1999 on a charge of drugs trading. His son, who ran the paper now, told me that the small amount of cannabis found in his father's Mercedes had been planted there by agents of Mian Nawaz Sharif, the then prime minister of Pakistan. It seemed like a typical Pakistani story of big men pursuing small private feuds and vendettas, and perhaps it wasn't entirely inaccurate: a few weeks after I left Pakistan, a special anti-narcotics court in Lahore sentenced Afridi to death. In any case, the smaller people were suffering: the staff had been working without salaries for three months.

But the shared austerity had made people jollier. The door to the room I usually sat in—really, a windowless box—opened every two minutes to reveal a new person with a joke, an anecdote, a filched cigarette, and a curious but friendly glance towards me, the visitor from India. A boy would regularly bring trays filled with chipped cups of milky tea which had been hastily poured. The cups were wet on the outside, and there were so many visitors that after three hours the dusty table glistened all over with small overlapping circles.

Jamal was as much of a cigarette-cadger and tea-drinker as anyone there. But he looked restless amid the bonhomie of his colleagues, and his face was alien to theirs—darker and blunter, not from this part of the world. I often felt his dull yellow eyes on me; there was, I sensed, something he wished to tell me in private, and when the moment came early one evening, it was this difference that he was keen to establish.

I hadn't been misled by his appearance. He was a Bengali, from Bangladesh, the country that had been East Pakistan until it came into being (with Indian help) as a separate nation in 1971. In 1975, as a young captain in the Bangladeshi army, he had taken part in the military coup against the government of Prime Minister Sheikh Mujibur Rahman. He had been present on the morning when Rahman and his family were gunned down at their official residence. 'An accident,' he said, 'we didn't mean to kill him.' Whether accidental or not, the moment was firmly in the past, part of Bangladesh's history. But Jamal had spent most of the quarter century since then dealing with the consequences.

He had spent four more years in Bangladesh, waging a futile insurgency against the government, before finally escaping to

Pakistan. There was no other choice: Pakistan, still bitter about its lost province, was the only country that wouldn't deport him straight back to Bangladesh where he was sure to be executed for Rahman's murder. He hadn't liked his new country one bit. He had arrived in Pakistan just as General Zia-ul-Haq was beginning his programme of Islamization; there was enough of the liberal Bengali, the reader of Tagore and Nazrul Islam, in him to be repelled by the brutal imposition of religion on everyday life. But he couldn't object too loudly; as a political refugee, he had to be grateful that he wasn't being hanged or shot. He managed as best he could, moving from job to job, city to city.

The story was refined and embellished over several evenings. I wasn't always sure how to respond to it, especially when he added that he felt he had a wonderful book inside him. But I didn't want to discourage or alienate him. He had known such a damaged life, only a kind of survival in Pakistan. And I felt he was on my side: a fellow stranger in Pakistan, adrift among the fanatics.

And Pakistan appeared, during my first days there, alarmingly filled with fanatics: there were the black-turbaned heavy-bearded leaders of the Taliban, arriving at their embassy in Islamabad in gleaming new Pajero cars; the retired general in Rawalpindi declaiming on the nobility of jihad; the crudely painted donation boxes for the jihad in Kashmir in the bazaars; the fundamentalist demagogues in small towns threatening to march upon Islamabad if sharia law and interest-free banking weren't immediately introduced; and the tribals in the so-called self-administering areas near the Afghan border cutting off hands in their attempts at proper Islamic justice. Almost every day, Sunnis murdered Shi'as and vice-versa, and a few young mujahideen achieved *shahadat*, or martyrdom, in Indian Kashmir. Against this background, it was easy to begin to sense, and fear, something hard and fierce even in the simple devotion of the skullcapped men half prostrate, on chilly evenings, on the streets of Peshawar.

Jihadis

But here I had to look out for my own prejudices. There had been many Muslims in the railway towns of North and Central India I had grown up in. I couldn't distinguish them from the low-caste Hindus among the railway labour gangs my father supervised. My father certainly had Muslim colleagues. But I cannot remember identifying any among the exhausted men in sweat-drenched white shirts and grey pants who returned home with my father for a cup of tea after a day out on the tracks, although the tea would have been served to them not in cups but in the special glasses kept aside in our kitchen for Muslims and low-caste Hindus.

Most of the Muslims were, in fact, very poor—much more so than us—and those were the ones I noticed. They lived in ghettos inside the older parts of the town, where, after the expansiveness of the British-built cantonment and Civil Lines and Railway Colony, the streets suddenly shrank. The houses were edged with open drains, the women disappeared behind sinisterly black burqas, flimsy rags curtained off the hanging carcasses at the butchers' shops, and the gaunt men with pointed beards looked quite capable of the brutality that our prejudices ascribed to them.

These prejudices were bred partly by our own lower middle class deprivations: anxieties about money, status and security that came to be related, in the usual unreflective way, to the alien-looking community in our midst. We weren't the kind of people who incited or took part in Hindu–Muslim riots, which in North India in the 1970s and 1980s occurred frequently, often cynically organized by out-of-power politicians wishing to destabilize an existing government, and which ended with the murders of scores of Muslims by an aggressively Hindu police. But we did accept the stereotype, and we had no trouble imagining the bearded Muslim as a violent aggressor who could murder a Hindu with as much relish as he might slaughter a cow.

Another, subtler cliché presented Muslims as backward-looking, a great drag on modernizing India, if not fifth columnists for Pakistan. Of course, the blunter dismissal was: Why don't these Muslims simply go to Pakistan? After all India had been partitioned in 1947 in order to create a new homeland for Indian Muslims. Pakistan was what most of them had asked for, so what were they doing in India?

It seems a crude question now, but it wasn't easy to answer then; and the assertion, made often by politicians and other privileged men, that India was a secular country which was open to people from all religions didn't convince us upper-caste Hindus who lived in straitened circumstances and practised as well as suffered discrimination. And so, feeling frustrated and demoralized ourselves, we unburdened upon the Muslims most of the pity and scorn with which we would have seen, if we could, our own lives. Hindu women probably deserved sympathy as much as Muslim women, but in our imagination it was Muslim women who led terribly oppressed lives.

The clichés bubbled up only when we noticed the Muslims. But mostly we didn't notice them—until the late 1980s, when Hindu nationalists began to agitate for the demolition of Babri mosque in Ayodhya, a town on the Gangetic plain in the state of Uttar Pradesh. It soon became a movement—and an argument—that swept across India. The Hindu nationalists claimed that the sixteenth-century Moghul conqueror of India, Babur, had built the mosque over the birthplace of Lord Rama after demolishing a Hindu temple on the same site. They saw a profound contempt for Hindus in Babur's decision, and they sought a kind of delayed retribution. They wanted the mosque, which was no longer used for prayers, demolished and a temple built in its place.

I was at university in Delhi by this time. On the campus, there were furious protests against what the Hindus in Ayodhya wanted to do. Student politicians organized demonstrations in which Hindus joined with Muslims and where one speaker after another denounced the Hindu nationalists for attempting to destroy the great Indian traditions of tolerance and accommodation. Still, in December 1992, the mosque was demolished by a Hindu mob. The student politicians in the campus raged for some weeks afterwards, but the Muslim students stayed away from their rallies. When I came across them in the dining room, I noticed they looked bitter, but I didn't feel involved. I had my own anxieties to deal with; a degree and then, with luck, a job that would help me climb out of the relative poverty my family had lived in for much of my childhood—relative, that is, to the newly moneyed middle class which was starting to flourish in India. Occasionally I would go to the after-dinner lectures by visiting left-wing journalists and academics—articulate, suave men who talked about the historical bonds between Hindus and Muslims and the uniquely syncretic civilization of India. These ideas about India's past and present didn't always match my experience—the sense I had of the distrust and hostility between Hindus and Muslims, and the keener sense I'd had, in the course of my travels through small-town India, of the stagnant resentments of the Muslim ghettos. But I didn't have the courage to contradict them then, and even now feel insecure before such powerful liberal pieties.

Pakistan has its own marginalized but vigorous liberals. They were the people who talked to me about the 'bearded fundos' and the imminent—or, according to some people, ongoing—Talibanization of Pakistan. It was a phrase I heard often, a new way of referring to troubles that had begun much earlier, in 1979, when Soviet troops entered Afghanistan to replace one faction of the ruling Afghan Communist Party with another, and the United States responded by arming anti-communist Afghans with the help of its ally, the military dictator of Pakistan, General Zia-ul-Haq.

Soon after his coup in 1977 against the elected government of Zulfikar Ali Bhutto, Zia had begun ostentatiously to declare his devotion to Islam. He announced his intention to create a pure Islamic society—that perennially undefined and therefore unfinished task which has given political legitimacy to many despots in Muslim countries. In April 1979 he hanged Bhutto—the populist demagogue who as prime minister used to describe Zia to visitors as 'my little monkey'.

Zia promptly began to channel military and other assistance from America and Saudi Arabia to the anti-communist radical Islamists based in Pakistan. He arranged for the smooth flow of mercenaries from Arab and other Muslim countries to Pakistan. He opened his country's borders to two million refugees escaping the proxy war in Afghanistan, and placed Pakistan in the forefront of what became an American-led global jihad against Soviet communism.

Pakistan was already quite an isolated country, as well as, almost from its beginning, an unhappy one. Very early in its history, its foundational myth had been broken: a shared religion, it turned out, couldn't solve the problem of how people with different ethnic and linguistic backgrounds were to live together. Urdu-speaking Muslims from India, arriving in large numbers in Sindh, found themselves resented by the poor Sindhis, who in turn felt themselves oppressed by the rich and dominant majority of Punjabi-speakers in the north. The Pakistani army behaved brutally towards the separatist Bengalis in East Pakistan, and then surrendered quickly to the invading Indian troops in the short war that followed in 1971. There was international shame and internal humiliation. The disastrous Pakistani obsession with controlling events in Afghanistan grew out of the urgent need to pacify the Pushtun separatists of the North-West Frontier.

India has its share of restless minorities, but it also has a

Jihadis

consistent political life. In Pakistan, the elected politicians have wrecked the country's frail democratic structures, with the help of the army officers and the bureaucrats who are the real rulers. Zia was anxious to present Pakistan to America as a needy frontline state against communist aggression, and to make himself invulnerable as a dedicated anti-communist and Islamic holy warrior.

He was not without his Pakistani supporters. His Islamic zeal was admired by the religious parties who received government patronage for their so far unsuccessful attempt to Islamize Pakistan, and at whose madrasas, or theological schools, thousands of young Afghan refugees were to be fed, housed and educated. He was popular among senior officers in the military, who were still smarting over the surrender of 90,000 soldiers to the Indian army in 1971. They sought to acquire, along with private fortunes, 'strategic depth' against India by supervising the jihad in Afghanistan.

Lt General Hamid Gul was one of the first jihadis in the military. He was much loved by Zia, who made him director of Military Intelligence and then Director-General of the ISI, the Inter-Services Intelligence Agency. In the 1980s Gul was one of the three or four most powerful men in Pakistan—people who, under Zia's patronage, could get away with just about anything.

But then in 1988 Zia and other senior army men died in a still mysterious air crash. Benazir Bhutto, the daughter of the man Zia had hanged, became prime minister of Pakistan. She got rid of Gul at the first available opportunity, in 1989. Gul turned into an intriguer: he led the frustrated power-hungry officers of the ISI who conspired successfully with a few politicians to bring down Benazir Bhutto in 1990.

I wanted to meet him, but he lived at the Chaklala airbase near Rawalpindi. I told him on the phone that my shadows might stop me travelling there. The galling awareness of his lost authority seemed present in his swift response. 'I'll see,' he said in a tight voice, 'who dares stops you from visiting my home.'

His house had Palladian columns—the mansions of military officers in Pakistan are always grand. The living room had framed photos of the Ka'ba on the walls and a suffocating excess of ornament: huge crystal decorations, shiny lifesize brass deer, green satin upholstery, rugs made from animal skins. A bearded man in a salwar kurta sat uneasily on the big sofa, and then stood up hurriedly when another man, beardless, with a clipped moustache and wearing a tweed jacket, strode into the room. This was Gul, the jihadi, though his style suggested his original career as a cavalry officer. At times during our conversation he sounded like a graduate of Sandhurst. However, the facts of his early life as he told them, very reluctantly, were that his family came from the remote hills of Swat, and that he'd gone to a village school and then a government-run college in Lahore.

These were humble origins when compared to the 'brown sahibs' Gul was known for attacking at every opportunity—the men Anglicized and groomed to assume power at grander institutions such as Aitchison College in Lahore, and St Patrick's College in Karachi. They partly accounted for Gul's immodest ambitions and claims. In February 1989, when the Soviet army withdrew from Afghanistan, he was, as director-general of the ISI, leading the jihad. In fact, according to him, his role in the jihad had begun even while he was a lowly brigadier. Three weeks after the Soviet intervention in 1979, he wrote and circulated a policy paper, in which he advocated that Pakistan support a low-intensity guerrilla war against the Soviet Union and their Afghan allies, and gradually take it right into the Muslim-majority Central Asian provinces of the Soviet Union.

The paper reached Zia who was impressed by Gul's energy and ambition. A meeting with the general followed. 'I told

General Zia,' Gul said, and the bearded man on the sofa nodded and smiled at the memory of the dead dictator, 'that if we defeated the Russians, and I was very optimistic that we would, then there was no reason why the borders of our great Islamic world should stop at the Amu Dariya.' (The Amu Dariya, or Oxus River, forms the boundary between Afghanistan and the former Soviet Union.)

Gul claimed his paper went on to be read by high-placed officials in the CIA, and formed the basis of later incursions into what William Casey, the director of the CIA, described as the 'soft underbelly of the Soviet Union'.

Much of this seemed like boasting. The Carter administration had long been waiting for the Soviets to slip up in Afghanistan. Zbigniew Brzezinski, National Security Advisor to President Carter, whose stated aim was to 'sow shit in the Soviet backyard', had arranged for clandestine aid to the radical Islamists in Pakistan a few months before Soviet troops arrived in Afghanistan. The Soviet intervention gave them the pretext they needed to up the ante. The day the Soviet army entered Afghanistan, Brzezinski wrote an exultant letter to Carter, 'Now we can give the Soviet Union its Vietnam War.' The CIA, under Casey, deepened this trap for the Soviets throughout the early and mid 1980s by providing billions of dollars worth of arms and aid.

In fact, Casey wanted the ISI to involve the Muslims of the Soviet Union in the jihad; he wasn't satisfied with the ISI-arranged smuggling of thousands of Qur'ans into what is now Uzbekistan and Tajikistan, or with the distribution of heroin among Soviet troops. An officer of the ISI I spoke to said that the ISI received plenty of unofficial encouragement from Casey to attempt more damaging stuff—but nothing that could be traced back to the CIA or the government of the United States.

Gul now had nothing but abuse for his former bankrollers in the CIA. 'A self-serving people. All they wanted was to turn

Afghanistan into a Vietnam for the Soviet Union, they used us for this purpose, and then they lost interest after the Soviets withdrew.'

This was a commonplace sentiment in Pakistan: you heard it from liberal journalists who from the beginning had highlighted the folly and risk of fighting other people's wars; you heard it from the jihadis hoping to fight another day. American involvement in Afghanistan and Pakistan had become a story about the cynicism of cold warriors such as Brzezinski and Casey.

The jihad that Gul imagined himself to be leading turned out to be under neither his nor the CIA's control. Many different realpolitik interests had brought it to Pakistan, and would, in time, take it away. The Americans wanted to rouse the Muslims of the world against the Soviet Union; the Saudi royal family, which matched American assistance dollar for dollar, wanted its own version of Sunni Islam, Wahhabism, to triumph over the then resurgent Shi'ism of Ayatollah Khomeini of Iran. Pakistan was merely a base for these larger battles, somewhere that CIA operatives could, for a while at least, mingle happily with such rich Arab jihadis as Osama Bin Laden.

After the Soviet withdrawal was decided upon in Geneva in 1987, American interest in both the jihad and Afghanistan dwindled. The CIA promptly scaled back and soon ended its aid to Pakistan and the mujahideen.

Left pretty much to their own devices, the ISI and Gul began to flounder. In 1989, he abandoned his usual mode of guerrilla warfare in Afghanistan, and conceived and supervised what turned out to be a disastrous frontal assault by the mujahideen on the communist-held city of Jalalabad. Four months later, the mujahideen had lost 3,000 men and were nowhere near taking the city. The Afghan communist government in Kabul lasted for another three years, during which period the mujahideen declared jihads against each other.

Jihadis

The divisions between the seven mujahideen parties recognized by the ISI had been deepening since 1979. The rifts between them owed less to ethnic and linguistic differences, and more to the inequitable way in which the ISI had parcelled out the largesse from America and Saudi Arabia. The ISI under Gul was most generous to a particularly brutal mujahideen leader called Gulbuddin Hekmatyar, whose wealth and power depended on the production and smuggling of heroin. The ISI expected Hekmatyar to install a pro-Pakistan government in Kabul after the fall of the communists. But Hekmatyar turned out to be unacceptable to most other mujahideen leaders, especially to those who had fought the Soviets without much help from America or Pakistan.

When the Tajik mujahideen commander, Ahmad Shah Massoud, finally drove out the communist government of Kabul in 1992, a full-scale civil war broke out in Afghanistan. Hekmatyar, backed by the ISI, rocket-bombed Kabul for months. More people died in the city during the fighting in the early 1990s than during the whole of the decade-long jihad against the Russians. Regional powers stepped in once again to bankroll various factions: the Saudis supported the Sunni fundamentalists, Iran backed the Shi'a Hazaras, Tajikistan and Uzbekistan had their own favourites among the Tajiks and Uzbeks. The ISI still hadn't lost faith in Hekmatyar when in 1994 the student militia of the Taliban suddenly emerged and conquered most of Afghanistan.

These were more than personal or professional misjudgements and failures. The work of Gul and men like him undermined a whole society. Reckless but powerful adventurers pursuing absurd fantasies of a pan-Islamic empire had taken a largely poor and illiterate country to the edge.

Gul himself had done well out of it all. There was the Palladian-fronted house in Rawalpindi, and also a farmhouse. Rumour had it that he owned more properties elsewhere.

And that winter, the winter before September 11, there were

still new jihads and jihadis to root for. 'These Americans now accuse Osama Bin Laden of terrorism. Once upon a time they used to call upon him in Peshawar and ask him to recruit more Arabs for the jihad,' said Gul, anxious, like all the jihadis I was to meet in Pakistan, to claim a special intimacy with Bin Laden. 'I met him in Sudan in 1993. Such a wise and intelligent man. So much spirituality on his face. But this is the effect of jihad. It is a very noble state to be in. That's why I look so young, although I am sixty-four years old. Jihad keeps me young, gives me a great purpose in life.'

Gul's enemies in Pakistan—and there were many—scoffed at his Islamic fervour. It was to them another kind of opportunism: a private pipeline to power and to some of the money that flowed in from rich Muslim countries for organizations devoted to Islamic causes. Listening to them you could easily begin to think of jihad as just another racket visited upon a poor backward country. Certainly, renewed faith alone didn't account for the many sectarian groups that had sprung up in the last twenty years, whose exploits—shoot-outs, bomb explosions, arson—dominated the national news.

The Shi'a groups were funded from Iran, the Sunnis from Saudi Arabia and Iraq. After the proxy war in Afghanistan, Pakistan played host to the traditional rivalries of Islam. And the many sects and ideologies of the Islamic world also travelled to it. The Muslim Brotherhood in Egypt influenced the leaders of the Jaamat-I-Islami, the biggest of Pakistan's religious parties— several of its leaders studied at Cairo. The Saudis arrived late, but their open-handed generosity ensured a speedy embrace of Wahhabism among the poorer members of the clergy: many Sunni madrasas, religious schools partly funded with Saudi money, now stand near the borders that Pakistan and Afghanistan share with the Shi'a-majority Iran.

Jihadis

Among these imported Islamic schools, those belonging to the Deobandis are the most powerful, and closest to the Wahhabis. The name comes from a small town near Delhi called Deoband. A madrasa was established there in 1866 as part of the insular Muslim response to British rule in the nineteenth century. It was set up by men who felt that Western-style education of the kind proposed by the British, and embraced by the Hindus, was going to uproot and fracture the Muslim community, and who were convinced that a training in the fundamentals of the Qur'an and the sharia would shield Indian Muslims from the corruptions of the modern world.

In the newspaper office in Peshawar, Jamal said, 'You must go to the Deobandi madrasas. That's where a lot of the Taliban were trained, and also many of those young Pakistani men who go to Afghanistan to fight for the Taliban. You'll find lots of fanatics there.'

I did want to find a few fanatics; I also wanted to travel to Afghanistan. On both fronts, however, my attempts were being thwarted. At the Taliban's chaotic embassy in Islamabad, my visa application, deposited and redeposited several times, seemed as much of an illusion as the existence of an Afghan state or government. It wasn't easy to find the jihadis. The names Jamal sold me—expensively: he said he hadn't been paid his salary and needed the money, and I didn't argue—turned out to be men who had long ago retired. All the leads offered to me by the other English-language journalists I knew came to nothing. I began hovering round the offices of the Urdu publications, many of which were sympathetic to the jihadis. It was at the office of a plump young editor in Islamabad, one of the professional cheerleaders of the jihad and another self-proclaimed friend of Osama Bin Laden, that I ran into Shafiq.

Shafiq looked very old, although he was only in his mid-forties. When the editor introduced him as a veteran of the jihad in Afghanistan, he raised the sleeves of his kurta and displayed a bullet wound in his left arm. He didn't speak much; his Urdu was a low growl—the furtive tone, it turned out, of a fixer. His demands for money were more extravagant than Jamal's; and we were forced to meet early in the morning or late at night, the only times when the spies were off duty. It was difficult to arrange these meetings—he claimed his mobile phone was tapped by the ISI—but he usually had the information I wanted.

It took him some time to come up with a name for Karachi: it wasn't his 'area', he said. And then he said, with the glint in his eyes that always appeared in expectation of money, that he had found someone special for me: an activist of the Sipah-e-Sahaba, one of the most dreaded anti-Shi'a groups in Pakistan whose acronym, SSP, featured often in the daily papers, usually in news reports of attacks by or on Shi'as. He would, he said, using the English words, provide me with 'good material'. All I had to do was shake off the spies and show up at the Deobandi madrasa in Binori Town.

One early morning, when the spies were still asleep, I took a flight from Peshawar to Karachi. I was relieved to find that no strange men in beat-up cars awaited me at the other end. Everywhere on the wide boulevard leading to the city centre there were signs of Karachi's financial eminence, in the billboards, the glass-fronted boutiques and the fancy patisseries. I had expected a meaner place, living up to its reputation as a setting for violent battles between militant groups of Muslim migrants from India and the police. But in this port city, with the spies gone, and the warm sea air and clear light and colonial buildings so much like those of Bombay, I suddenly felt freer than I ever had before in Pakistan.

I felt as a Pakistani visitor to the city might; and it was as a Pakistani journalist from London that I introduced myself to

Rahmat. The deception was necessary, Shafiq had told me: my connection to India would throw Rahmat and he would not want to talk. In any case, it gave me a new assurance the evening I went to the Binori Town madrasa. In my salwar kurta, bought earlier in the day, I could have been any one of the hundreds of young men coming in and out of the evening *namaaz*.

Rahmat was waiting for me, as Shafiq had said he would, at a small shop selling Afghan caps and Qur'ans just inside the tall gateway to the madrasa. He was younger than I had expected, and his grimy white kurta, worn plastic slippers and dense beard only highlighted his exceptional good looks, his delicate cheekbones and shyly quizzical eyes.

We sat and talked in one of the garishly lit shops and cafes that hemmed in the madrasa. Initially I felt a little disappointed. Shafiq had exaggerated: Rahmat wasn't a student but an odd-job man at the Binori Town madrasa. As for the Sipah-e-Sahaba, he had never belonged to it, though some members of the group had helped him and his family after his brother had been arrested and charged with murdering a Shi'a landlord.

The murder had happened near Rahmat's ancestral village in the Punjab, where his father ran an auto-repair shop. Rahmat had been languishing there, with his parents, four brothers and two sisters, waiting for a job to come his way after his schooling at a local madrasa near the city of Faislabad. Things hadn't been so bad in the 1980s, in the days of Zia-ul-Haq's Islamization, when you could still get a job after a madrasa education. But Rahmat had gone to the madrasa after that time, and had come out of it to join the hundreds of thousands of unemployable young men in Pakistan. Some of his friends had got enough money together to travel to the Gulf, and he had been hoping to follow them. Then one day his brother murdered the landlord.

There had been ongoing difficulties with the landlord, who was a much-hated figure among his tenants, for the mistresses he kept in semi-servitude as well as for his financial crookedness. He had bungled the records of Rahmat's family's ownership of a piece of fertile land. Rahmat's father and his brothers had been powerless to argue. But then he had tried to manipulate the mortgage on Rahmat's father's auto-repair shop. That was what had enraged Rahmat's brother.

Rahmat said, '*Zamindar bada powerful banda tha*, the landlord was a powerful man.' The many relatives of the dead man came in a Pajero and flogged his father in front of the family and destroyed the auto-repair shop. The police ransacked his house a few times and even locked Rahmat up for a few days, although he had been away in the fields with a friend at the time of the murder.

The revolving disco-like lights on the ceiling glistened on Rahmat's perspiring face as he spoke. The shop was busy. It seemed, rather incongruously, part of the celebration of wealth and leisure I had seen elsewhere in the city. The solemn-faced skullcapped visitors to the mosque inside the madrasa were easily outnumbered by the paunchy men in tight jeans and T-shirts striding quickly to the shops and returning to their Mercedes with small mountains of shiny sweetboxes.

Only the men at the mosque in the nearby town helped his family, Ramat said. They employed his teenage brother at their own madrasa; they used their contacts in the police to get the pressure taken off Rahmat's family. Rahmat vaguely understood that they were members of the SSP, and opposed to Shi'as, but he hadn't given it much thought. Then one evening in 1995 one of the SSP men, not much older than Rahmat, who often led the *namaaz* on Fridays, called for him.

When he arrived at the mosque on his bicycle, he found a small crowd of young men already there, including a few from his village, people who had also been tormented by the now-dead landlord. None of them knew why they had been summoned. Then the man who had called for them came in, accompanied by an Afghan wearing a black turban, and addressed them briefly.

He said that the guest with him had come all the way from Afghanistan where a new jihad had commenced. There were many corrupt men like the landlords of Punjab in Afghanistan: they called themselves mujahideen, as though they were engaged in jihad, but they were worse than bandits and rapists. Now a new force had arisen to vanquish them and establish the law of the Prophet. The soldiers fighting the jihad were young Talibs, students, but Allah was with them.

It was the first time Rahmat had heard about the students—the Taliban. There had been several Afghans at his madrasa, but he had kept away from them. The Afghan refugees had a bad reputation in his part of Pakistan; they were seen as liars and thieves. His father dealt with them all the time in his auto-repair shop. The heavy trucks they drove from Afghanistan damaged the roads, and the drivers were often high on opium.

So when the Afghan man began to speak, Rahmat was sceptical. He spoke Urdu with a heavy Pushtu accent that, Rahmat remembered, made some of the men smile. But the Afghan was serious. He didn't waste much time: he said he had come to ask for volunteers for the jihad in Afghanistan. He couldn't promise much in return, except food and shelter; the way of jihad was not strewn with roses. But it was a holy duty for Muslims, and *shahadat*, martyrdom, was all they could expect from it.

Most of the young men weren't interested. But Rahmat, with a brother in jail and the auto-repair shop—the sole source of his family's income—now gone, couldn't turn away so easily from what the Afghan was offering. His father and his brothers wondered what he was getting into but didn't try to stop him. He went with other young men in a chartered bus to Quetta in

Baluchistan. They crossed the border into Afghanistan illegally, at night. On the other side, along with Pushtun Afghans, there were many more Pakistanis. They were taken to a training camp situated in a rocky valley near the border, where there were men from Chechnya, Kashmir and Uzbekistan. There were even Pakistani army officers. It was in this training camp that he had grown his beard, not under any pressure—although men in Afghanistan were required to wear four-inch long beards—but out of his wish to be a good Muslim.

Rahmat had been at the camp for less than two weeks when his group was summoned to the western provinces where the Taliban were fighting to capture the city of Herat. By the time Rahmat got there, it was already under the control of the Taliban. He and his fellow mujahideen were like conquerors in the city. But it was a strange place for them. It was very cold, and the locals spoke Persian, not Urdu or Pushtu; they even looked like Iranians. Even more alien were the young Pushtun men of the Taliban who went around shutting down schools, smashing TVs and VCRs, and tearing up photographs. One of them discovered a semi-nude photo of an Indian film actress in the tent Rahmat shared with eleven or twelve other Pakistanis. There was awkwardness between the Afghan and the Pakistani volunteers for some time after that.

He didn't like the rough ways of the Taliban: they were backward people, he thought. They were cruel to their women and religious minorities and military opponents—someone from his village had been forced to participate in a massacre of civilians from the Shi'a Hazara community in central Afghanistan. He was a bit frightened of them. But he couldn't deny that they had brought peace to Afghanistan, and when the Pakistanis he was with spoke of imposing a similar peace in Pakistan, where there was so much injustice and banditry, it seemed like an attractive idea.

Jihadis

Rahmat didn't stay long in Afghanistan as he was wanted as a witness at the trial of his brother. Back in his village he met up again with the men at the mosque. It was with one of them that he'd gone to the Binori Town madrasa three years before we met. There was some money to be made in doing menial jobs for the students and teachers; he could eat cheaply and he could always find a place to sleep. Things were better here than in the Punjab where his brother was still in jail and his father close to death.

Rahmat had shaken his head when I first asked him if he wanted to eat anything. But when I ordered another plate of halwa, he was quick to reach out and place his hand on the arm of the waiter, startling him slightly. After the food came— an oily plateful of what looked to my furtive, vegetarian eyes like mutton—he became more expansive and his Urdu, studded up to this point with Punjabi slang, became more formal, full of difficult Arabic and Persian words. He spoke of the greatness and necessity of jihad, of how Muslims were being oppressed everywhere, in Kashmir, Afghanistan, Chechnya, Egypt, Palestine, how the Jews in Israel could get away with anything because they were supported by Western powers.

I had heard, and was to hear, a lot of this talk from both the leaders and the foot soldiers of the jihad. You had to be careful neither to dismiss it nor to swallow it whole. It was easy to see through the self-aggrandizement and deceptions of people like Hamid Gul. But the oppression and injustice that Rahmat spoke of were more than just rhetorical flourishes picked up from the teachers at his madrasa and the ISI officers at the training camp in Afghanistan; they were the basis of his own experience of the world.

Rahmat was like the young men of my own class in small-town India in the 1980s and early 1990s—people for whom the world didn't seem to have a place. The idea of religion as

157

redemption, the unquestioning submission to one creed or philosophy—these were the same demands that my own background had made of me, and it had taken some effort, and much luck, to be able to move away from them, to redefine myself as an individual, and to enter into new, more complicated affiliations with the larger world.

Others weren't as lucky: these were people whose frustration and rage over their many deprivations could easily be appropriated into ideological crusades. It was among the young unemployed in India that the Hindu nationalist movement (also largely funded, like the jihad, from abroad—by rich Hindus in the US and UK) found its foot soldiers: the men who formed the mobs, who were in charge of the dirty stuff, of the lynchings and destruction.

Hindu disaffection, however, was of a different order. The young Hindus I knew were frustrated by their exclusion from the middle class; they did not, despite their rhetoric of an Indian golden age, seek to radically change the ways of the world, or hold up alternative visions, as Mahatma Gandhi once had, of what a good and true life was, and could be. Even the most extreme Hindu ideologues did not, in the end, wish, like the jihadis, to challenge or reject the knowledge and power of the West. They were content to take the world as they found it, dominated by the West, and then find a niche for themselves in it: they were above all sly materialists. This pragmatic collaboration with the West is what has produced the new Hindu renaissance of the last 150 years—a regeneration of which the software tycoons of Silicon Valley and the Indian writers in English are related aspects. Gandhi's ambition—to form a society as different as possible from the one in the West—had few takers left in India. Ironically, his distrust and fear of Western modernity was now amplified best by the radical Islamists of Pakistan, where the westernized post-colonial elite—those men from the posh colleges that Hamid Gul despised, who now spoke helplessly of the Talibanization of Pakistan—had discredited itself.

This is why, while India daily moves closer to the West, Pakistan seems much further away from it. It is also why Rahmat, although he believed me to be a Muslim, saw me essentially as an alien, someone far away from him, a resident of London, the city of Sodom and Gomorrah. It's why I was startled when Rahmat looked up from his plate of mutton and rice and asked me if the women in London went around with their legs exposed.

It was a question that came from my own past: the kind of thing I would turn around in my mind, when I was still a boy in isolated towns, with no TV or cinema around to inhibit my imagination. It was unsettling to think how quickly that past had vanished; how dramatically my circumstances had changed. No one before me in my family had ever left India. I now spend a lot of my time in London, and travel to many different parts of the world. I write for American and British newspapers and magazines; depend upon them, in fact, for a living.

Globalization has opened up the West; there is more space in it for people like me—people who would have had to struggle harder for a similar space in their native countries. I still feel myself on the margins, writing about subjects that appear remote from the preoccupations around me, the obsession with food, sex, money, movies and celebrities that is reflected in the weekend papers in Britain. But the first cultural shock has worn off. As an Indian writing in English I am a child, however strange, of the West. England is, after all, the place I have chosen to be; and I have, in time, come to see something brittle and self-righteous in my exasperation with articles about new restaurants and breast implants.

In any case, I spend most of my time in London at my desk and have only a shallow relationship with the world around me.

When I first arrived I was unsettled by the devout Muslims I saw in the streets of east London. However, as so often happens, the more money you have the more liberal you grow, the more in tune you are with the cosmopolitan city and its bland middle-class tolerance. In London, experiencing security and stability for the first time in my life, I became someone without a past; and as the months passed the Muslims faded into the promiscuous bustle of gay discos, Balti restaurants, and bagel shops.

But this kind of westernization can be superficial; you can quickly lapse into an older cultural conservatism. In London one evening I stood behind a group of white-haired Hindu women who had just come out of a sari shop. I couldn't help sharing the distaste they felt at the sight of tall English girls in tight black dresses stumbling out of the Vibe Bar on Brick Lane, chased by drunken boys in bright shirts.

Your political loyalties can also be more complicated than those ascribed to you by other people. This explains my unease when I visited the American embassy in Islamabad a few days after meeting Rahmat. The stern experts on the Taliban and Islamic fundamentalism there kept using the words 'us' and 'them' while impressing upon me the urgency of forcing 'those guys', the Taliban, to give up their special guest, Bin Laden. Although I, with my beard and Afghan cap, looked like one of 'them'—the desperate men just outside the embassy's fort-like walls—the Americans had no doubt where I belonged: I was one of 'us', part of a powerful imperial civilization that, in this vulnerable outpost, was denoted by bowling alleys, cocktail bars, and the framed photos of barbecue parties on office walls.

No ambiguities existed for the diplomats: they defended the government they worked for with as much passion and vigour as the jihadis—the 'them' of their vocabulary—spoke of jihad; and they could make you feel that the war they were fighting was also your war, and the side we were all on had both truth and power behind it.

It was hard to demur when you considered the opposition. Far from offering a blueprint for a new civilization or society, the Taliban seemed perversely intent on destroying the few bits and pieces of Afghanistan's cultural heritage that had managed to survive the long war. I was in India when the news of the Taliban's intention to destroy all Buddhist statues in Afghanistan first broke. I still hadn't gone to Afghanistan and I wasn't sure what was going on. I rang a Pakistani journalist in Peshawar. He confirmed some of the theories I had seen in the Pakistani papers on the Internet: the Taliban were frustrated by the sanctions imposed on them by the UN, and wanted to draw international attention to the plight of Afghans facing drought and starvation. There was a struggle going on between the hardliners and moderates within the Taliban, and this time the former had won.

The journalist wasn't sure about the statues. The huge Buddhas in Bamiyan had been around for centuries; they could not be removed. But the museum in Kabul, which held the best representatives of Indo-Greek sculpture, had been looted long ago, first by the mujahideen who took over the city after the fall of the communist regime in 1992, and then by the Taliban in 1996. There was not much left there. For years now, statues had been smuggled out of Afghanistan and transported as far as New York and Tokyo, although you could still find an occasional example in the bazaars of Peshawar.

As it happened, I had already seen some of these statues in a house in an upper-class suburb of Peshawar. They belonged to General Naseerullah Babur, another of Pakistan's powerful military men, and Benazir Bhutto's 'favourite uncle'. He wouldn't say how he had got hold of the statues—which were displayed in glass cases in his living room and many of which I recognized from photographs—and only mumbled something about finding them during excavations. But it wasn't hard to guess; and later I discovered that the manner in which he had acquired the statues was as much of an open secret as his original sponsorship of the Taliban.

Babur's connection with Afghanistan began when he was Governor of the North-West Frontier Province in the 1970s. It was then he first met the Afghan Islamists who later became famous names in the jihad, and introduced them to American diplomats in Islamabad.

He was also responsible for suppressing a particularly savage civil war in Karachi between local Sindhis and Muslim migrants from India. As Babur told me his stories, his broad Pushtun face often cracked into a childlike smile. He came over as the retired man who has made his little pile a bit dubiously but is nevertheless eager to establish his role in great events; or like the brave Pushtun of legend, as an admiring taxi driver described him to me, who travelled around Karachi during the worst violence in an open, unescorted jeep.

In 1993 Benazir Bhutto came back into power, three years after being overthrown by the ISI and Hamid Gul, and Babur became Minister for the Interior in her government. Afghanistan was close to collapse. Its roads, bridges, schools, orchards and irrigation systems lay in ruins. Even more disastrous was the moral breakdown that had taken place in the years after the Soviet withdrawal in 1989. The law-enforcement systems of a modern state had barely existed outside the cities at any time in the country's history; now civil war and the displacement of millions of people had undermined the tribal and religious codes that served in their place. Warlords and gangsters flourished in the vacuum. Gulbuddin Hekmatyar, the mujahid favoured by the ISI, had already branched off into heroin manufacturing and smuggling; many other mujahideen commanders took to smuggling and highway robbery. Men with guns stood at improvised checkposts on all major roads. The situation was particularly bad in the Pushtun-majority provinces of southern Afghanistan, where commanders raped young boys and women and plundered at will.

One day in 1994, in a village near Kandahar, a Pushtun man in his thirties called Mohammed Omar heard about two women who had been abducted and raped by local commanders. Like many young Pushtuns from his village, Omar, the son of landless peasants, had participated in the jihad against local and foreign communists. He had been wounded several times and had lost his right eye. After the Soviet withdrawal he had gone back to teaching at his village madrasa. He was deeply aggrieved by the anarchy around him, and often talked to his friends in the village about how they could bring it to an end and establish the law of the Qur'an. The rapes finally moved him to action. He went to the local madrasas and raised a band of thirty students for a rescue mission. The students got hold of about sixteen rifles. They went and freed the women and hanged the commanders from the barrel of a tank. A few months later, there was another incident in which two commanders fought a gun battle in the streets of Kandahar over a boy both wished to rape. Once again, Omar showed up with his students, freed the boy and executed the commanders.

These were the stories Rahmat heard in his mosque in the Punjab; Babur heard the same stories in Islamabad. The fame of the Taliban grew quickly. Afghans everywhere began appealing to them for protection from the warlords. Soon requests for help—along with large cash donations—came to the Taliban from the traders and smugglers who needed peace and open roads in southern Afghanistan for the transport of goods to Iran and the central Asian republics.

Babur had long been looking into the possibility of building new roads, and oil and gas pipelines, through Afghanistan to reach the central Asian republics of the former Soviet Union.

There had been keen interest from multinational oil companies. But Kabul was still being fought over. The ISI, which both Babur and Bhutto distrusted, insisted on supporting Hekmatyar, who was not a leader who could impose the stability that was needed to conduct business in Afghanistan. The only other route to central Asia went through southern Afghanistan, but that route was infested with bandits.

Babur thought up a plan of rebuilding the road from Pakistan to Herat in north-western Afghanistan with funding from international agencies. In October 1994 he took a group of Western and Chinese diplomats on an exploratory trip to Herat. Later that month, Babur attempted something riskier: he arranged for thirty Pakistani trucks to drive through Afghanistan to the capital of Turkmenistan, Ashkhabad.

Babur told me that he was advised against the trip. The commanders who controlled the roads in southern Afghanistan were reportedly very angry with him. They hadn't been told about the diplomats' visit and they assumed Babur was supporting the Taliban, who just a few days previously had captured a massive arsenal built up during the days when the CIA sent arms to the mujahideen.

Babur said, 'I went ahead. It was an experiment. I thought, let's see what happens.'

A few miles outside Kandahar, the convoy was stopped by local commanders. They ordered the Pakistani drivers to park in a nearby village. There were some Pakistani army officers on the convoy, but they were outnumbered and did not resist. Instead they relayed the commanders' demands to their superiors in Islamabad: money, a share of the goods in the convoy, and a promise to stop supporting the Taliban.

For three days, Pakistani officials in Islamabad wondered what to do. A commando operation to rescue the convoy was discussed and finally dropped. Then Babur asked the Taliban to help.

Jihadis

The students carried out an assault on the village where the convoy was parked, and chased out the commanders and their men. That same evening they attacked Kandahar and after two days of fighting conquered the city and expelled the remaining warlords from the area.

This was the beginning of the military campaign that brought almost all of Afghanistan under Taliban control in the space of just two years. Early in 1995, they took Herat; a year later, they were in Kabul. They didn't do it all by themselves: thousands of Pakistanis like Rahmat volunteered to fight with them; bribes raised from shippers and smugglers neutralized most of the warlords; and Babur put considerable Pakistani expertise at the Taliban's disposal.

He sent Pakistani engineers to replace the phone system, to repair Kandahar airport and to improve the roads; and although Babur wouldn't deny or confirm it to me, and only broke into his impish smile again, Pakistani army regulars fought alongside the Taliban and high-ranking officers planned their campaigns. Babur himself closely monitored the capture of Kabul in 1996, from which he carried away, like the invaders of the past, his own booty: the statues of the Buddha and Bodhisattva that now adorned his living room.

Five years later, the 'boys', as Babur called the Taliban, had grown more ambitious. They weren't content, as in the old days, to expel the warlords and institute a kind of rough and ready justice. They now wanted to create the purest Islamic society in the world. Their leaders called themselves mullahs, although few of them had the necessary educational qualifications—Mohammed Omar had in fact gone a step further and anointed himself Amir-ul-Momineem, Commander of the Faithful. They designed a new flag for Afghanistan. Men from the Department of Prevention of Vice and Promotion of Virtue went around checking the length of beards and beating up women without male escorts.

Babur disapproved of their restrictions on women. But they no longer turned to men like Babur for advice. They had their own supporters: the mullahs of rural Afghanistan, and the jihadis, Islamist politicians and ISI officers of Pakistan.

And they had their sympathizers: Ishrat was one of them, although he hadn't lived in Afghanistan since 1981, when as a sixteen-year-old refugee he made the long journey from the southern province of Helmand to Pakistan. He went to a local school in Peshawar during the anti-Soviet jihad and picked up enough English to be able to act as a guide and interpreter to foreign journalists. Ishrat was, Shafiq told me, the best person to take to Afghanistan; his English was excellent and he knew his way around not only the police and customs men, but also the potentially troublesome tribals in the border areas.

'You must write the truth,' he kept saying, 'and see things in context. Don't be influenced by what you read in the Western media.' There was, he said, nothing unprecedented about the Taliban's restrictions on women, their harshness towards petty criminals or their religious strictures: the tribal system that had ruled the lives of the majority of Afghans had always been severe.

Ishrat was a short man. The beard hanging from his small face seemed very long and the salwar kurtas he wore were always too big for his thin body. In his admiration for the Taliban there seemed to me to be something of the fascination that the physically unprepossessing have for demonstrations of brute power and strength.

He made me uneasy, but I was stuck with him. And there was a discomfiting kernel of truth in his wildest assertions. Ishrat was obsessed with the attention given by the West to the destruction of the giant Buddhas in Bamiyan. 'Why do Western people care so much about old Buddhist statues no one worships? Why are they not writing front page articles about the millions of starving and dying people in Afghanistan? They want to give money for the statues and take them to their museums, but what about human beings?'

I wasn't sure of my own feelings. I had visited the refugee camps near Peshawar where families huddled under tiny plastic tents on exposed flat ground, next to narrow lanes muddied with soapy water and urine. I had read the alarming NGO reports about famine and mass starvation in Afghanistan. I knew about the UN's failure to fundraise even $221m as humanitarian aid for Afghanistan.

I had also just started writing a book about the Buddha, and had been reading with some fascination about the way merchant caravans had travelled with his ideas from North India to central Asia. In Pakistan, I'd visited some of the sites where the merchants had built great monasteries. I hadn't been much interested in Bamiyan: the giant statues looked ugly in the photographs, and there was Robert Byron's testimony from the early 1930s about them lacking 'even the dignity of labour'. Nevertheless, their antiquity gave them a kind of poise—for fifteen centuries, standing quietly in a broad mountain valley, they had withstood the change of seasons and religions. The news of their defacement appalled me, but then, as the days passed, I got tired of the outrage and scorn. There seemed something too easy and glib about the demonizing of the Taliban. In India, the loudest protests had come from the same Hindu nationalists who had demolished the Babri mosque in Ayodhya in 1992. In the angry editorials in the British papers, the Taliban once again appeared as particularly vicious barbarians from the Middle Ages instead of the very recent product of the West's unthoughtful meddling in a remote and not well-understood society. At least this was how they increasingly seemed to me. So when Ishrat said, 'It is all hypocrisy, the Western people are afraid of Islam, they want to protect the statues, but they had never heard of these statues, they don't know anything about Afghanistan, they are not interested in whether people live or die there,' I kept quiet.

In Afghanistan, Ishrat was always eager to bring my attention to the Taliban's successes. 'You have heard of the Afridis? Pushtun tribe people. They controlled the drug business. Poppy grown in Afghanistan, turned into heroin in Pakistan and then smuggled out to Europe and America through Iran and Karachi. No one was writing about that. American's favourite mujahideen, Hekmatyar, was running dozens of heroin laboratories. Now Taliban has banned poppy, the smugglers are angry at them, but they say heroin is against Islam. They lose money because of their faith. But still no one is writing. They all talk about Osama Bin Laden. But who is Bin Laden? He is America's man, America made him who he is.'

Ishrat's garrulousness made him assertive. He wanted me to go to Jalalabad and talk to Hindus and Sikhs who would confirm his account of the great peace and stability brought to the country by the Taliban. But that wasn't what I wanted to do. I told him I wanted to go to the villages.

'What will you do in the villages?' Ishrat said. 'There is nothing there.' I thought he was resisting me because his contacts were all in the cities. But in the end he backed down and said he knew someone I could talk to.

He kept up his pro-Taliban propaganda in the taxi on the way to a village near Jalalabad. Pointing to an ancient-looking cassette of Indian film music on the dashboard, he said, 'See, Afghans can listen to music. All you Western journalists are saying Taliban banned music.' But then a checkpost approached in the distance. The taxi driver reached for the cassette and stuffed it quickly into the pocket of his frayed jacket before the boys with black turbans and Kalashnikovs could strut over to the car and put their tender-skinned faces through the window and utter severe-sounding questions.

Jihadis

Ishrat was quiet after that. The sun rose higher and the light steadily grew harsh, draining colour even out of the roadside tents of the nomads. There was little traffic: a few big trucks that the straggly families by the road would try to wave down—Ishrat identified them as Pakistan-bound refugees from the Tajik-majority northern provinces—and more frequently, Toyota pickups, fast and dangerous on the broken road, with black-turbaned men holding Kalashnikovs crammed uncomfortably in the back.

The Toyotas—famously the vehicles with which the Taliban had achieved their military victory in Herat—kicked up swaying clouds of dust that were then quietly absorbed into the stubborn white haze. There was more dust once we turned off the road to Jalalabad, and the car began to rock and shudder down a rutted dirt path. The dust blew in through the rolled-up windows and settled in a film on the battered brown leather of the car seats; it powdered the beards of Ishrat and the taxi driver; it blotted out the occasional groups of children and chador-draped women carrying dung cakes on their heads; and it scared off the scrawny goats sitting in the narrow shade of the mud wall before which we suddenly stopped.

A low wooden door opened and a tall man with a long white beard came out and embraced Ishrat. His quick quizzical glance at me modulated into a smile as Ishrat spoke to him in Pushtu and explained my presence.

The man took me through the empty hay-littered courtyard to what seemed like a special room for visitors. He said very little either to Ishrat or to me. He brought me water in a shallow trough and indicated a place in the courtyard—before a furrowed drain that ran around the compound—where I could wash my face and hands. He returned shortly afterwards with some green tea. The tea tasted slightly of dust, and made the bone china cup—an unexpected thing in the bare room—seem as if it had been sitting unused for a long time.

I felt expectant; also slightly exhausted by the drive and by my nervousness of the Taliban men in the Toyotas. Ishrat hadn't promised much in the car. He had told me the name of our host—Faiz. He had filled me in on Faiz's involvement in the anti-Soviet jihad, and the injuries—always glamorous items in these accounts of the mujahideen—he had sustained during a mortar attack by the communists.

It was of that life that Faiz spoke to me intermittently that afternoon and evening in the cool bare room, Ishrat translating, the driver looking on blankly. He spoke not as a man who thought himself successful would, with pride or nostalgia. He spoke—leaning against the wall, his knees drawn up, narrow eyes wandering around the room—with the neutral air of a man who had lived his life in the only way he could.

He could barely remember his childhood, when his father owned a few cows and goats. But he spoke vividly of the time in the 1970s when the desert-like area around him was irrigated with Soviet assistance, and orange and olive orchards came up on the previously uncultivable land. His family was one of the beneficiaries. There had been brief moment of relative prosperity: that was when the house we were sitting in was built, and Faiz's elder brother was sent to Kabul to be educated.

Trouble happened very soon afterwards. Faiz couldn't remember the date, but his brother in Kabul was probably killed in 1978, during the purges that followed the communist coup. He was suspected of being an Islamist, although he was only a student and kept away from politics.

The communists came to the province, rounded up and killed a few mullahs, and arrested anyone they suspected of being counter-revolutionary. Then the Russians arrived.

Ishrat, translating and embellishing at the same time, told me of the Afghan rage and contempt for foreign invaders, and how every Afghan spontaneously joined the uprising against the

Russians. But this didn't match what he translated immediately afterwards: how Faiz had stayed away from the young men in the province who went to fight the Russians. He was married by then, with a young son and the orchards to look after.

But then the bombing began, from the Russian helicopters, in response to guerrilla attacks on communist convoys. Many of the cultivated fields near the highway to Kabul were mined, and once the canals were destroyed it became harder and harder to keep the orchards going.

Faiz's parents, on their way to Jalalabad for a wedding, were killed when the bus they were travelling on was hit by a stray mortar. There were other tragedies. His son turned out to be 'insane'—Ishrat used the Urdu word, 'Paagal'—and Faiz took him to various shrines, including a well-known one near Jalalabad which was famed for curing insanity, and made him wear various amulets. But none of these helped.

Faiz's two brothers were already with the mujahideen when he began fighting alongside them. It wasn't a full-time job. He joined specific expeditions, mostly ambushes of government convoys. He was home the rest of the time, taking care of his diminishing farmland.

It was Ishrat who volunteered the information, in Urdu, while Faiz looked on uncomprehendingly, that Faiz had earned a reputation as a brave man very early in the war. It was why he had been smuggled across the border and into a hospital in Peshawar after he suffered serious abdominal injuries during a mortar attack on his position in the mountains around Jalalabad.

Pakistan—where he met Ishrat—was a revelation for Faiz. It was where he first saw how the jihad against the communists had turned into a big business. Some of the so-called leaders of the Afghan mujahideen, living in grand villas in Hayatabad, were not even known to him by name. But there they were, handling the disbursement of arms and aid to the refugees and the mujahideen.

They made him think with pity and rage about the young men he was fighting with—people who started out with just a few .303 rifles among them until they managed to ambush an arms convoy and equip themselves with the latest Soviet equipment.

By the time Faiz got back to Afghanistan, the jihad against the Russians was almost over. A local mujahideen commander was already ruling over his province, and so peace came quickly and lasted longer in his part of Afghanistan. White men from UN agencies came to repair the irrigation canals; many of the destroyed orchards and fields were replanted.

Faiz wasn't one of the lucky farmers. None of the canals close to him were repaired. He had to go back to where his father had started out. He made a living out of selling the milk of the few cows and goats he had left over from the days of the jihad; he also made a bit of money by working as a labourer.

This was at a time when great wealth was being created all around him. Most of the restored fields grew poppy, under orders from the mujahideen commander, who lived in a mansion and maintained a private army. He wasn't as bad as the warlords in Helmand province; he wasn't a bandit or rapist. In fact, he was quite helpful to people who had fought in the jihad. But everyone knew he was involved in smuggling and drugs: the big business Faiz had seen in Pakistan had come to Afghanistan. Flights came to Jalalabad from Dubai loaded with colour TV sets that were then smuggled into Pakistan on big trucks. The opium went out to labs in southern Afghanistan and then, as heroin, to Iran.

This was why Faiz had first thought well of the Taliban when they came up from the south and chased out the commander. He didn't mind their severity; only people in the cities chafed at their restrictions on women. But they didn't alter the essential things. The smuggling continued. Poppy cultivation had stopped only recently, and he knew of people who were still at it. A few well-connected merchants and traders in Jalalabad grew rich. Most other people became poorer; his two brothers had to leave with their families for Pakistan where they worked as truck drivers. And there was the harassment. Young men showed up at his house trying to draft his son into the war against the Tajiks in the north, and had to be persuaded that he was unfit to be a soldier. He also didn't like their dependence on Arab and Pakistani jihadis, many of whom he saw in the province. Foreigners had done enough damage in Afghanistan; it was time for them to leave the country and its people alone.

Dismay appeared on Ishrat's face as he translated this, and a brief argument broke out between him and Faiz. I couldn't follow most of it, and I didn't trust the account I got from Ishrat who claimed to be arguing that the Arabs and Pakistanis helping the Taliban were fellow Muslims, and not infidels like the Russians and Americans.

I had wondered all afternoon about that emptiness of the big-seeming house, the absence of Faiz's wife and his son. I now saw two emaciated cows stumbling into the courtyard, followed by a thin stubble-faced man with a stick: this was Faiz's 'insane' son, explained Ishrat. He tethered the cows to an iron picket and then walked out of sight. A little later, I heard pots and pans being shuffled in an adjacent room and then I saw a chador-clad figure move briskly across the courtyard to throw some hay before the cows, and then swiftly retreat. She had been there all through the afternoon, possibly sleeping or lying down silently on the ground.

I asked Ishrat if it was possible to talk to her for a few minutes. He was quick to pick up on the hesitation in my voice. 'Why do you want to talk to her?' he asked.

I didn't have to respond. Faiz, who had gone out, came back into the room at that very moment. The lantern he held filled the room with the smell of kerosene. Ishrat explained my request to him in Pushtu. I saw his face tense.

The answer was no. Ishrat said, speaking once again on his own, that local custom did not permit strange men to talk to women. Faiz interrupted him and said that he could convey my question to his wife and bring back her reply.

It was better than nothing, so I asked the obvious question about life for women under the Taliban. It took a while for Ishrat to translate this, and I wasn't sure if he had done so accurately until the answer came back with a slightly more relaxed Faiz.

Faiz laughed as he spoke, and even Ishrat smiled as he translated. The thing she disliked most about Taliban rule was when she had to travel by bus to the nearby towns. The roads were bad; the buses were few; and the journeys were worst for the women who were forced to sit squashed at the back, separate from the men in the front of the bus.

The light outside the room grew softer; it was in the grey-blue dusk that Ishrat and Faiz went out to offer namaaz. I watched them from the room: two silently vigorous figures on the scruffy floor of the courtyard, bending and straightening up almost in unison, expressing a common faith, but so apart in their experiences: Ishrat, the fixer for foreign journalists in Peshawar, in touch with and amplifying ever-new ideologies and passions, and Faiz the retired fighter, all his previous disappointments and griefs bleached by his present struggles for survival, by the bare house and courtyard, and the greater blankness outside.

That kind of steady grinding-down of individual lives seems to go on all the time in places like Afghanistan and Pakistan. A few days after that evening with Faiz and Ishrat I was in Peshawar and heard about Jamal from one of the other men I'd met at the offices of *The Frontier Post*. Terrible things had happened to Jamal and the paper. A few days after my visit, a letter had come in by email. It started innocuously enough but then went on to insult Prophet Mohammed in the grossest terms. Jamal approved it for publication without reading it through to the end. No one else noticed before it was pounced upon by one of the fundamentalist organizations who were always waiting to undermine the English-language press. A mob came and set fire to the press. The police arrested several journalists; the editor managed to escape the police and went into hiding with his fellow tribesmen somewhere near the Khyber Pass. Most of the journalists had now been released but Jamal was in prison, awaiting trial for blasphemy.

The punishment for blasphemy in Pakistan was death. But Jamal was already close to dying. The journalist was surprised to learn that I didn't know—hadn't guessed from his dull yellow eyes—about Jamal's heroin addiction. It had begun soon after he arrived in Peshawar and got to know some drug dealers; he had been in and out of several hospitals.

No one could do anything for him now, the journalist said. I was shocked at his callousness at first, and then I felt guilty. In London I had received a couple of emails from Jamal about the book he wanted to write. I hadn't responded, as the book seemed to me a doomed idea.

The journalist, who himself had only just escaped the fury of the fundamentalists, was only being truthful, and I didn't feel that I could offer to help. I was a Hindu and an Indian. How could I get involved with an assassin, a heroin-addict and a blasphemer in Pakistan?

'They are all such fanatics here!' Jamal had said at our first meeting and I had been grateful for the sentiment then. But I had felt myself change during the weeks in Pakistan, after I recovered from the first few days of instinctive fear. There had been an unexpected moment towards the end of my stay. I had gone to see a Moghul mosque in Peshawar. The spies hadn't followed me into the courtyard, where a few men sat in the late afternoon sun, and I felt I was alone until I saw an old man sleeping in one dark corner. He was obviously an Afghan refugee. His long white beard and sharp features made me think he was from Herat, or the western provinces close to Iran. His head, resting on a silk-wrapped bundle, displayed the fine profile of monks and wayfarers in Persian and Moghul miniatures; and watching him in the decaying old building—where the inlaid tiles were all faded or chipped, the broad-blade fans swayed dangerously as they spun—I suddenly felt myself pulled centuries back. I had a sense, fleeting but vivid and exhilarating, of the greatness of the old global civilization of Islam, of the splendour of once-famous and now devastated cities—Herat, Balkh, Baghdad—of the whole life and world the religion had once created.

That world was now in turmoil; it had been broken into by the invincible modern civilization of the West. From the outside it seemed capable only of producing fanaticisms of the kind that had crushed Jamal, and it was hard not to be repelled by it.

'The foreigners should leave us alone,' Faiz had said, 'we will find our own way.' But countless men had tried and failed, many societies had been exposed to new kinds of pain, and it still wasn't clear what that way could be.

I had thought Jamal an ally, someone on my side. But I belonged to another, more fortunate world. The American diplomats in Islamabad had guessed correctly: I already had my side chosen for me. Jamal's fate was tied to the faceless people on the other side—people who were persecutors as much as victims. I couldn't see how things, given the way they were now, could work out for them. They could be cruel and unreasonable—'fanatics'. And yet I wanted them to flourish. I wanted them to have as much dignity and freedom as I had been allowed, even though I increasingly doubted whether the kind of life I lived was what they longed for, or could be content with.

Two Indians
on America
Amit Chaudhuri

Ramachandra Guha

(2002)

Amit Chaudhuri

When we were children, we played cowboys and Indians sometimes. We rather liked being cowboys; we instructed ourselves that the Indians were 'Red' Indians—the term 'American Indian' was still not in currency—not remotely like us, who enacted our make-believe in the large basement garages of a building on Malabar Hill in South Bombay. It was while looking for us, we noted, that Columbus had lighted upon America. The enormity of the accident—and the relatively unacknowledged but not inconsiderable part we had played in it!

In many places and ways, Bombay echoed, and still echoes, America. This is not to say it is an imitation; its America is to be found there, in its streets, and nowhere else. But this echo also sets it apart from every other Indian city; gives it its own melancholy destiny to fulfil.

There is, first of all, the allure of tall buildings. They cluster around Nariman Point—what might probably be called Bombay's 'financial district': the Air India building (where a bomb went off in 1993), the Indian Express building, the Oberoi Towers. This is reclaimed land; I remember when Nariman Point was still a 'point', a strip of land petering out into rocks and the sea. But tall buildings are everywhere in South Bombay. Some of them are as famous as famous people; a few, like some Bombay celebrities, have less than impeccable reputations. Some time in the late Seventies or early Eighties a building called Kanchenjunga, designed by the architect Charles Correa, came up on the hilly incline of Peddar Road, a giant, off-white rectangular box, with large perforations made in it, coloured violently red on the inside (the perforations were the balconies of duplex flats). For a long time, no one occupied those flats. The building had been erected on a disputed site. No matter; the building became a star—if a slightly shunned one—and a part of the skyline of jostling high and low, young and old structures, the all-night party of the

Two Indians on America

Bombay skyline. Years later, occupants appeared on the balconies; but you are not really meant to see people in the tall Bombay buildings.

There is more than a hint of New York here. The tall buildings are, literally, 'upstarts'; they are mainly post-Independence social climbers; their altitude suggests the precedence of desire over the genteel evasions of the colonial age.

But, in the perpetual sunshine, in the sea, in the palm trees, is also something of California. The pleasures of the body; the body standing in the sun.

And so, all those beaches; in Chowpatty, Juhu, Marve, not to speak of the Governor's private beach, which children from the Cathedral School used to visit once a year. The children taken for pony rides; the men, some of them frauds, racketeers or embezzlers, gambolling on the sand; semi-nude, back to a second infancy. The image crystallizes for me Bombay's mixture of the childlike and the grown-up, of naivety and ruthlessness, a mixture that, as I now know, is also peculiarly American. Childhood fantasy and adult knowingness, innocence and violence, inhabiting the same space, even the same mind and body.

I was introduced to America through the comic book. My Bengali parents had taught me no English before I went to school; settled outside Bengal, in Bombay, they had longed to make me intimate with the Bengali language. I was admitted into the school—on what basis, I don't know; I knew no English. The headmistress suggested an unusual two-pronged approach to my mother: to familiarize me with the language by giving me both Ladybird and comic books to read. Through the Ladybird books I was brought to a world of English families and landscapes; this education in English continued with Enid Blyton, whose cocooned universe contained strange cruelties and snobberies as well as buttered scones and picnic hampers.

That world, although close to us historically in many ways,

felt remote; but American comic books, which taught me to read, somehow entered our lives in Bombay and became indistinguishable from them; we didn't know where one ended and the other began. The much thumbed and perused copy, in the 'circulating library', of the Archie Comics Digest; the thin line separating us from Riverdale. The monthly purchase of Gold Key comics; the 'friendly' ghosts and witches; Richie Rich, that Fitzgeraldian cartoon character, who, with swimming pools, butlers, chauffeurs, was still not completely happy. Superheroes who led dull lives as employees in tall buildings, to whom the simple act of putting on spectacles conferred an impenetrable aura of ordinariness and guaranteed a foolproof disguise; or led reclusive lives as tycoons in opulent mansions with vast underground garages in which a single car was kept; or even, like Elastic Man, turned sad, congenital deformities into a prodigious talent for fighting crime. If Gregor Samsa had been born in America, would his 'metamorphosis' have made him famous, like Spiderman or the Incredible Hulk?

Our American childhood in Bombay happened during the Cold War, when one part of the world was under the canopy of Brezhnev's enormous eyebrows. We were in that part of the world. Although India is a democracy, it was certainly a political and strategic ally of Russia; Russia gave us an idea of moral and economic rectitude, while America provided us with a sort of illicit entertainment. As for Soviet entertainment, there were the astonishing films. We went to watch Sovexport films for two reasons. The first was that Russian films emerged from a more consciously artistic tradition of cinema than anything to be found in Hollywood. The other reason was less high-minded: our political friendship led to an odd indulgence on the part of the National Board of Film Censors, and the nudity in bad Sovexport films went largely uncut. The cuts in Hollywood films were clumsily, even insultingly, made—a woman might be unbuttoning her blouse; she seemed to suffer a brief spasm or convulsion; then she was seen to be buttoning her blouse. We, in the Seventies, studied that spasm closely but hopelessly. Nakedness in American movies was kept from us by a wall of propriety harder to penetrate than the Iron Curtain.

Superheroes; but also villains. For a generation, Henry Kissinger was the most hated man in India. In 1975, Sanjay Gandhi would overtake him in loathsomeness; but that bureaucratic suit, those thick glasses and that heavy accent would always make Indians shudder. And Nixon, too, who, with Kissinger, presided over the Bangladesh war; the way the American government always seemed to be on the wrong side of everything. Nevertheless, the young men and women queued up for application forms at the USIS in Marine Lines. The lines were long and exhausting; later, they left for the States. Returning for holidays, the men wore shorts, and T-shirts with the logos of obscure universities. Even their fathers began to wear shorts. On the rear windows of cars in Bombay, they pasted stickers with the names of those unheard-of universities, which others would be obliged to memorize in a traffic jam. What was it that took them there? Was it a desire for success and assimilation that Europe could not offer? And was it the ability, and desire, to merge (but not quite) with those crowds in Manhattan, or settle down in some suburb, or relocate themselves in the vast spaces in between?

Ramachandra Guha

At a garden party in Calcutta sometime in the late Fifties, a football kicked by the host's son broke a whisky bottle. Fragments of glass entered the exposed arm of the Consul General of the United States of America, who was taken to the hospital to be stitched up. As he went off, the biologist J. B. S. Haldane broke an embarrassed silence with this comment: 'A little Bengali communist has successfully attacked an American imperialist.'

By the time I moved to Calcutta twenty years later, a communist government had come to power in Bengal. One of its first acts was to name the street on which the US Consulate stood after Ho Chi Minh. Otherwise too the intellectual climate was suffused with hostility to America. Our heroes were Marx and Mao, and, moving on, writers who had taken our side in the Cold War, such as Jean Paul Sartre and Gabriel García Márquez.

I became a member of the local British Council, but would not enter the library of the United States Information Service. Then my wife got a scholarship to Yale, and I reluctantly followed. I reached New Haven on a Friday, and was introduced to the Dean of the School where I was to teach. On Sunday I was taking a walk through the campus when I saw the Dean park his car, take a large carton out of the boot, and carry it across the road to the School and up three flights to his office.

That sight of the boss as his own coolie was a body blow to my anti-Americanism. My father and grandfather had both been heads of Indian research laboratories; any material they took to work or back—even a slim file with a single piece of paper in it—would be placed in the car by one flunkey and carried inside by another. (Doubtless the Warden of an Oxford College can likewise call upon a willing porter.) Over the years, I have often been struck by the dignity of labour in America, by the ease with which high-ranking Americans carry their own loads, fix their own fences, and mow their own lawns. This, it seems to me, is part of a wider absence of caste or class distinctions. Indian intellectuals have tended to downplay these American achievements: the respect for the individual, the remarkable social mobility, the searching scrutiny to which public officials and state agencies are subjected. They see only the imperial power, the exploiter and the bully, the invader of faraway lands and the manipulator of international organizations to serve the interests of the American economy. The Gulf War, as one friend of mine put it, was undertaken 'in defence of the American way of driving'.

On the world stage America is not a pretty sight. Even between its various wars of adventure, its arrogance is on continuous display. The United States has disregarded strictures passed on it by the International Court of Justice, and defaulted on its financial obligations to the United Nations. It has violated the global climate change treaty, and the global biodiversity treaty. It has not signed the agreement to abolish the production of landmines. The only international treaties it signs and honours are those it can both draft and impose on other countries, such as the agreement on Intellectual Property Rights.

The truth about America is that it is at once deeply democratic and instinctively imperialist. This curious coexistence of contrary values is certainly exceptional in the history of the world. Other democratic countries, such as Sweden or Norway at the present time, are not imperialist. Scandinavian countries honour their international obligations, and (unlike the Americans) generously support social welfare programmes in the poorer parts of the world. Other imperialist countries, such as France and Great Britain in the past, were not properly democratic. In the heyday of European expansion men without property and all women did not have the vote. Even after suffrage was extended British governments were run by an oligarchy. The imagination boggles at the thought of a Ken Starr examining the sexual and other peccadilloes of a Benjamin Disraeli.

Historically, anti-Americanism in India was shaped by an aesthetic distaste for America's greatest gift—the making of money. When Jawaharlal Nehru first visited the United States in 1949, as Prime Minister of a free India, he was given a banquet in New York where the host told him: 'Mr Neroo, there are fifty billion dollars sitting around this table…' Naturally, the Brahmin schooled by British socialists was less than impressed.

Within India, the austere socialism of Nehru's day has now been replaced by the swaggering buoyancy of consumer capitalism. In cultural terms, America, rather than Britain, has become the locus of Indian emulation. Politically, too, the countries are closer than ever before. Yet the new enchantment with America—which is perhaps most manifest amongst politically minded Hindus—seems to have as shallow a foundation as the older disgust. Subliminally, but sometimes also on the surface, it is premised on the belief that America and its ally Israel have taken a tough line with the Muslims. (They take no nonsense from the Palestinians, as we should take no nonsense from the Pakistanis.) The prosperous Indian community in America models itself on the Jewish diaspora, whose influence it hopes one day to equal, and even exceed.

The current admiration for the United States has all to do with power. Strategic thinkers in New Delhi have little time for America's experiments with transparency of governance; they ask only that it recognize India as the 'natural' leader of this part of the world—as, in fact, the United States of South Asia. That it already is. Like its new-found political mentor, India is more reliably democratic than the other countries of South Asia; at the same time, it seeks to bully and dominate them. At least in the short term, the prestige attached to the term 'democracy' in the post Cold War (and post September 11) world will make India even more insolent in its dealings with its neighbours. Echoing a famous President of Mexico, King Gyanendra might well say: 'Poor Nepal! So far from God, so near to the Republic of India.'

Pariah

Viramma

(1997)

I am the midwife here. I was born in the village of Velpakkam in Tamil Nadu, and when I married, I came to Karani, my husband's village. I was still a child then. I am a farm worker and, like all my family, I am a serf, bonded to Karani's richest landowner. We are Pariahs. We live apart from the other castes; we eat beef, we play the drums at funerals and weddings because only we can touch cow hide; we work the land. My son Anbin corrects me when I say 'Pariah'; he says we should use the word 'Harijan'. Every day people from the political parties come to the village and tell us to demand higher wages, to fight the caste system. And they mean well. But how would we survive? We have no land, not even a field.

We midwives help women during labour and are paid twenty rupees a month by the state. When a woman goes into labour, her relatives come and find me: 'Eldest sister-in-law! The woman's in pain at home!' So I drop everything; I go and see her, examine her, turn her round one way, then the other; I pester her a bit and then tell her more or less when the child is going to be born. And cut the cord with a knife and tell one of the other women attending to find a hoe and a crowbar and to dig a hole in the channel near the house. I wait for the placenta to come out and go and bury it immediately. Then I take care of the mother. I stretch her out on a mat, propped up with pillows, wash the baby with soap and hot water and lay it down next to its mother. Then I put a sickle and some margosa leaves at the head of the mat, so spirits don't come near them—those rogue spirits love to prowl around the lanes in the evening or at night, eating any food left lying on the ground and trying to possess people.

It's well known that they follow us everywhere we go, when we're hoeing or planting out; when we're changing our sanitary towels; when we're washing our hair. They sense that we're going to visit a woman in labour and then they possess us. That's why we put down the sickle and the margosa leaves. After the birth

Pariah

I'll visit the mother quite often, to make sure everything's going all right. If impurities have stayed in the womb, I'll cook the leaves of the 'cow's itch' plant, extract the juice and make the mother drink it three times.

That's how a birth happens here. We Pariahs prefer to have babies at home. I tell the nurse if the newborns are boys or girls, and she goes and enters them in the registers at Pondicherry hospital. In the past, we'd take women to hospital only in emergencies. We went there in an ox-cart or a rickshaw, and often the woman died on the way. Nowadays doctors visit the villages and give medicines and tonics to women when they pregnant. In the sixth or seventh month they're meant to go to dispensary for a check-up. A nurse also comes to the village. Yes, everything has changed now.

I had my twelve children alone; I didn't let anyone near me. 'Leave me in peace,' I always said to the nurses. It will come out on its own! Why do you want to rummage around in there?' I always give birth very gently—like stroking a rose. It never lasts long: I'm not one of those women whose labours drag on all night, for days even.

When I'm giving birth I first make a point of preparing a tray for Ettiyan—the god of death's assistant—and his huge men, with their thick moustaches and muscly shoulders. On the tray I put green mangoes, coconuts and other fruit as well as some tools: a hoe, a crowbar, a basket, so that they can set to work as soon the child comes out of the sack in our womb. Yes! I've seen enough to know what I'm talking about. I've had a full bushel of children! Everything we eat goes into that sack: that's how the child grows. Just think what a mystery it is. With the blood he collects over ten months, Isvaran [the god Siva] moulds a baby in our womb. Only he can do that. Otherwise how could a sperm become a child?

I've always had plenty of milk. It used to flow so much the

187

front of my sari was all stiff. It's well known that we breastfeed our children for a long time. That prevents us from having another child immediately. If we were always pregnant, how could we work and eat? Rich women can stretch their legs and take a rest. But to get my rice, I have to work: planting out, hoeing, grazing the cows, collecting wood. When we've got a little one in our arms, it's the same: we take it everywhere, and we worry, because while we're working we don't really know what it's doing, where it is. That's why we try to wait at least three years, until the child grows up, walks and can say, 'Dad', 'Mum', 'That's our cow'. That's what we take as a sign. Then we can start 'talking' again, 'doing it'. If we time it like this, the child will be strong and chubby.

But Isvaran has given me a baby a year. Luckily my blood has stayed the same; it hasn't turned, and my children have never been really emaciated. Of course that also depends on the way you look after them. For me, that used to be my great worry! I managed to feed them all well. As soon as I had a little money, I'd buy them sweets. I'd make them rice whenever I could, some *dosai*, some *idli*. I'd put a little sugar in cow's milk... That's how I took care of them. There are some women who just let their children be without giving them regular meals. Human beings can only live if you put at least a little milk in their mouths when they're hungry! It happens with us that some women skip their children's mealtimes when they're working. But how do you expect them to grow that way?

Isvaran has done his work well; he's put plenty of children in my womb: beautiful children, born in perfect health. It's only afterwards that some have died. One of diarrhoea, another of apoplexy. All of them have walked! Two of my children even came to the peanut harvest. I pierced their noses to put a jewel in. I plaited their hair and put flowers in it and pretty *potteu* on their foreheads, made with paste. I took good care of my little

Pariah

ones. I never neglected them. I dressed them neatly. If high-caste people saw them running in the street, they'd talk to them kindly, thinking that they were high-caste children.

How many children have I had? Wait… I've had twelve. The first was a girl, Muttamma. Then a boy, Ganesan. After that, a girl, Arayi. *Ayo!* After that I don't remember any more. But I've definitely had twelve: we registered them at the registry office. Yes, when there's a birth, you have to go there and declare it. 'Here sir, I've had a boy or a girl and I name it Manivelu, Nataraja or Perambata.' Down there they enter all that into a big ledger. *Ayo!* If we went to that office, perhaps they could tell us how many children I've had and their names as well. *Ayo!* Look at that, I don't remember any more. They're born: they die. I've haven't got all my children's names in my head: all I have left are Miniyamma, my fourth child; Anbin, my eighth; and Sundari, my eleventh.

A pregnant woman is prey to everything that roams around her: ghosts, ghouls, demons, the evil spirits of people who have committed suicide or died violent deaths. She has to be very careful, especially if she is a Pariah. We Pariah women have to go all over the place, grazing the cattle, collecting wood. We're outside the whole time, even when the sun's at its height. Those spirits take advantage of this: they grab us and possess us so we fall ill, or have miscarriages. Something like that happened to me when I was pregnant with my second child.

One of my nephews died suddenly, the day after his engagement. One night when I was asleep I saw him sitting on me—I felt him! My husband told me that I had squeezed him very tight in my arms, that I'd been delirious and mumbling something. The following day we decided that the boy needed something, and that's why he'd come. My husband went to get bottles of arrack and palm wine. I arranged the offerings in the middle of the house: betel, areca nuts, lime, a big banana leaf

189

with a mountain of rice, some salt fish, some toast, a cigar, bottles of alcohol, a jar of water and a beautiful oil lamp. In the meantime my husband went to find the priest from the temple of Perumal [Vishnu]—he's the one responsible for funerals. The priest asked us to spread river sand next to the offerings. He called on Yama, the god of death, and drew the sign of Yama in the sand. We ate that evening as usual and went to sleep in a corner. You must never sleep opposite the door, because a spirit might slap you when it comes in if it finds you in its way. You have to be brave when a spirit arrives! In fact you won't see it; you only hear its footsteps, like the sound of little bells, *djang, djang*, when an ox-cart goes by. It goes *han! han! han!* as if it's craving something. It always comes with its messengers, all tied to each other with big ropes. You hear them walking with rhythmic, heavy steps: *ahum! ahum! ahum!*

We were very afraid. As soon as the spirit came in, the lamp went out in a flash, even though it was full of oil. We heard it walking about and eating its fill and then suddenly it fled. We heard it running away very fast. When day broke soon after it had gone, we rushed to see what had happened. The rice was scattered everywhere. On the sand we found a cat's paw-print, and part of Yama's sign had been rubbed out. The spirit had come in the form of a cat! While we were waiting for the priest to come, we collected the offerings in a big wicker basket. The priest himself was very satisfied and said that the spirit wouldn't come back. But I fell ill soon after and had a miscarriage.

There are worse spirits, though: the *katteri*, for example, who spy on women when they are pregnant. You have to be very careful with them. There are several sorts of *katteri*: Rana Katteri, who has bleeding wounds and drinks blood; or Irsi Katteri, the foetus eater—she's the one who causes miscarriages. As soon as she catches the smell of a foetus in a woman's womb, she's there, spying, waiting for her chance. We can tell immediately that it's

Pariah

that bitch at work if there are black clots when a baby aborts: she sucks up the good blood and leaves only the bad.

My first three children were born at my mother's house. Their births went well, and they died in good shape. It was the spirit living in that house who devoured them. My grandfather knew about sorcery. People came to see him; they used to say that he called up the spirit, talked to it and asked it to go along with him when he went out. It lived with him, basically. When my grandfather died, we tried to drive it away but it was no use; it used to come back in the form of my grandfather; it joined in conversations, calling my grandmother by her name like her dead husband used to. And my grandmother used to answer back, 'Ah! The only answer I'll give you is with my broom, you dog! I recognize you! I know who you are! Get out of here!' It would just throw tamarind seeds at her face. When a sorcerer came from Ossur to try and get rid of it, it turned vicious. The sorcerer told us he couldn't do anything against it. The spirit had taken root in that ground. It was old and cunning: we were the ones who had to go. It destroyed everything! Everything! A garlic clove couldn't even grow! My father had to sell his paddy field. I gave birth three times there: none of those children survived. The spirit ate them as and when they were born. Nothing prospered. That's how it is with the spirits.

All my children have been buried where they died: the first ones at Velpakkam, the others at Karani. My mother insisted we burn the first-born and throw her ashes in the river so a sorcerer didn't come and get them. The ashes or bones of first-borns are coveted by magicians. A tiny bit of ash or hair is enough for them. You see them with a hoe on their shoulder prowling around where a first-born has been burnt or buried. We made sure that everything disappeared. We have a saying that if you dissolve the ashes completely in water, you'll immediately have another child.

Until they grow up, we mothers always have a fire in our belly for our children: we must feed them, keep them from sickness, raise them to become men or women who can work. One of my three sisters died of a kind of tuberculosis. She had been married and she left a son. I brought him up after her death, but like his mother, he was often ill. Before she died, my sister had prayed that he would become strong, so I took up her prayers. I went into three houses and in each one I asked for a cubit of fabric. I put the three bits of fabric on the ground and laid the child on them. Then I went into three other houses and exchanged the child for three measures of barley, saying, 'The child is yours; the barley is mine.' Of course afterwards I would get the child back. Then I went to three other houses to collect handfuls of dirt. I mixed the three handfuls, spread them out and rolled the baby in them, saying, 'Your name will be Kuppa! You are Kuppa! You have been born of dirt!' Then I pierced his nostril with a silver thread which I twisted into a ring. That worked very well for him! He's still alive and he still wears that ring in his nose today.

What is more important for us women than children? If we don't draw anything out of our womb, what's the use of being a woman? A woman who has no son to put a handful of rice in her mouth, no daughter to close her eyes, is an unhappy woman. She or her parents must have failed in their dharma. I have been blessed in that way: Isvaran has filled my womb. Ah, if all my children were alive, they'd do all the trades in the world! One would be a labourer, another a carpenter. I would have made one of them study. We could have given two daughters away in marriage and enjoyed our grandchildren. I would be able to go and rest for a month with each of my sons. Yes, we would have been proud of our children.

Translated by Will Hobson

Serendip
Ian Jack

(1998)

Ian Jack

The people of Sri Lanka (or Ceylon as it was then known) first saw the power of steam in ships, and then the railways came. Much later, in 1981, I met a madman on the platform of Colombo railway station, the narrow-gauge side. The Tamil war on the island was just beginning. I was working for a Sunday newspaper in London at the time and had filed my copy for the week. Now, on a Sunday afternoon, I could relax. I decided to take a look at the little branch line, rumoured to be still worked by steam locomotives, which runs up from the capital to the town of Ratnapura and the tea and rubber estates in the foothills. That was how I met Mr Goonawardene.

No trains were expected. The station was deserted. He must have been watching me for some time from his position behind the pillar. He may even have seen in my behaviour a kindred spirit; the way, for example, I walked up and down the platform peering over the edge for tell-tale signs of locomotive cinders on the tracks—what could that be but derangement? His approach was startlingly direct.

'Sir, sir, allow me to introduce myself. My name is Goonawardene and I am a racialist.'

He was a thin man in grubby white clothes and black lacing shoes which lacked shoelaces. He wanted to tell me his theory of the world, how it had developed and where it had gone wrong.

The guilty party, he said, was Western science. Out of science had come industry and medicine. The industrial countries of the West had enormous appetites for raw materials—cotton, tea, sugar, rubber, oil—and to feed these appetites they had behaved like capricious gods, plucking people from one country and dumping them in another without a thought for tomorrow. Think of it! Africans dispatched by sea to the Caribbean to cut sugar; Indians exported by sea to Africa to build railways; and here, in Sri Lanka, Tamilians shipped by ferry from India to pick tea. Then Western medicine had come along with its bag of tricks and permitted all these black and brown people to multiply; 'to breed like microbes', was how Mr Goonawardene put it.

He shaped a globe with his hands and waggled his fingers to show it pulsating. I imagined a round Dutch cheese alive with grubs. 'A mess, a most terrible mess. Blacks, whites, browns, yellows, all mixed up. They must be sent back to where they came from and then we shall have some peace.' His fingers stopped moving. The globe was now calm and orderly. 'That is why I call myself a racialist.'

I was anxious to get away. 'Well,' I said, 'no trains to Ratnapura today. I should be getting back to the hotel.'

But it was not so easy. 'No, no, train is coming soon. A little train, lots of smoke. You'll like it.' He dusted a station bench with his sleeve. 'Sit, please sir, sit.'

We sat. Mr Goonawardene leaned forward, as though he had noticed me for the first time as a person as well as an audience. 'Which is your country?'

'Britain.'

He broke into a broad smile. 'Ah, then you are the guilty-party-in-chief. Step forward into the dock. I shall be the prosecutor. Now tell me, Mr Britisher, who perfected the steam engine?'

'James Watt.'

'Correct. A Scotchman, born I believe in the seaport of Greenock. A great man. It may be that he and Isaac Newton are the only two British scientists of what we may call world class, at least until the atomic age. Now give me the place and date of the first railway in the world.'

'Stockton and Darlington. Was it in 1825?'

'Very correct. George Stephenson was the engineer. Imagine! A boy who worked at a coal mine, who could neither read nor write by the age of eighteen, and yet he built the world's first really successful steam locomotives. But I can see you know everything, your knowledge is A1.'

We sat together like a schoolmaster and his successful pupil. Then Mr Goonawardene winked and became playful. Could I tell him who had perfected the internal-combustion engine? I fumbled; not Henry Ford?

'No, no. Herr Rudolph Diesel, 1897. And Diesel was a native of which country?'

I guessed Germany and Mr Goonawardene said that was right, though in fact Herr Diesel had been born in Paris. The inventor died in mysterious circumstances, vanishing from the deck of a cross-channel steamer in the year before the outbreak of the First World War. Mr Goonawardene suspected suicide. 'Like many great men he may have suffered mania and depression. I am also suffering from the same condition and I have been tempted by the same fate. But do you see what I am trying to tell you?'

His arms went out to make a see-saw. 'Britishers invent the steam engine. Britain goes up. Germans invent the petrol engine. Germans and their cousins the Americans go up. Britain comes down.' These days, he said, only backward places such as Colombo ever saw a steam locomotive and even here they were rare.

The afternoon wore on. It was a grey day in the tropics. A curtain of rain swept in from the Indian Ocean and hammered on the station roof. Mr Goonawardene began to shiver.

'When is the train coming, Mr Goonawardene?'

'Soon, soon.'

A lie; but he couldn't let me go, our quiz was too delightful a conversational form. What tune had the band played when the Titanic went down? Who was the most powerful man in Stalinist Russia? ('Stalin?' Tsk, tsk! 'Beria, the head of the secret police?' Tsk, tsk again. No, it was Maxim Litvinov, the Soviet ambassador in London and Washington, though I can't now remember why.) And then he named three prominent Britons: a journalist, a peer and a politician. Did I know these people? I said I knew of them. Then would I write to them on his behalf?

Serendip

'I want them to set up a commission of enquiry, to come to Colombo and establish my sanity.' For the past twenty years he had lived in the Angoda lunatic asylum—it was, he said, 'a fine three-storey building of the British period'—but he had never believed, because he knew so much, that he could really be insane. 'And you must admit,' he said finally, 'that I am knowing a pretty damn lot, isn't it?'

No train ever came, at least on the narrow-gauge side. My companion went home to his asylum and I returned to my room overlooking the ocean at the Galle Face Hotel. There were ships on the horizon, their shapes occasionally blurred by the rain which came and went in squalls and dark patches which moved across the sea. They were square shapes. I imagined a flat hull loaded with containers and not the raked funnels and curving sterns of my childhood. That night, remembering Mr Goonawardene and the ships, I wrote to my father, who was dying.

It was not a good letter. Nobody had told my father he hadn't long to live, though perhaps in his conscious moments he understood this well enough. My letter was part of a cheerful pretence. I knew that more than fifty years before he had sailed into Colombo as a junior engineer on a cargo steamer, the SS *Nuddea*, and so I described Colombo: how a lighthouse still stood in the main street, how the tea now went by containers, how some people still remembered the British India Steam Navigation Company, the line which had owned the *Nuddea*, though the puritanical black-and-white funnels of its ships no longer popped up above the dock's high walls. In my father's time it had been one of the biggest shipping companies in the world. I made a few jokes—cheerfulness, that was the thing—and hoped that he was feeling better.

He died a couple of months later. For most of his life he had worked as a steam mechanic, a fitter, one of the men who were on the downswinging end of Mr Goonawardene's see-saw. One of Watt's children; I had never heard him mention Herr Diesel, though the German had perfected his engine five years before my father was born. The saddest change in him, my mother said, was the way that, long before the end, he had completely lost interest in the world. He had read a few sentences of my letter from Colombo and then lain it down on the bedspread and said nothing. 'And you know what your father was like,' my mother said, 'he was always so interested in things.' I remembered a saying of his, spoken from the heart of a man who had grown up among the gossip of a small Scottish town: 'Stupid folk talk about other folk. Intelligent folk talk about things.'

Five years later I came back to Sri Lanka. The Tamil war was now in full swing. Tamil guerrillas had beaten back the Sri Lankan army in the north of the island. Troops were regularly ambushed or blown up by landmines, and the Sinhalese in the south were frightened and angry. Bombs went off in Colombo, while in the countryside entire villages were rounded up and massacred, Sinhalese by the Tamils and Tamils by the Sinhalese. Tourists and businessmen no longer came. Colombo's hotels were empty. At the Galle Face they said I could have any room—even the Royal Scandinavian Suite—for less than half the listed price.

Mr Goonawardene's diagnosis looked in the case of his own country to have been right. Ethnic differences within the same nation had exploded into savagery (though science and the West could hardly be blamed; Sri Lanka's Tamil separatists were not those Tamils imported from India by the British to pick tea; they had arrived long before European colonization). But where was Mr Goonawardene? Now, on another Sunday with another newspaper story safely filed, I went down to the railway station again. Nobody in the stationmaster's office had seen him. What kind of man was I looking for?

'Thin and old,' I said, 'and slightly mad, but he knows a lot.

He said he came here often in the afternoons—the platforms on the narrow-gauge side.'

'We have seen no such person.'

Sitting alone in the wide open spaces of the Royal Scandinavian Suite and listening to the sea, I began to think I'd made him up. The next day, I asked at the British Council library. The women behind the counter said she thought she knew who I meant. He had died a year back. 'He came here every morning to read the *Encyclopaedia Britannica* and the London newspapers. He wrote a lot in his notebook. He was interested in everything, all kinds of facts.'

That was all she remembered: Mr Goonawardene as a heap of facts who was locked up every night in the Angoda asylum. He had left no other trace of personality. An old version of Europe—the Europe of Watt and the British India Steam Navigation Company, the Europe of curiosity and enquiry—had sailed to Sri Lanka and planted seeds in him. And the seeds had sprouted to cover his personality like bindweed. His was a seaborne disease.

The Tutor
Nell Freudenberger

(2003)

She was an American girl, but one who apparently kept Bombay time, because it was three-thirty when she arrived for their one o'clock appointment. It was a luxury to be able to blame someone else for his wasted afternoon, and Zubin was prepared to take full advantage of it. Then the girl knocked on his bedroom door.

He had been in the preparation business for four years, but Julia was his first foreign student. She was dressed more like a Spanish or an Italian girl than an American, in a sheer white blouse and tight jeans that sat very low on her hips, perhaps to show off the tiny diamond in her belly button. Her hair was shiny, reddish-brown—chestnut you would call it—and she'd ruined her hazel eyes with a heavy application of thick, black eyeliner.

'I have to get into Berkeley,' she told him.

It was typical for kids to fixate on one school. 'Why Berkeley?'

'Because it's in San Francisco.'

'Technically Berkeley's a separate city.'

'I know that,' Julia said. 'I was born in San Francisco.'

She glanced at the bookshelves that covered three walls of his room. He liked the kids he tutored to see them, although he knew his pride was irrelevant: most didn't know the difference between Spender and Spenser, or care.

'Have you *read* all of these?'

'Actually that's the best way to improve your verbal. It's much better to see the words in context.' He hated the idea of learning words from a list; it was like taking vitamin supplements in place of eating. But Julia looked discouraged, and so he added: 'Your dad says you're a math whiz, so we don't need to do that.'

'He said that?'

'You aren't?'

Julia shrugged. 'I just can't believe he said "whiz".'

'I'm paraphrasing,' Zubin said. 'What were your scores?'

The Tutor

'Five-sixty verbal, seven-sixty math.'

Zubin whistled. 'You scored higher than I did on the math.'

Julia smiled, as if she hadn't meant to, and looked down. 'My college counsellor says I need a really good essay. Then my verbal won't matter so much.' She dumped out the contents of an expensive-looking black leather knapsack, and handed him the application, which was loose and folded into squares. Her nails were bitten, and decorated with half-moons of pale pink polish.

'I'm such a bad writer though.' She was standing expectantly in front of him. Each time she took a breath, the diamond in her stomach flashed.

'I usually do lessons in the dining room,' Zubin said.

The only furniture in his parents' dining room was a polished mahogany table, covered with newspapers and magazines, and a matching sideboard—storage space for jars of pickle, bottles of Wild Turkey from his father's American friends, his mother's bridge trophies, and an enormous, very valuable Chinese porcelain vase, which the servants had filled with artificial flowers: red, yellow and salmon-coloured cloth roses beaded with artificial dew. On nights when he didn't go out, he preferred having his dinner served to him in his room; his parents did the same.

He sat down at the table, but Julia didn't join him. He read aloud from the form. 'Which book that you've read in the last two years has influenced you most, and why?'

Julia wandered over to the window.

'That sounds okay,' he encouraged her.

'I hate reading.'

'Talk about the place where you live, and what it means to you.' Zubin looked up from the application. 'There you go. That one's made for you.'

She'd been listening with her back to him, staring down Ridge Road toward the Hanging Garden. Now she turned around—did a little spin on the smooth tiles.

'Can we get coffee?'

'Do you want milk and sugar?'

Julia looked up, as if shyly. 'I want to go to Barista.'

'It's loud there.'

'I'll pay,' Julia said.

'Thanks. I can pay for my own coffee.'

Julia shrugged. 'Whatever—as long as I get my fix.'

Zubin couldn't help smiling.

'I need it five times a day. And if I don't get espresso and a cigarette first thing in the morning, I have to go back to bed.'

'Your parents know you smoke?'

'God, no. Our driver knows—he uses it as blackmail.' She smiled. 'No smoking is my dad's big rule.'

'What about your mom?'

'She went back to the States to find herself. I decided to stay with my dad,' Julia added, although he hadn't asked. 'He lets me go out.'

Zubin couldn't believe that any American father would let his teenage daughter go out at night in Bombay. 'Go out where?'

'My friends have parties. Or sometimes clubs—there's that new place, Fire and Ice.'

'You should be careful,' Zubin told her.

Julia smiled. 'That's so Indian.'

'Anyone would tell you to be careful—it's not like the States.'

'No,' Julia said.

He was surprised by the bitterness in her voice. 'You miss it.'

'I am missing it.'

'You mean now in particular?'

Julia was putting her things back into the knapsack haphazardly—phone, cigarettes, datebook, chapstick. She squinted at the window, as if the light were too bright. 'I mean, I don't even know what I'm missing.'

The Tutor

Homesickness was like any other illness: you couldn't remember it properly. You knew you'd had the flu, and that you'd suffered, but you didn't have access to the symptoms themselves: the chills, the swollen throat, the heavy ache in your arms and legs as if they'd been split open and something—sacks of rock—had been sewn up inside. He had been eighteen, and in America for only the second time. It was cold. The sweaters he'd bought in Bombay looked wrong—he saw that the first week—and they weren't warm enough anyway. He saw the same sweaters, of cheap, shiny wool, in too-bright colours, at the 'international' table in the Freshman Union. He would not sit there.

His room-mate saw him go out in his T-shirt and windcheater, and offered to loan him one of what seemed like dozens of sweaters: brown or black or wheat-coloured, the thickest, softest wool Zubin had ever seen. He went to the Harvard Coop, where they had a clothing section, and looked at the sweaters. He did the calculation several times: the sweaters were 'on sale' for eighty dollars, which worked out to roughly 3,300 rupees. If it had been a question of just one he might have managed, but you needed a minimum of three. When the salesperson came over, Zubin said that he was just looking around.

It snowed early that year.

'It gets like, how cold in the winter in India?' his room-mate Bennet asked.

Zubin didn't feel like explaining the varied geography of India, the mountains and the coasts. 'About sixty degrees Fahrenheit,' he said.

'*Man,*' said Bennet. Jason Bennet was a nice guy, an athlete from Natick, Massachusetts. He took Zubin to eat at the lacrosse table, where Zubin looked not just foreign, but as if he were another species—he weighed at least ten kilos less than the smallest guy, and felt hundreds of years older. He felt as if he were surrounded by enormous and powerful children. They were hungry, and then they were restless; they ran around and around in circles, and then they were tired. Five nights a week they'd pledged to keep sober; on the other two they drank systematically until they passed out.

He remembered the day in October that he'd accepted the sweater (it was raining) and how he'd waited until Jason left for practice before putting it on. He pulled the sweater over his head and saw, in the second of woolly darkness, his father. Or rather, he saw his father's face, floating in his mind's eye like the Cheshire Cat. The face was making an expression that Zubin remembered from the time he was ten, and had proudly revealed the thousand rupees he'd made by organizing a betting pool on the horse races among the boys in the fifth standard.

He'd resolved immediately to return the sweater, and then he had looked in the mirror. What he saw surprised him: someone small but good-looking, with fine features and dark, intense eyes, the kind of guy a girl, not just a girl from home but any girl— an American girl—might find attractive.

And he wanted one of those: there was no use pretending he didn't. He watched them from his first-floor window, as close as fish in an aquarium tank. They hurried past him, laughing and calling out to one another, in their boys' clothes: boots, T-shirts with cryptic messages, jeans worn low and tight across the hips. You thought of the panties underneath those jeans, and in the laundry room you often saw those panties: impossibly sheer, in incredible colours, occasionally, delightfully torn. The girls folding their laundry next to him were entirely different from the ones at home. They were clearly free to do whatever they wanted— a possibility that often hit him, in class or the library or on the historic brick walkways of the Radcliffe Quad, so intensely that he had to stop and take a deep breath, as if he were on the point of blacking out.

He wore Jason's sweater every day, and was often too warm; the classrooms were overheated and dry as furnaces. He almost never ran into Jason, who had an active and effortless social schedule to complement his rigorous athletic one. And so it was a surprise, one day in late October, to come back to the room and find his room-mate hunched miserably over a textbook at his desk.

'Midterms,' Jason said, by way of an explanation. Zubin went over and looked at the problem set, from an introductory physics class. He'd taken a similar class at Cathedral; now he laid out the equations and watched as Jason completed them, correcting his room-mate's mistakes as they went along. After the third problem Jason looked up.

'Man, thanks.' And then, as if it had just occurred to him. 'Hey, if you want to keep that—'

He had managed so completely to forget about the sweater that he almost didn't know what Jason meant.

'It's too small for me anyway.'

'No,' Zubin said.

'Seriously. I may have a couple of others too. Coach has been making us eat like hogs.'

'Thanks,' Zubin said. 'But I want something less preppy.'

Jason looked at him.

'No offence,' Zubin said. 'I've just been too fucking lazy. I'll go tomorrow.'

The next day he went back to the Coop with his almost-new textbooks in a bag. These were for his required classes (what they called the Core, or general knowledge), as well as organic chemistry. If you got to the reserve reading room at nine, the textbooks were almost always there. He told himself that the paperbacks for his nineteenth-century novel class weren't worth selling—he'd bought them used anyway—and when he took the rest of the books out and put them on the counter, he realized he had forgotten *The Norton Anthology of American Literature* in his dorm room. But the books came to $477.80 without it.

He took the T downtown to a mall where he bought a down jacket for $300, as warm as a sleeping bag, the same thing the black kids wore. He got a wool watchman's cap with a Nike swoosh.

When he got home, Jason laughed. 'Dude, what happened? You're totally ghetto.' But there was approval in it. Folding the brown sweater on Jason's bed, Zubin felt strong and relieved, as if he had narrowly avoided a terrible mistake.

Julia had been having a dream about losing it. There was no sex in the dream; she couldn't remember whom she'd slept with, or when. All she experienced was the frustrating impossibility of getting it back, like watching an earring drop and scatter in the bathroom sink, roll and clink down the drain before she could put her hand on it. The relief she felt on waking up every time was like a warning.

She had almost lost it in Paris, before they moved. He was German, not French, gangly but still handsome, with brown eyes and blondish hair. His name was Markus. He was a year ahead of her at the American School and he already knew that he wanted to go back to Berlin for university, and then join the Peace Corps. On the phone at night, he tried to get her to come with him.

At dinner Julia mentioned this idea to her family.

'*You* in the Peace Corps?' said her sister Claudia, who was visiting from New York. 'I wonder if Agnès B. makes a safari line?'

When Claudia came home, she stayed with Julia on the fourth floor, in the *chambre de bonne* where she had twin beds and her Radiohead poster, all her CDs organized by record label and a very old stuffed monkey named Frank. The apartment was half a block from the Seine, in an old hotel on the Rue des Saint-Pères; in the living room were two antique chairs, upholstered in red-and-gold striped brocade, and a porcelain clock with shepherdesses on it. The chairs and the clock were Louis XVI, the rugs were from Tehran, and everything else was beige linen.

Claudia, who now lived with her boyfriend in a railroad apartment on the Lower East Side, liked to pretend she was poor. She talked about erratic hot water and rent control and cockroaches, and when she came to visit them in Paris she acted surprised, as if the houses she'd grown up in—first San Francisco, then Delhi, then Dallas, Moscow and Paris—hadn't been in the same kind of neighbourhood, with the same pair of Louis XIV chairs.

'I can't believe you have a Prada backpack,' she said to Julia. Claudia had been sitting at the table in the kitchen, drinking espresso and eating an orange indifferently, section by section. 'Mom's going crazy in her old age.'

'I bought it,' Julia said.

'Yeah but, with what?'

'I've been selling my body on the side—after school.'

Claudia rolled her eyes and took a sip of her espresso; she looked out the window into the little back garden. 'It's so *peaceful* here,' she said, proving something Julia already suspected: that her sister had no idea what was going on in their house.

It started when her father's best friend, Bernie, left Paris to take a job with a French wireless company in Bombay. He'd wanted Julia's father to leave with him, but even though her father complained all the time about the oil business, he wouldn't go. Julia heard him telling her mother that he was in the middle of an important deal.

'This is the biggest thing we've done. I love Bernie—but he's afraid of being successful. He's afraid of a couple of fat Russians.'

Somehow Bernie had managed to convince her mother that Bombay was a good idea. She would read the share price of the wireless company out loud from the newspaper in the mornings, while her father was making eggs. It was a strange reversal; in the past, all her mother had wanted was for her father to stay at home. The places he travelled had been a family joke, as if he were trying to outdo himself with the strangeness of the cities— Istanbul and Muscat eventually became Tbilisi, Ashkhabad, Tashkent. Now, when Julia had heard the strained way that her mother talked about Bernie and wireless communication, she had known she was hearing part of a larger argument—known enough to determine its size, if not its subject. It was like watching the exposed bit of a dangerous piece of driftwood, floating just above the surface of a river.

Soon after Claudia's visit, in the spring of Julia's freshman year, her parents gave her a choice. Her mother took her to Galeries Lafayette, and then to lunch at her favourite crêperie on the Ile Saint-Louis where, in between *galettes tomate-fromage* and *crêpe pomme-chantilly*, she told Julia about the divorce. She said she had found a two-bedroom apartment in the West Village: a 'feat', she called it.

'New York will be a fresh start—psychologically,' her mother said. 'There's a bedroom that's just yours, and we'll be a five-minute train ride from Claudie. There are wonderful girls' schools—I know you were really happy at Hockaday.'

'No I wasn't.'

'Or we can look at some co-ed schools. And I'm *finally* going to get to go back for my masters—' She leaned forward confidentially. 'We could both be graduating at the same time.'

'I want to go back to San Francisco.'

'We haven't lived in San Francisco since you were three.'

'So?'

The sympathetic look her mother gave her made Julia want to yank the tablecloth out from underneath their dishes, just to hear the glass breaking on the rustic stone floor.

'For right now that isn't possible,' her mother said. 'But there's no reason we can't talk again in a year.'

The Tutor

Julia had stopped being hungry, but she finished her mother's crêpe anyway. Recently her mother had stopped eating anything sweet; she said it 'irritated her stomach' but Julia knew the real reason was Dr Fabrol, who had an office on the Ile Saint-Louis very near the crêperie. Julia had been seeing Dr Fabrol once a week during the two years they'd been in Paris; his office was dark and tiny, with a rough brown rug and tropical plants which he misted from his chair with a plastic spritzer while Julia was talking. When he got excited he swallowed, making a clicking sound in the back of his throat.

In front of his desk Dr Fabrol kept a sandbox full of little plastic figures: trolls with brightly coloured hair, toy soldiers, and a little dollhouse people dressed in American clothes from the Fifties. He said that adults could learn a lot about themselves by playing '*les jeux des enfants*'. In one session, when Julia couldn't think of anything to say, she'd made a ring of soldiers in the sand, and then without looking at him, put the mother doll in the centre. She thought this might be over the top even for Dr Fabrol, but he started arranging things on his desk, pretending he was less interested than he was so that she would continue. She could hear him clicking.

The mother doll had yellow floss hair and a full figure and a red-and-white polka-dotted dress with a belt, like something Lucille Ball would wear. She looked nothing like Julia's mother—a fact that Dr Fabrol obviously knew, since Julia's mother came so often to pick her up. Sometimes she would be carrying bags from the nearby shops; once she told them she'd just come from an exhibit at the new Islamic cultural centre. She brought Doctor Fabrol a postcard of a Phoenician sarcophagus.

'I think this was the piece you mentioned?' Her mother's voice was louder than necessary. 'I think you must have told me about it—the last time I was here to pick Julia up?'

'Could be, could be,' Dr Fabrol said, in his stupid accent. They both watched Julia as if she were a TV and they were waiting to find out about the weather. She couldn't believe how dumb they must have thought she was.

Her father asked her if she wanted to go for an early morning walk with their black labrador, Baxter, in the Tuileries. She would've said no—she wasn't a morning person—if she hadn't known what was going on from the lunch with her mother. They put their coats on in the dark hall with Baxter running around their legs, but by the time they left the apartment, the sun was coming up. The river threw off bright sparks. They crossed the bridge, and went through the archway into the courtyard of the Louvre. There were no tourists that early but a lot of people were walking or jogging on the paths above the fountain.

'Look at all these people,' her father said. 'A few years ago, they wouldn't have been awake. If they were awake they would've been having coffee and a cigarette. Which reminds me.'

Julia held the leash while her father took out his cigarettes. He wasn't fat but he was tall and pleasantly big. His eyes squeezed shut when he smiled, and he had a beard, mostly grey now, which he trimmed every evening before dinner with special scissors. When she was younger, she had looked at other fathers and felt sorry for their children; no one else's father looked like a father to her.

In the shade by the stone wall of the Tuileries, with his back to the flashing fountain, her father tapped the pack, lifted it to his mouth and pulled a cigarette out between his lips. He rummaged in the pocket of his brown corduroys for a box of the tiny wax matches he always brought back from India, a white swan on a red box. He cupped his hand, lit the cigarette and exhaled away from Julia. Then he took back Baxter's leash and said: 'Why San Francisco?'

The Tutor

She wasn't prepared. 'I don't know.' She could picture the broad stillness of the bay, like being inside a postcard. Was she remembering a postcard?

'It's quiet,' she said.

'I didn't know quiet was high on your list.'

She tried to think of something else.

'You know what I'd like?' her father asked suddenly. 'I'd like to watch the sunrise from the Golden Gate—do you remember doing that?'

'Yes,' Julia lied.

'I think you were in your stroller.' Her father grinned. 'That was when you were an early riser.'

'I could set my alarm.'

'You could set it,' her father teased her.

'I'm awake now,' she said.

Her father stopped to let Baxter nose around underneath one of the grey stone planters. He looked at the cigarette in his hand as if he didn't know what to do with it, dropped and stamped it out, half smoked.

'Can I have one?'

'Over my dead body.'

'I'm not sure I want to go to New York.'

'You want to stay here?' He said it lightly, as if it were a possibility.

'I want to go with you,' she said. As she said it, she knew how much she wanted it.

She could see him trying to say no. Their shadows were very sharp on the clean paving stones; above the bridge, the gold Mercury was almost too bright to look at.

'Just for the year and a half.'

'*Bombay*,' her father said.

'I liked India last time.'

Her father looked at her. 'You were six.'

'Why are you going?'

'Because I hate oil and I hate oilmen. And I hate these goddamn *kommersants*. If I'd done it when Bernie first offered—' Her father stopped. 'You do not need to hear about this.'

Julia didn't need to hear about it; she already knew. Her father was taking the job in Bombay—doing exactly what her mother had wanted him to do—just as her parents were getting a divorce. The only explanation was that he'd found out about Dr Fabrol. Even though her mother was going to New York (where she would have to find another psychologist to help her get over Julia's), Julia could see how her father wouldn't want to stay in Paris. He would want to get as far away as possible.

Julia steered the conversation safely toward business: 'It's like, mobile phones, right?'

'It is mobile phones.' Her father smiled at her. 'Something you know about.'

'I'm not *that* bad.'

'No, you're not.'

They'd walked a circle in the shade, on the promenade above the park. Her father stopped, as if he wasn't sure whether he wanted to go around again.

'It's not even two years,' Julia said. There was relief just in saying it, the same kind she'd felt certain mornings before grade school, when her mother had touched her head and said *fever*.

Her father looked at the Pont Neuf; he seemed to be fighting with himself.

'I'd rather start over in college—with everybody else,' she added.

Her father was nodding slowly. 'That's something we could explain to your mother.'

As you got older, Zubin noticed, very occasionally a fantasy that you'd been having forever came true. It was disorienting, like waking up in a new and better apartment, remembering that you'd moved, but not quite believing that you would never go back to the old place.

That was the way it was with Tessa. Their first conversation was about William Gaddis; they had both read *Carpenter's Gothic*, and Zubin was halfway through *JR*. In fact he had never finished *JR*, but after the party he'd gone home and lay on his back in bed, semi-erect but postponing jerking off with the relaxed and pleasant anticipation of a sure thing, and turned fifty pages. He didn't retain much of the content of those pages the next morning, but he remembered having felt that Gaddis was an important part of what he'd called his 'literary pedigree', as he and Tessa gulped cold red wine in the historic, unheated offices of the campus literary magazine. He even told her that he'd started writing poems himself.

'Can I read them?' she asked. As if he could show those poems to anyone!

Tessa moved closer to him; their shoulders and their hips and their knees were pressed together.

'Sure,' he said. 'If you want.'

They had finished the wine. Zubin told her that books were a kind of religion for him, that when things seemed unbearable the only comfort he knew was to read. He did not tell her that he was more likely to read science fiction at those times than William Gaddis; he hardly remembered that himself.

'What do you want to do now?' he'd asked, as they stepped out on to the narrow street, where the wind was colder than anything he could have imagined at home. He thought she would say she had class in the morning, or that it was late, or that she was meeting her room-mate at eleven, and so it was a surprise to him when she turned and put her tongue in his mouth. The wind disappeared then, and everything was perfectly quiet. When she pulled away, her cheeks and the triangle of exposed skin between her scarf and her jacket were pink. Tessa hung her head, and in a whisper that was more exciting to him than any picture he had ever seen, print or film, said: 'Let's go back to your room for a bit.'

He was still writing to Asha then. She was a year below him in school, and her parents had been lenient because they socialized with his parents (and because Zubin was going to Harvard). They had allowed him to come over and have a cup of tea, and then to take Asha for a walk along Marine Drive, as long as he brought her back well before dark. Once they had walked up the stairs from Hughes Road to Hanging Garden and sat on one of the benches, where the clerks and shop-girls whispered to each other in the foliage. He had ignored her flicker of hesitation and pointed down at the sun setting over the city: the Spenta building with a pink foam of cloud behind it, like a second horizon above the bay. He said that he wouldn't change the worst of the concrete-block apartments, with their exposed pipes and hanging laundry and waterstained, crumbling facades, because of the way they set off plain Babulnath Temple, made its tinselled orange flag and bulbous dome rise spectacularly from the dense vegetation, like a spaceship landed on Malabar Hill.

He was talking like that because he wanted to kiss her, but he sometimes got carried away. And when he noticed her again he saw that she was almost crying with the strain of how to tell him that she had to get home right now. He pointed to the still-blue sky over the bay (although the light was fading and the people coming up the path were already dark shapes) and took her hand and together they climbed up to the streetlight, and turned left toward her parents' apartment. They dropped each other's hand automatically when they got to the driveway, but Asha was so relieved that, in the mirrored elevator on the way up, she closed her eyes and let him kiss her.

That kiss was the sum of Zubin's experience, when he lost it with Tessa on Jason Bennet's green futon. He would remember forever the way she pushed him away, knelt in front of him and, with her jeans unbuttoned, arched her back to unhook her bra and free what were still the breasts that Zubin held in his mind's eye: buoyant and pale with surprising long, dark nipples.

Clothed, Tessa's primary feature was her amazing acceptability; there was absolutely nothing wrong with the way she looked or dressed or the things she said at the meetings of the literary magazine. But when he tried to remember her face now, he came up with a white oval into which eyes, a nose and a pair of lips would surface only separately, like leftover Cheerios in a bowl of milk.

When he returned from the States the second time, Asha was married to a lawyer and living in Cusrow Baug. She had twin five-year-old boys, and a three-year-old girl. She had edited a book of essays by famous writers about Bombay. The first time he'd run into her, at a wine tasting at the Taj President, he'd asked her what she was doing and she did not say, like so many Bombay women he knew, that she was married and had three children. She said: 'Prostitution.' And when he looked blank, she laughed and said, 'I'm doing a book on prostitution now. Interviews and case histories of prostitutes in *Mumbai*.'

When their city and all of its streets had been renamed overnight, in '94, Zubin had had long discussions with Indian friends in New York about the political implications of the change. Now that he was back those debates seemed silly. The street signs were just something to notice once and shake your head at, like the sidewalks below them—constantly torn up and then abandoned for months.

His mother was delighted to have him back. 'We won't bother you,' she said. 'It will be like you have your own artist's loft.'

'Maybe I should start a salon,' Zubin joked. He was standing in the living room, a few weeks after he'd gotten back, helping himself from a bottle of Rémy Martin.

'Or a saloon,' his father remarked, passing through.

He didn't tell his parents that he was writing a book, mostly because only three of the thirty poems he'd begun were actually finished; that regrettable fact was not his fault, but the fault of the crow that lived on the sheet of tin that was patching the roof over his bedroom window. He'd learned to ignore the chainsaw from the new apartment block that was going up under spindly bamboo scaffolding, the hammering across the road, the twenty-four-hour traffic and the fishwallah who came through their apartment blocks between ten and ten-thirty every morning, carrying a steel case on his head and calling '*hell-o, hell-o, hell-o.*' These were routine sounds, but the crow was clever. It called at uneven intervals, so that just as Zubin was convinced it had gone away, it began again. The sound was mournful and rough, as depressing as a baby wailing; it sounded to Zubin like despair.

When he'd first got back to Bombay, he'd been embarrassed about the way his students' parents introduced him: 'BA from Harvard; Henry fellow at Oxford; PhD from Columbia.' He would correct them and say that he hadn't finished the PhD (in fact, he'd barely started his dissertation) when he quit. That honesty had made everyone unhappy, and had been bad for business. Now he said his dissertation was in progress. He told his students' parents that he wanted to spend a little time here, since he would probably end up in the States.

The parents assumed that he'd come back to get married. They pushed their children toward him, yelling at them: 'Listen to Zubin; he's done three degrees—two on scholarship—not lazy and spoiled like you. Aren't I paying enough for this tutoring?' They said it in Hindi, as if he couldn't understand.

The kids were rapt and attentive. They did the practice tests he assigned them; they wrote the essays and read the books. They didn't care about Harvard, Oxford and Columbia. They were thinking of Boston, London and New York. He could read their minds. The girls asked about particular shops; the boys wanted to know how many girlfriends he had had, and how far they'd been willing to go.

None of his students could believe he'd come back voluntarily. They asked him about it again and again. How could he tell them that he'd missed his bedroom? He had felt that if he could just get back there—the dark wood floor, the brick walls of books, the ancient roll-top desk from Chor Bazaar—something would fall back into place, not inside him but in front of him, like the lengths of replacement track you sometimes saw them fitting at night on dark sections of the Western Railway commuter line.

He had come home to write his book, but it wasn't going to be a book about Bombay. There were no mangoes in his poems, and no beggars, no cows or Hindu gods. What he wanted to write about was a moment of quiet. Sometimes sitting alone in his room there would be a few seconds, a silent pocket without the crow or the hammering or wheels on the macadam outside. Those were the moments he felt most himself; at the same time, he felt that he was paying for that peace very dearly—that life, his life, was rolling away outside.

'But why did you wait three years?' his mother asked. 'Why didn't you come home right away?'

When he thought about it now, he was surprised that it had taken only three years to extract himself from graduate school. He counted it among the more efficient periods of his life so far.

He saw Julia twice a week, on Tuesdays and Thursdays. One afternoon when his mother was hosting a bridge tournament, he went to her house for the first time. A servant showed him into her room and purposefully shut the door, as if he'd had instructions not to disturb them. It was only four o'clock but the blinds were drawn. The lights were on and the door to her bathroom was closed; he could hear the tap running. Zubin sat at a small, varnished desk. He might have been in any girl's room in America: stacks of magazines on the book shelf, tacked-up posters of bands he didn't know, shoes scattered across a pink rag-rug and pieces of pastel-coloured clothing crumpled in with the sheets of the bed. A pair of jeans was on the floor where she'd stepped out of them, and the denim held her shape: open, round and paler on the inside of the fabric.

Both doors opened at once. Zubin didn't know whether to look at the barefoot girl coming out of the bathroom, or the massive, bearded white man who had appeared from the hall.

'Hi Daddy,' Julia said. 'This is Zubin, my tutor.'

'We spoke on the phone, sir,' said Zubin, getting up.

Julia's father shook hands as if it were a quaint custom Zubin had insisted on. He sat down on his daughter's bed, and the springs protested. He looked at Zubin.

'What are you working on today?'

'Dad.'

'Yes.'

'He just got here.'

Julia's father held up one hand in defence. 'I'd be perfectly happy if you didn't get into college. Then you could just stay here.'

Julia rolled her eyes, a habit that struck Zubin as particularly American.

'We'll start working on her essay today.' Zubin turned to Julia: 'Did you do a draft?' He'd asked her the same thing twice a week for the past three, and he knew what the answer would be. He wouldn't have put her on the spot if he hadn't been so nervous himself. But Julia surprised him: 'I just finished.'

'What did you write about?' her father asked eagerly.

'The difficulties of being from a broken home.'

The Tutor

'Very interesting,' he said, without missing a beat.

'I couldn't have done it without you.'

'I try,' he said casually, as if this were the kind of conversation they had all the time. 'So maybe we don't even need Zubin—if you've already written your essay?'

Julia shook her head: 'It isn't good.'

Zubin felt he should say something. 'The new format of the SAT places much greater emphasis on writing skills.' He felt like an idiot.

Julia's father considered Zubin. 'You do this full-time?'

'Yes.'

'Did you always want to be a teacher?'

'I wanted to be a poet,' Zubin said. He could feel himself blushing but mostly he was surprised, that he had told these two strangers something he hadn't even told his parents.

'Do you write poems now?'

'Sometimes,' Zubin said.

'There are some good Marathi poets, aren't there?'

'That's not what I'm interested in.' Zubin thought he'd spoken too forcefully, but it didn't seem to bother Julia's father.

'I'll leave you two to work now. If you want, come to dinner some time—our cook makes terrible Continental food, because my daughter won't eat Indian.'

Zubin smiled. 'That sounds good—thank you, Sir.'

'Mark,' Julia's father said, closing the door gently behind him.

'Your dad seems cool.'

Julia was gathering up all of her clothes furiously from the bed and the floor. She opened her closet door—a light went on automatically—and threw them inside. Then she slammed it. He didn't know what he'd done wrong.

'Do you want me to take a look at what you have?'

'What?'

'Of the essay.'

221

'I didn't write an essay.'

'You said—'

Julia laughed. 'Yeah.'

'How do you expect to get into Berkeley?'

'You're going to write it.'

'I don't do that.' He sounded prim.

'I'll pay you.'

Zubin got up. 'I think we're finished.'

She took her hair out of the band and redid it, her arms above her head. He couldn't see any difference when she finished. 'A hundred dollars.'

'Why do you want me to write your essay?'

Suddenly Julia sank down on to the floor, hugging her knees. 'I have to get out of here.'

'You said that before.' He wasn't falling for the melodrama. 'I'll help you do it yourself.'

'A thousand. On top of the regular fee.'

Zubin stared. 'Where are you going to get that much money?'

'Half a *lakh*.'

'That calculation even I could have managed,' Zubin said, but she wasn't paying attention. She picked up a magazine off her night table, and flopped down on the bed. He had the feeling that she was giving him time to consider her offer and he found himself—in that sealed-off corner of his brain where these things happened—considering it.

With $200 a week, plus the $1,000 bonus, he easily could stop all the tutoring except Julia's. And with all of that time, there would be no excuse not to finish his manuscript. There were some prizes for first collections in England and America; they didn't pay a lot, but they published your book. Artists, he thought, did all kinds of things for their work. They made every kind of sacrifice—financial, personal, moral—so as not to compromise the only thing that was truly important.

The Tutor

'I'll make a deal with you,' Zubin said.

Julia looked bored.

'You try it first. If you get really stuck—then maybe. And I'll help you think of the idea.'

'They *give* you the idea,' she said. 'Remember?'

'I'll take you to a couple of places. We'll see which one strikes you.' This, he told himself, was hands-on education. Thanks to him, Julia would finally see the city where she had been living for nearly a year.

'Great,' said Julia sarcastically. 'Can we go to Elephanta?'

'Better than Elephanta.'

'To the Gateway of India? Will you buy me one of those big, spotted balloons?'

'Just wait,' said Zubin. 'There's some stuff you don't know about yet.'

They walked from his house past the Hanging Garden, to the small vegetable market in the lane above the Walkeshwar Temple. They went down a flight of uneven steps, past small, open electronic shops where men clustered around televisions waiting for the cricket scores. The path wound between low houses, painted pink or green, a primary school and a tiny, white temple with a marble courtyard and a black *nandi* draped in marigolds. Two vegetable vendors moved to the side to let them pass, swivelling their heads to look, each with one hand lightly poised on the flat basket balanced on her head. Inside the baskets, arranged in an elegant multicoloured whorl, were eggplants, mint, tomatoes, Chinese lettuces, okra, and the smooth white pumpkins called *dudhi*. Further on a poster man had laid out his wares on a frayed, blue tarpaulin: the usual movie stars and glossy deities, plus kittens, puppies and an enormous white baby, in a diaper and pink headband. Across the bottom of a composite photo—an English cottage superimposed on a Thai beach, in the shadow of Swiss mountains dusted with yellow and purple wild flowers and bisected by a torrential Amazonian waterfall—were the words, HOME IS WHERE. WHEN YOU GO THERE, THEY HAVE TO LET YOU IN. Punctuation aside, it was difficult for Zubin to imagine a more depressing sentiment.

'You know what I hate?'

Zubin had a strange urge to touch her. It wasn't a sexual thing, he didn't think. He just wanted to take her hand. 'What?'

'Crows.'

Zubin smiled.

'You probably think they're poetic or something.'

'No.'

'Like Edgar Allen Poe.'

'That was a raven.'

'Edgar Allen Po*etic*.' She giggled.

'This kind of verbal play is encouraging,' Zubin said. 'If only you would apply it to your practice tests.'

'I can't concentrate at home,' Julia said. 'There are too many distractions.'

'Like what?' Julia's room was the quietest place he'd been in Bombay.

'My father.'

The steps opened suddenly on to the temple tank: a dark green square of water cut out of the stone. Below them, a schoolgirl in a purple jumper and a white blouse, her hair plaited with two red ribbons, was filling a brass jug. At the other end a labourer cleared muck from the bottom with an iron spade. His grandmother had brought him here when he was a kid. She had described the city as it had been: just the sea and the fishing villages clinging to the rocks, the lush, green hills, and in the hills these hive-shaped temples, surrounded by the tiny coloured houses of the priests. The concrete block apartments were still visible on the Malabar side of the tank, but if you faced the sea you could ignore them.

The Tutor

'My father keeps me locked up in a cage,' Julia said mournfully.

'Although he lets you out for Fire and Ice,' Zubin observed.

'He doesn't. He ignores it when I go to Fire and Ice. All he'd have to do is look in at night. I don't put pillows in the bed or anything.'

'He's probably trying to respect your privacy.'

'I'm his *kid*. I'm not supposed to have privacy.' She sat down suddenly on the steps, but she didn't seem upset. She shaded her eyes with her hand. He liked the way she looked, looking—more serious than he'd seen her before.

'Do you think it's beautiful here?' he asked.

The sun had gone behind the buildings, and was setting over the sea and the slum on the rocks above the water. There was an orange glaze over half the tank; the other, shadowed half was green and cold. Shocked-looking white ducks with orange feet stood in the shade, each facing a different direction, and on the opposite side two boys played an impossibly old-fashioned game, whooping as they rolled a worn-out bicycle tire along the steps with a stick. All around them bells were ringing.

'I think lots of things are beautiful,' Julia said slowly. 'If you see them at the right time. But you come back and the light is different, or someone's left some trash, or you're in a bad mood—or whatever. Everything gets ugly.'

'This is what your essay is about.' He didn't think before he said it; it just came to him.

'The Banganga Tank?'

'Beauty,' he said.

She frowned.

'It's your idea.'

She was trying not to show she was pleased. Her mouth turned up at the corners, and she scowled to hide it. 'I guess that's Okay. I guess it doesn't really matter what you choose.'

Julia was a virgin, but Anouk wasn't. Anouk was Bernie's daughter; she lived in a fancy house behind a carved wooden gate, on one of the winding lanes at Cumbala Hill. Julia liked the ornamental garden, with brushed-steel plaques that identified the plants in English and Latin, and the blue ceramic pool full of lumpy-headed white-and-orange goldfish. Behind the goldfish pond was a cedar sauna, and it was in the sauna that it had happened. The boy wasn't especially cute, but he was distantly related to the royal house of Jodhpur. They'd only done it once; according to Anouk that was all it took, before you could consider yourself ready for a real boyfriend at university.

'It's something to get over with,' Anouk said. 'You simply hold your breath.' They were listening to the Shakira album in Anouk's room, which was covered with pictures of models from magazines. There were even a few pictures of Anouk, who was tall enough for print ads, but not to go to Europe and be on runways. She was also in a Colgate commercial that you saw on the Hindi stations. Being Anouk's best friend was the thing that saved Julia at the American School, where the kids talked about their fathers' jobs and their vacation houses even more than they had in Paris. At least at the school in Paris they'd gotten to take a lot of trips—to museums, the Bibliothèque Nationale, and Monet's house at Giverny.

There was no question of losing her virginity to any of the boys at school. Everyone would know about it the next day.

'You should have done it with Markus,' Anouk said, for the hundredth time, one afternoon when they were lying on the floor of her bedroom, flipping through magazines.

Julia sometimes thought the same thing; it was hard to describe why they hadn't done it. They'd talked about it, like they'd talked about everything, endlessly, late at night on the phone, as if they were the only people awake in the city. Markus was her best friend—still, when she was sad, he was the one she wanted to talk to—but when they kissed he put his tongue too far into her mouth and moved it around in a way that made her want to gag. He was grateful when she took off her top and let him put his hand underneath her bra, and sometimes she thought he was relieved too, when she said no to other things.

'You could write him,' Anouk suggested.

'I'd love him to come visit,' Julia allowed.

'Visit and come.'

'Gross.'

Anouk looked at her sternly. She had fair skin and short hair that flipped up underneath her ears. She had cat-shaped green eyes exactly like the ones in the picture of her French grandmother, which stared out of an ivory frame on a table in the hall.

'What about your tutor?'

Julia pretended to be horrified. 'Zubin?'

'He's cute, right?'

'He's about a million years older than us.'

'How old?'

'Twenty-nine, I think.'

Anouk went into her dresser and rummaged around. 'Just in case,' she said innocently, tossing Julia a little foil-wrapped packet.

This wasn't the way it was supposed to go—you weren't supposed to be the one who got the condom—but you weren't supposed to go to high school in Bombay, to live alone with your father, or to lose your virginity to your SAT tutor. She wondered if she and Zubin would do it on the mattress in his room, or if he would press her up against the wall, like in 9 1/2 *Weeks*.

'You better call me, like, the second after,' Anouk instructed her.

She almost told Anouk about the virginity dream, and then didn't. She didn't really want to hear her friend's interpretation.

It was unclear where she and Markus would've done it, since

at that time boys weren't allowed in her room. There were a lot of rules, particularly after her mother left. When she was out, around eleven, her father would message her mobile, something like: WHAT TIME, MISSY? or simply, ETA? If she didn't send one right back, he would call. She would roll her eyes, at the cafe or the party or the club, and say to Markus, 'My dad.'

'Well,' Markus would say. 'You're his daughter.'

When she came home, her father would be waiting on the couch with a book. He read the same books over and over, especially the ones by Russians. She would have to come in and give him a kiss, and if he smelled cigarettes he would ask to see her bag.

'You can't look in my bag,' she would say, and her father would hold out his hand. 'Everybody else smokes,' she told him. 'I can't help smelling like it.' She was always careful to give Markus her Dunhills before she went home.

'Don't you trust me?' she said sometimes (especially when she was drunk).

Her father smiled. 'No. I love you too much for that.'

It was pouring and the rain almost shrieked on Zubin's tin roof, which still hadn't been repaired. They were working on reading comprehension; a test two years ago had used Marvell's 'To His Coy Mistress'. Zubin preferred 'The Garden', but he'd had more success teaching 'To His Coy Mistress' to his students; they told him it seemed 'modern'. Many of his students seemed to think that sex was a relatively new invention.

'It's a persuasive poem,' Zubin said. 'In a way, it has something in common with an essay.'

Julia narrowed her eyes. 'What do you mean, persuasive?'

'He wants to sleep with her.'

'And she doesn't want to.'

'Right,' Zubin said.

'Is she a virgin?'

The Tutor

'You tell me.' Zubin remembered legions of teachers sing-songing exactly those words. 'Look at line twenty-eight.'

'That's disgusting.'

'Good,' he said. 'You understand it. That's what the poet wanted—to shock her a little.'

'That's so manipulative!'

It was amazing, he thought, the way Americans all embraced that kind of psychobabble. *Language* is manipulative, he wanted to tell her.

'I think it might have been very convincing,' he said instead.

'*Vegetable* love?'

'It's strange, and that's what makes it vivid. The so-called metaphysical poets are known for this kind of conceit.'

'That they were conceited?'

'Conceit,' Zubin said. 'Write this down.' He gave her the definition; he sounded conceited.

'*The sun is like a flower that blooms for just one hour,*' Julia said suddenly.

'That's the opposite,' Zubin said. 'A comparison so common that it doesn't mean anything—you see the difference?'

Julia nodded wearily. It was too hot in the room. Zubin got up and propped the window open with the wooden stop. Water sluiced off the dark, shiny leaves of the magnolia.

'What is that?'

'What?'

'That thing, about the sun.'

She kicked her foot petulantly against his desk. The hammering outside was like an echo, miraculously persisting in spite of the rain. 'Ray Bradbury,' she said finally. 'We read it in school.'

'I know that story,' Zubin said. 'With the kids on Venus. It rains for seven years, and then the sun comes out and they lock the girl in the closet. Why do they lock her up?'

'Because she's from Earth. She's the only one who's seen it.'
'The sun.'
Julia nodded. 'They're all jealous.'

People thought she could go out all the time because she was American. She let them think it. One night she decided to stop bothering with the outside stairs; she was wearing new jeans that her mother had sent her; purple cowboy boots and a sparkly silver halter top that showed off her stomach. She had a shawl for outside, but she didn't put it on right away. Her father was working in his study with the door cracked open.

The clock in the hall said 10.20. Her boots made a loud noise on the tiles.

'Hi,' her father called.

'Hi.'

'Where are you going?'

'A party.'

'Where?'

'Juhu.' She stepped into his study. 'On the beach.'

He put the book down and took off his glasses. 'Do you find that many people are doing Ecstasy—when you go to these parties?'

'Dad.'

'I'm not being critical—I read an article about it in *Time*. My interest is purely anthropological.'

'Yes,' Julia said. 'All the time. We're all on Ecstasy from the moment we wake up in the morning.'

'That's what I thought.'

'I have to go.'

'I don't want to keep you.' He smiled. 'Well I do, but—' Her father was charming; it was like a reflex.

'See you in the morning,' she said.

The worst thing was that her father *knew* she knew. He might have thought Julia knew even before she actually did; that was when he started letting her do things like go out at 10.30, and smoke on the staircase outside her bedroom. It was as if she'd entered into a kind of pact without knowing it; and by the time she found out why they were in Bombay for real, it was too late to change her mind.

It was Anouk who told her, one humid night when they were having their tennis lesson at Willingdon. The air was so hazy that Julia kept losing the ball in the sodium lights. They didn't notice who'd come in and taken the last court next to the parking lot until the lesson was over. Then Anouk said: 'Wow, look—*Papa*!' Bernie lobbed the ball and waved; as they walked toward the other court, Julia's father set up for an overhead and smashed the ball into the net. He raised his fist in mock anger, and grinned at them.

'Good lesson?'

'Julia did well.'

'I did not.'

'Wait for Bernie to finish me off,' Julia's father said. 'Then we'll take you home.'

'How much longer?'

'When we're finished,' said Bernie sharply.

'*On sort ce soir.*'

'*On va voir,*' her father said. Anouk started to say something and stopped. She caught one ankle behind her back calmly, stretched, and shifted her attention to Julia's father. 'How long?'

He smiled. 'Not more than twenty.'

They waited in the enclosure, behind a thin white net that was meant to keep out the balls, but didn't, and ordered fresh lime sodas.

'We need an hour to get ready, at least.'

'I'm not going.'

'Yes you are.'

Anouk put her legs up on the table and Julia did the same and they compared: Anouk's were longer and thinner, but Julia's had a better shape. Julia's phone beeped.

'It's from Zubin.'

Anouk took the phone.

'It's just about my lesson.'

Anouk read Zubin's message in an English accent: CAN WE SHIFT FROM FIVE TO SIX ON THURSDAY?

'He doesn't talk like that,' Julia said, but she knew what Anouk meant. Zubin was the only person she knew who wrote SMS in full sentences, without any abbreviations.

Anouk tipped her head back and shut her eyes. Her throat was smooth and brown and underneath her sleeveless white top, her breasts were outlined, the nipples pointing up. 'Tell him I'm hot for him.'

'You're a flirt.'

Anouk sat up and looked at the court. Now Bernie was serving. Both men had long, dark stains down the fronts of their shirts. A little bit of a breeze was coming from the trees behind the courts; Julia felt the sweat between her shoulders. She thought she'd gone too far, and she was glad when Anouk said, 'When are they going to be finished?'

'They'll be done in a second. I think they both just play 'cause the other one wants to.'

'What do you mean?'

'I mean, my dad never played in Paris.'

'Mine did,' Anouk said.

'So maybe he just likes playing with your dad.'

Anouk tilted her head to the side for a minute, as if she were thinking. 'He would have to though.'

The adrenaline from the fight they'd almost had, defused a minute before, came flooding back. She could feel her pulse in her wrists. 'What do you mean?'

The Tutor

Her friend opened her eyes wide. 'I mean, your dad's probably grateful.'

'Grateful for *what*?'

'The job.'

'He had a good job before.'

Anouk blinked incredulously. 'Are you serious?'

'He was the operations manager in Central Asia.'

'Was,' Anouk said.

'Yeah, well,' Julia said. 'He didn't want to go back to the States after my mom did.'

'My God,' Anouk said. 'That's what they told you?'

Julia looked at her. *Whatever you're going to say, don't say it.* But she didn't say anything.

'You have it backwards,' Anouk said. 'Your mother left because of what happened. She went to America, because she knew your father couldn't. There was an article about it in *Nefte Compass*—I couldn't read it, because it was in Russian, but my dad read it.' She lifted her beautiful eyes to Julia's. 'My dad said it wasn't fair. He said they shouldn't've called your dad a crook.'

'Four–five,' her father called. 'Your service.'

'But I guess your mom didn't understand that.'

Cars were inching out of the club. Julia could see the red brake lights between the purple blossoms of the hedge that separated the court from the drive.

'It doesn't matter,' Anouk said. 'You said he wouldn't have gone back anyway, so it doesn't matter whether he *could* have.'

A car backed up, beeping. Someone yelled directions in Hindi.

'And it didn't get reported in America or anything. My father says he's lucky he could still work in Europe—probably not in oil, but anything else. He doesn't want to go back to the States anyway—*alors, c'est pas grand chose*.'

The game had finished. Their fathers were collecting the balls from the corners of the court.

'Ready?' her father called, but Julia was already hurrying across the court. By the time she got out to the drive she was jogging, zigzagging through the cars clogging the lot, out into the hot night-time haze of the road. She was lucky to find an empty taxi. They pulled out into the mass of traffic in front of the Hagi Ali and stopped. The driver looked at her in the mirror for instructions.

'Malabar Hill,' she said. 'Hanging Garden.'

Zubin was actually working on the essay, sitting at his desk by the open window, when he heard his name. Or maybe hallucinated his name: a bad sign. But it wasn't his fault. His mother had given him a bottle of sambuca, which someone had brought her from the duty-free shop in the Frankfurt airport.

'I was thinking of giving it to the Mehtas but he's stopped drinking entirely. I could only think of you.'

'You're the person she thought would get the most use out of it,' his father contributed.

Now Zubin was having little drinks (really half drinks) as he tried to apply to college. He had decided that there would be nothing wrong with writing a first draft for Julia, as long as she put it in her own words later. The only problem was getting started. He remembered his own essay perfectly, unfortunately on an unrelated subject. He had written, much to his English teacher's dismay, about comic books.

'Why don't you write about growing up in Bombay? That will distinguish you from the other applicants,' she had suggested.

He hadn't wanted to distinguish himself from the other applicants, or rather, he'd wanted to distinguish himself in a much more distinctive way. He had an alumni interview with an expatriate American consultant working for Arthur Anderson in Bombay; the interviewer, who was young, Jewish and from New York, said it was the best college essay he'd ever read.

The Tutor

'Zu-*bin*.'

It was at least a relief that he wasn't hallucinating. She was standing below his window, holding a tennis racket. 'Hey Zubin—can I come up?'

'You have to come around the front,' he said.

'Will you come down and get me?'

He put a shirt over his T-shirt, and then took it off. He took the glass of sambuca to the bathroom sink to dump it, but he got distracted looking in the mirror (he should've shaved) and drained it instead.

He found Julia leaning against a tree, smoking. She held out the pack.

'I don't smoke.'

She sighed. 'Hardly anyone does any more.' She was wearing an extremely short white skirt. 'Is this a bad time?'

'Well—'

'I can go.'

'You can come up,' he said, a little too quickly. 'I'm not sure I can do antonyms now though.'

In his room Julia gravitated to the stereo. A Brahms piano quartet had come on.

'You probably aren't a Brahms person.'

She looked annoyed. 'How do *you* know?'

'I don't,' he said. 'Sorry—are you?'

Julia pretended to examine his books. 'I'm not very familiar with his work,' she said finally. 'So I couldn't really say.'

He felt like hugging her. He poured himself another sambuca instead. 'I'm sorry there's nowhere to sit.'

'I'm sorry I'm all gross from tennis.' She sat down on his mattress, which was at least covered with a blanket.

'Do you always smoke after tennis?' he couldn't help asking.

'It calms me down.'

'Still, you shouldn't—'

'I've been having this dream,' she said. She stretched her legs out in front of her and crossed her ankles. 'Actually it's kind of a nightmare.'

'Oh,' said Zubin. Students' nightmares were certainly among the things that should be discussed in the living room.

'Have you ever been to New Hampshire?'

'What?'

'I've been having this dream that I'm in New Hampshire. There's a frozen pond where you can skate outside.'

'That must be nice.'

'I saw it in a movie,' she admitted. 'But I think they have them—anyway. In the dream I'm not wearing skates. I'm walking out on to the pond, near the woods, and it's snowing. I'm walking on the ice but I'm not afraid—everything's really beautiful. And then I look down and there's this thing—this dark spot on the ice. There are some mushrooms growing, on the dark spot. I'm worried that someone skating will trip on them, so I bend down to pick them.'

Her head was bent now; she was peeling a bit of rubber from the sole of her sneaker.

'That's when I see the guy.'

'The guy.'

'The guy in the ice. He's alive, and even though he can't move, he sees me. He's looking up and reaching out his arms and just his fingers are coming up—just the tips of them through the ice. Like white mushrooms.'

'Jesus,' Zubin said.

She misunderstood. 'No—just a regular guy.'

'That's a bad dream.'

'Yeah well,' she said proudly. 'I thought maybe you could use it.'

'Sorry?'

'In the essay.'

The Tutor

Zubin poured himself another sambuca. 'I don't know if I can write the essay.'

'You have to.' Her expression changed instantly. 'I have the money—I could give you a cheque now even.'

'It's not the money.'

'Because it's dishonest?' she said in a small voice.

'I—' But he couldn't explain why he couldn't manage to write even a college essay, even to himself. 'I'm sorry.'

She looked as if she'd been about to say something else, and then changed her mind. 'Okay,' she said dejectedly. 'I'll think of something.'

She looked around for her racket, which she'd propped up against the bookshelf. He didn't want her to go yet.

'What kind of a guy is he?'

'Who?'

'The guy in the ice—is he your age?'

Julia shook her head. 'He's old.'

Zubin sat down on the bed, at what he judged was a companionable distance. 'Like a senior citizen?'

'No, but older than you.'

'Somewhere in that narrow window between me and senior citizenship.'

'You're not old,' she said seriously.

'Thank you.' The sambuca was making him feel great. They could just sit here, and get drunk and do nothing, and it would be fun, and there would be no consequences; he could stop worrying for tonight, and give himself a little break.

He was having that comforting thought when her head dropped lightly to his shoulder.

'Oh.'

'Is this okay?'

'It's okay, but—'

'I get so tired.'

'Because of the nightmares.'

She paused for a second, as if she was surprised he'd been paying attention. 'Yes,' she said. 'Exactly.'

'You want to lie down a minute?'

She jerked her head up—nervous all of a sudden. He liked it better than the flirty stuff she'd been doing before.

'Or I could get someone to take you home.'

She lay down and shut her eyes. He put his glass down carefully on the floor next to the bed. Then he put his hand out; her hair was very soft. He stroked her head and moved her hair away from her face. He adjusted the glass beads she always wore, and ran his hand lightly down her arm. He felt that he was in a position where there was no choice but to lift her up and kiss her very gently on the mouth.

'Julia.'

She opened her eyes.

'I'm going to get someone to drive you home.'

She got up very quickly and smoothed her hair with her hand.

'Not that I wouldn't like you to stay, but I think—'

'Okay,' she said.

'I'll just get someone.' He yelled for the servant.

'I can get a taxi,' Julia said.

'I know you *can*,' he told her. For some reason, that made her smile.

In September she took the test. He woke up early that morning as if he were taking it, couldn't concentrate, and went to Barista, where he sat trying to read the same *India Today* article about regional literature for two hours. She wasn't the only one of his students taking the SAT today, but she was the one he thought of, at the 8.40 subject change, the 10.00 break, and at 11.25, when they would be warning them about the penalties for continuing to write after time was called. That afternoon he thought she would ring him to say how it had gone, but she didn't, and it wasn't until late that night that his phone beeped and her name came up: JULIA: VERBAL IS LIKE S-SPEARE: PLAY. It wasn't a perfect analogy, but he knew what she meant.

He didn't see Julia while the scores were being processed. Without the bonus he hadn't been able to give up his other clients, and the business was in one of its busy cycles; it seemed as if everyone in Bombay was dying to send their sixteen-year-old child halfway around the world to be educated. Each evening he thought he might hear her calling up from the street, but she never did, and he didn't feel he could phone without some pretence.

One rainy Thursday he gave a group lesson in a small room on the first floor of the David Sassoon library. The library always reminded him of Oxford, with its cracked chalkboards and termite-riddled seminar tables, and today in particular the soft, steady rain made him feel as if he were somewhere else. They were doing triangles (isosceles, equilateral, scalene) when all of a sudden one of the students interrupted and said: 'It stopped.'

Watery sun was gleaming through the lead glass windows. When he had dismissed the class, Zubin went upstairs to the reading room. He found Bradbury in a tattered ledger book and filled out a form. He waited while the librarian frowned at the call number, selected a key from a crowded ring, and, looking put-upon, sent an assistant into the reading room to find 'All Summer in a Day' in the locked glass case.

It had been raining for seven years; thousands upon thousands of days compounded and filled from one end to the other with rain, with the drum and gush of water, with the sweet crystal fall of showers and the concussion of storms so heavy they were tidal waves come over the islands.

He'd forgotten that the girl in the story was a poet. She was different from the other children, and because it was a science fiction story (this was what he loved about science fiction) it wasn't an abstract difference. Her special sensitivity was explained by the fact that she had come to Venus from Earth only recently, on a rocket ship, and remembered the sun—it was like a penny—while her classmates did not.

Zubin sat by the window in the old seminar room, emptied of students, and luxuriated in a feeling of potential he hadn't had in a long time. He remembered when a moment of heightened contrast in his physical surroundings could produce this kind of elation; he could feel the essay wound up in him like thread. He would combine the Bradbury story with the idea Julia had had, that day at the tank. Beauty was something that was new to you. That was why tourists and children could see it better than other people, and it was the poet's job to keep seeing it the way the children and the tourists did.

He was glad he'd told her he couldn't do it because it would be that much more of a surprise when he handed her the pages. He felt noble. He was going to defraud the University of California for her gratis, as a gift.

He intended to be finished the day the scores came out and, for perhaps the first time in his life, he finished on the day he'd intended. He waited all day, but Julia didn't call. He thought she would've gone out that night to celebrate, but she didn't call the next day, or the next, and he started to worry that she'd been wrong about her verbal. Or she'd lied. He started to get scared that she'd choked—something that could happen to the best students, you could never tell which. After ten days without hearing from her, he rang her mobile.

'Oh yeah,' she said. 'I was going to call.'

'I have something for you,' he said. He didn't want to ask about the scores right away.

She sighed. 'My dad wants you to come to dinner anyway.'

'Okay,' Zubin said. 'I could bring it then.'

There was a long pause, in which he could hear traffic. 'Are you in the car?'

'Uh-huh,' she said. 'Hold on a second?' Her father said something and she groaned into the phone. 'My dad wants me to tell you my SAT scores.'

'Only if you want to.'

'Eight hundred math.'

'Wow.'

'And six-ninety verbal.'

'You're kidding.'

'Nope.'

'Is this the Julia who was too distracted to do her practice tests?'

'Maybe it was easy this year,' Julia said, but he could tell she was smiling.

'I don't believe you.'

'Zu*bin*!' (He loved the way she added the extra stress.) 'I *swear*.'

They ate *coquilles St Jacques* by candlelight. Julia's father lit the candles himself, with a box of old-fashioned White Swan matches. Then he opened Zubin's wine and poured all three of them a full glass. Zubin took a sip; it seemed too sweet, especially with the seafood. 'A toast,' said Julia's father. 'To my daughter the genius.'

Zubin raised his glass. All week he'd felt an urgent need to see her; now that he was here he had a contented, peaceful feeling, only partly related to the two salty dogs he'd mixed for himself just before going out.

'Scallops are weird,' said Julia. 'Do they even have heads?'

'Did any of your students do better?' her father asked.

'Only one, I think.'

'Boy or girl?'

'Why does that matter?' Julia asked. She stood up suddenly: she was wearing a sundress made of blue-and-white printed Indian cotton, and she was barefoot. 'I'll be in my room if anyone needs me.'

Zubin started to get up.

'Sit,' Julia's father said. 'Finish your meal. Then you can do whatever you have to do.'

'I brought your essay—the revision of your essay,' Zubin corrected himself, but she didn't turn around. He watched her disappear down the hall to her bedroom: a pair of tan shoulders under thin, cotton straps.

'I first came to India in 1976,' her father was saying. 'I flew from Moscow to Paris to meet Julia's mom, and then we went to Italy and Greece. We were deciding between India and North Africa—finally we just tossed a coin.'

'Wow,' said Zubin. He was afraid Julia would go out before he could give her the essay.

'It was February and I'd been in Moscow for a year,' Julia's father said. 'So you can imagine what India was like for me. We were staying in this pension in Benares—Varanasi—and every night there were these incredible parties on the roof.

'One night we could see the burning ghats from where we were—hardly any electricity in the city, and then this big fire on the ghat, with the drums and the wailing. I'd never seen anything like that—the pieces of the body that they sent down the river, still burning.' He stopped and refilled their glasses. He didn't seem to mind the wine. 'Maybe they don't still do that?'

'I've never been to Benares.'

Julia's father laughed. 'Right,' he said. 'That's an old man's India now. And you're not writing about India, are you?'

Writing the essay, alone at night in his room, knowing she was out somewhere with her school friends, he'd had the feeling, the delusion really, that he could hear her. That while she was standing on the beach or dancing in a club, she was also telling him her life story: not the places she'd lived, which didn't matter, but the time in third grade when she was humiliated in front of the class; the boy who wrote his number on the inside of her wrist; the weather on the day her mother left for New York. He felt that her voice was coming in the open window with the noise of the motorbikes and the televisions and the crows, and all he was doing was hitting the keys.

Julia's father had asked a question about India.

'Sorry?' Zubin said.

He waved a hand dismissively in front of his face. 'You don't have to tell me—writers are private about these things. It's just that business guys like me—we're curious how you do it.'

'When I'm here, I want to write about America and when I'm in America, I always want to write about being here.' He wasn't slurring words, but he could hear himself emphasizing them: 'It would have made *sense* to stay there.'

'But you didn't.'

'I was homesick, I guess.'

'And now?'

Zubin didn't know what to say.

'Far be it from me, but I think it doesn't matter so much, whether you're here or there. You can bring your home with you.' Julia's father smiled. 'To some extent. And India's wonderful—even if it's not your first choice.'

It was easy if you were Julia's father. He had chosen India because he remembered seeing some dead bodies in a river. He had found it 'wonderful'. And that was what it was to be an American. Americans could go all over the world and still be Americans; they could live just the way they did at home and nobody wondered who they were, or why they were doing things the way they did.

'I'm sure you're right,' Zubin said politely.

Finally Julia's father pressed a buzzer and a servant appeared to clear the dishes. Julia's father pushed back his chair and stood up. Before disappearing into his study, he nodded formally and said something—whether 'Good night,' or 'Good luck,' Zubin couldn't tell.

Zubin was left with a servant, about his age, with big, southern features and stooped shoulders. The servant was wearing the brown uniform from another job: short pants and a shirt that was tight across his chest. He moved as if he'd been compensating for his height his whole life, as if he'd never had clothes that fit him.

'Do you work here every day?' Zubin asked in his school-book Marathi.

The young man looked up as if talking to Zubin was the last in a series of obstacles that lay between him and the end of his day.

'*Nahin,*' he said. '*Mangalwar ani guruwar.*'

Zubin smiled—they both worked on Tuesdays and Thursdays. 'Me too,' he said.

The servant didn't understand. He stood holding the plates, waiting to see if Zubin was finished and scratching his left ankle with his right foot. His toes were round and splayed, with cracked nails and a glaucous coating of dry, white skin.

'Okay,' Zubin said. '*Bas.*'

Julia's room was, as he'd expected, empty. The lights were burning and the stereo was on (the disc had finished), but she'd left the window open; the bamboo shade sucked in and out. The mirror in the bathroom was steamed around the edges—she must've taken a shower before going out; there was the smell of some kind of fragrant soap and cigarettes.

He put the essay on the desk where she would see it. There were two Radiohead CDs, still in their plastic wrappers, and a

The Tutor

detritus of pens and pencils, hairbands, fashion magazines—French *Vogue*, *Femina* and *YM*—gum wrappers, an OB tampon and a miniature brass abacus, with tiny ivory beads. There was also a diary with a pale blue paper cover.

The door to the hall was slightly open, but the house was absolutely quiet. It was not good to look at someone's journal, especially a teenage girl's. But there were things that would be worse—jerking off in her room, for example. It was a beautiful notebook with a heavy cardboard cover that made a satisfying sound when he opened it on the desk.

'It's empty.'

He flipped the diary closed but it was too late. She was climbing in through the window, lifting the shade with her hand.

'That's where I smoke,' she said. 'You should've checked.'

'I was just looking at the notebook,' Zubin said. 'I wouldn't have read what you'd written.'

'My hopes, dreams, fantasies. It would've been good for the essay.'

'I finished the essay.'

She stopped and stared at him. 'You wrote it?'

He pointed to the neatly stacked pages, a paper island in the clutter of the desk. Julia examined them, as if she didn't believe it.

'I thought you weren't going to?'

'If you already wrote one—'

'No,' she said. 'I tried but—' She gave him a beautiful smile. 'Do you want to stay while I read it?'

Zubin glanced at the door.

'My dad's in his study.'

He pretended to look through her CDs, which were organized in a zippered binder, and snuck glances at her while she read. She sat down on her bed with her back against the wall, one foot underneath her. As she read she lifted her necklace and put it in her mouth, he thought unconsciously. She frowned at the page.

245

It was better if she didn't like it, Zubin thought. He knew it was good, but having written it was wrong. There were all these other kids who'd done the applications themselves.

Julia laughed.

'What?' he said, but she just shook her head and kept going.

'I'm just going to use your loo,' Zubin said.

He used it almost blindly, without looking in the mirror. Her towel was hanging over the edge of the counter, but he dried his hands on his shirt. He was drunker than he'd thought. When he came out she had folded the three pages into a small square, as if she were getting ready to throw them away.

Julia shook her head. 'You did it.'

'It's okay?'

Julia shook her head. 'It's perfect—it's spooky. How do you even know about this stuff?'

'I was a teenager—not a girl teenager, but you know.'

She shook her head. 'About being an American I mean? How do you know about that?'

She asked the same way she might ask who wrote *The Fairie Queene* or the meaning of the word 'synecdoche'.

Because I am not any different, he wanted to tell her. He wanted to grab her shoulders: *If we are what we want, I am the same as you.*

But she wasn't looking at him. Her eyes were like marbles he'd had as a child, striated brown and gold. They moved over the pages he'd written as if they were hers, as if she were about to tear one up and put it in her mouth.

'This part,' Julia said. 'About forgetting where you are? D'you know, that *happens* to me? Sometimes coming home I almost say the wrong street—the one in Paris, or in Moscow when we used to have to say "*Pushkinskaya*".'

Her skirt was all twisted around her legs.

'Keep it,' he said.

'I'll write you a cheque.'

'It's a present,' Zubin told her.

'Really?'

He nodded. When she smiled she looked like a kid. 'I wish I could do something for *you*.'

Zubin decided that it was time to leave.

Julia put on a CD—a female vocalist with a heavy bass line. 'This is too sappy for daytime,' she said. Then she started to dance. She was not a good dancer. He watched her fluttering her hands in front of her face, stamping her feet, and knew, the same way he always knew these things, that he wasn't going anywhere at all.

'You know what I hate?'

'What?'

'Boys who can't kiss.'

'All right,' Zubin said. 'You come here.'

Her bed smelled like the soap—lilac. It was amazing, the way girls smelled, and it was amazing to put his arm under her and take off each thin strap and push the dress down around her waist. She made him turn off the lamp but there was a street lamp outside; he touched her in the artificial light. She looked as if she were trying to remember something.

'Is everything okay?'

She nodded.

'Because we can stop.'

'Do you have something?'

It took him a second to figure out what she meant. 'Oh,' he said. 'No—that's good I guess.'

'I have one.'

'You do?'

She nodded.

'Still. That doesn't mean we have to.'

'I want to.'

'Are you sure?'

'If you do.'

'If I do—yes.' He took a breath. 'I want to.'

She was looking at him very seriously.

'This isn't—' he said.

'Of course not.'

'Because you seem a little nervous.'

'I'm just thinking,' she said. Her underwear was light blue, and it didn't quite cover her tan line.

'About what?'

'America.'

'What about it?'

She had amazing gorgeous perfect new breasts. There was nothing else to say about them.

'I can't wait,' she said, and he decided to pretend she was talking about this.

Julia was relieved when he left and she could lie in bed alone and think about it. Especially the beginning part of it: she didn't know kissing could be like that—sexy and calm at the same time, the way it was in movies that were not *9 1/2 Weeks*. She was surprised she didn't feel worse; she didn't feel regretful at all, except that she wished she'd thought of something to say afterwards. *I wish I didn't have to go*, was what he had said, but he put on his shoes very quickly. She hadn't been sure whether she should get up or not, and in the end she waited until she heard the front door shut behind him. Then she got up and put on a T-shirt and pyjama bottoms, and went into the bathroom to wash her face. If she'd told him it was her first time, he would've stayed longer, probably, but she'd read enough magazines to know that you couldn't tell them that. Still, she wished he'd touched her hair the way he had the other night, when she'd gone over to his house and invented a nightmare.

Zubin had left the Ray Bradbury book on her desk. She'd

thanked him, but she wasn't planning to read it again. Sometimes when you went back you were disappointed, and she liked the rocket ship the way she remembered it, with silver tail fins and a red lacquer shell. She could picture herself taking off in that ship—at first like an airplane, above the hill and the tank and the bay with its necklace of lights—and then straight up, beyond the sound barrier. People would stand on the beach to watch the launch: her father, Anouk and Bernie, everyone from school, and even Claudia and her mother and Dr Fabrol. They would yell up to her, but the yells would be like the tails of comets, crusty blocks of ice and dust that rose and split in silent, white explosions.

She liked Zubin's essay too, although she wasn't sure about the way he'd combined the two topics; she hoped they weren't going to take points off. Or the part where he talked about all the different perspectives she'd gotten from living in different cities, and how she just needed one place where she could think about those things and articulate what they meant to her. She wasn't interested in 'articulating'. She just wanted to get moving.

Zubin walked all the way up Nepean Sea Road, but when he got to the top of the hill he wasn't tired. He turned right and passed his building, not quite ready to go in, and continued in the Walkeshwar direction. The market was empty. The electronics shops were shuttered and the 'Just Orange' advertisements twisted like kites in the dark. There was the rich, rotted smell of vegetable waste, but almost no other trash. Foreigners marvelled at the way Indians didn't waste anything, but of course that wasn't by choice. Only a few useless things flapped and flattened themselves against the broad, stone steps: squares of folded newsprint from the vendors' baskets, and smashed matchbooks—extinct brands whose labels still appeared underfoot: 'export quality premium safety matches' in fancy script.

At first he thought the tank was deserted, but a man in shorts was standing on the other side, next to a small white dog with stand-up, triangular ears. Zubin picked a vantage point on the steps out of the moonlight, sat down and looked out at the water. There was something different about the tank at night. It was partly the quiet; in between the traffic sounds a breeze crackled the leaves of a few, desiccated trees, growing between the paving stones. The night intensified the contrast, so that the stones took on a kind of sepia, sharpened the shadows and gave the carved and whitewashed temple pillars an appropriate patina of magic. You could cheat for a moment in this light and see the old city, like taking a photograph with black-and-white film.

The dog barked, ran up two steps and turned expectantly toward the tank. Zubin didn't see the man until his slick, seal head surfaced in the black water. Each stroke broke the black glass; his hands made eddies of light in the disturbed surface. For just a moment, even the apartment blocks were beautiful.

Dervishes

Rory Stewart

(2002)

'**D**ervish are an abomination,' said Navaid.

'What do you mean by a Dervish?' I asked.

'Dervish? Don't you know? It's a very old concept. Fakir? Pir-Baba? Sufi? Silsilah Malang—that beggar doing magic tricks…?' Navaid was staring at a man who was sitting cross-legged in the street with a ten foot black python wrapped round his neck. 'That beggar—medieval mystics like Shahbaz Qalander—the people who live and dance at his tomb. They are all Dervish.'

When I first met Navaid at the tomb of Datta Ganj Baksh a week earlier, he had been examining the same snake man. Now Navaid was standing very still, stroking his white beard. The python was asleep and so was its owner and no one except Navaid seemed to notice them. For the last ten years he had spent his days at the mosques of the old city of Lahore. He had neither a family nor a job. His voice was quick, anxious, slightly high-pitched, as though he were worried I would leave before he had finished his sentence.

'You foreigners love the idea of Dervish—whirling Dervish, wandering Dervish, howling Dervish—exotic—like belly dancers and dancing camels,' he insisted, '—surely you understand what I mean?'

'But what's that beggar there got in common with a medieval Sufi poet?'

'One thing anyway—they are both irrelevant,' replied Navaid. 'They have nothing to do with Islam or Pakistan. They barely exist any more and, if they do, they don't matter. Forget about Dervish.'

Two weeks later I was walking alone along a canal in the Southern Punjab. It had been five months since I started walking across Asia but I had only been in the Punjab for a few days. The arid mountains of Iran had been replaced by a flat, fertile land and I was struggling to turn my limited Persian into Urdu. I was also getting used to new clothes. I was trying to dress in a way that did not attract attention. I was, like everyone else, wearing a loose, thin Pakistani salwar kameez suit and because of the 120 degree heat, a turban. I had swapped my backpack for a small cheap shoulder bag and I carried a traditional iron-shod staff. In Iran I was frequently accused of being a smuggler, a resistance fighter or a grave robber. In the Punjab, because of my clothes, black hair, and fair skin I was often mistaken for one of the millions of Afghani refugees now living in Pakistan. Afghanis have a reputation as dangerous men and this may partly have explained why I had not (so far) felt threatened, walking alone along the Punjab canals.

A snake was swimming down the canal, its head held high over its own reflection, shedding bars of water thick with sunlight in its wake. In a hollow between the towpath and the wheat field was a stunted peepul tree draped with green cloth and beneath it the earth grave of a 'Dervish'. A thin bare-chested man dragged a bucket through the canal, staggered to the edge of the path and threw water on the dry track. I watched him weaving up and down the grass bank towards me. The history of his labour was laid across the path in thick bars of colour. In front of him, where I was walking, was pale sand; at his feet was a band of black mud. Behind him stripe after stripe, each slightly paler than its successor, faded through orange clay until, where he had worked an hour before, nothing remained but pale sand. This was his job in the Canal Department.

'*Salaam alaikum.*'

'*Wa alaikum as-salaam,*' he replied. 'Where are you going?'

'To the canal rest-house.'

'Respected one,' he smiled and his voice was nervous, 'most kind one. Give me a sacred charm.'

'I'm sorry, I don't have one.'

'Look at me. This work. This sun.' He was still smiling.

'I'm very sorry. *Hoda Hafez*, God be with you.'

I turned away and he grabbed me by the arm. I hit him with my stick. He backed off and we looked at each other. I hadn't hurt him but I was embarrassed.

Navaid had warned me I would be attacked walking across Pakistan. 'Violent? Pakistan is a very violent country—the Baluch caught a young Frenchman who was trying to walk here last year and killed him. Or look at today's newspaper—you can be killed by your father for sleeping around, you can be killed by other Muslims for being a Shi'a, you can be killed for being a policeman, you can be killed for being a tourist.'

But I could see that the man I'd hit wasn't dangerous.

He was now smiling apologetically, 'Please, sir, at least let me have some of your water.'

I poured some water from my bottle into his hands. He bowed to me, passed it in front of his lips and then brushed it through his hair.

'And now a charm: a short one will be enough…'

'No, I'm sorry. I can't.'

I couldn't. I wouldn't play the role of a holy man. '*Hoda hafez.*' A hundred yards further on I looked back through the midday glare and saw him still staring at me. He had, it seemed, perhaps because I was walking in Pakistani clothes, mistaken me for what Navaid would call a wandering Dervish.

An hour later, I turned off the tow-path down a tree-lined avenue. There was a peepul, with its pointed leaves, trembling forty feet above. This one had outgrown its pink bark but its trunk was thin, its canopy small. It looked as though it had been planted when the canal was completed in 1913, and it would probably outlast the canal, since part of the peepul under which the Buddha achieved enlightenment, 2,500 years ago, is still alive in Sri Lanka. Further on, among the banyans, the ruby flowers of the Dak trees, and the yellow of the laburnum, was the electric blue spray of a Brazilian jacaranda imported I assumed by some extravagant engineer. Two men and two boys were sitting on the lawn.

'*Salaam alaikum.*'

'*Wa alaikum as-salaam.* We had been told to expect someone. Please sit down.' I sat on the charpoy string bed and we looked at each other. They knew nothing about me and I knew nothing about them. They were looking at a twenty-eight-year-old Briton, seated on a colonial lawn, in a turban and a sweat-soaked salwar kameez shirt. I was looking at a man, also in salwar kameez, but with a ball-point pen in his breast pocket—an important symbol in an area where less than half the men can write their own name. The other man, standing on the balls of his bare feet, staring at me with his hands forward like a wrestler, looked about sixty. He had shoulder-length grey, curly hair and a short beard. He was wearing an emerald green kemis shirt and a dark green sarong, a silver ankle ring, four long bead necklaces and an earring in his left ear. I asked if I could boil some water.

'*Acha, acha*, boil water,' said the old man with the earring and immediately loped off in a half-run, with his hands still held in front of him, to the peepul tree. I watched him build a fire and shout to a boy to bring a bucket of water from the canal. He and the column of smoke seemed small beneath the Buddha's tree. The man in green returned with the handleless pot of boiling water in his hands. When I took it from him, I burned my fingers and nearly dropped the pot. He asked if I'd like some honey and I said I would very much.

Ten minutes later, he returned breathless and sweating with part of a cone of dark wild honey in his hands.

'Where did you get it from?'

'From there,' he pointed to the peepul, 'I just climbed up there to get it.' I thought I could see where the cone must be—it was on a branch, some way out, about forty feet above the ground. It was a difficult climb for a sixty-year-old, even without the bees.

'What do you do?'

'Me?' He laughed and looked at the others, who laughed also. 'Why, I'm a Malang—a Dervish, a follower of Shahbaz Qalander of Sewhan Sharif.'

'And what does it mean to be a Dervish follower of Shahbaz Qalander of Sewhan Sharif?'

'Why, to dance and sing.' And he began to hop from foot to foot, clicking his fingers in the air, and singing in a high-pitched voice:

Shudam Badnam Dar Ishq,
Biya Paarsa Ikanoon,
The Tarsam Za Ruswaee,
Bi Har Bazaar Me Raqsam.

Come, behold how I am slandered for my love of God
But slander means nothing to me,
That's why I'll dance in the crowd, my friend
And prance throughout the bazaar.

'Who wrote that?'

'My sheikh, my master, Shahbaz Qalander, when he lived in the street of the whores.'

'And where are you from?'

'Me? Well my family is originally from Iran not Pakistan—we came like Shahbaz Qalander.'

Laal Shahbaz Qalander was a twelfth-century mystic, what Navaid would call a Dervish. He belonged to a monastic order, wandered from Iran to Pakistan preaching Islam, performed miracles, wrote poems like the one above, and was buried in a magnificent medieval tomb in Sewhan Sharif, a city founded by Alexander the Great. His name, Laal Shahbaz, they say records his brilliant red clothes and his spirit, free as the Shahbaz falcon. He is one of the most famous of a group of mystics who arrived in Pakistan between the eleventh and fourteenth centuries. Their poetry and teachings often celebrate an intoxication with and almost erotic love of God that appears at times to transcend all details of religious doctrine. Their mystical ideas seem to have passed, like the use of rosary beads and the repetition of a single phrase for meditation, from the sub-continent through the Islamic world, and from the crusaders into Christianity. It is they, not the Arab conquerors of the earlier centuries who are credited with peacefully converting the Hindus of Pakistan to Islam. Indeed, if the shirt of the man in front of me was like Shahbaz's red, not green, he would look, with his long hair and jewelry, exactly like a Hindu sadhu. And he is one of half a million Pakistanis who gather at Shahbaz's tomb once a year to celebrate with dancing and singing.

'Do you not have land?' I asked, 'Work as a farmer?

'I used to but I gave it all away—I have nothing now.'

'Nothing?'

'I need nothing else. As the prophet says, "Poverty is my pride,"' he replied, smiling so broadly that I wasn't sure whether I believed him.

When it was time to go, the Dervish accompanied me to the gate hobbling slightly on his bare feet.

'Have you always been a Dervish?' I asked.

'No, I was a civil servant in the Customs Department. I worked in the baggage inspection hall of Lahore airport for fifteen years.'

At the canal bank, I took out some money to thank him for the cooking and the honey. But he was horrified.

'Please,' I said, employing a Persian euphemism, 'take it for the children.'

'There are no children here,' the Dervish said firmly. 'Good luck and goodbye.' He shook my hand and, bringing his palm up to his chest, added in a friendlier voice, 'God be with you— walking is a kind of dancing too.'

When I walked back into Lahore, I met a very different kind of Muslim civil servant. 'Umar is a most influential person,' said Navaid. 'He knows everyone in Lahore, parties all night—meets Imran Khan all the time. And you must see his library. He will explain to you about Islam.'

I was invited to Umar's house at ten at night because he had had three parties to attend earlier in the evening. As I arrived, I saw a heavily built, bearded man in his mid-thirties stepping down from a battered transit van. He was talking on his mobile and holding up his arms so his driver could wrap a baggy, brown pinstriped jacket round him but he managed to hold out a hand to greet me. Still clutching my hand, he led me into a government bungalow of a very similar age and style to the canal rest-house. We removed our shoes and entered a small room, with shelves of English-language books covering all the walls and no chairs. Umar put down the phone, sat on the floor and invited me to sit beside him.

'*Salaam alaikum*, good evening. Please make yourself comfortable. I will tell the servant to get a blanket for you. This is my son, Salman,' he added. The eight year old was playing a video game. He waved vaguely but his focus was on trying to persuade a miniature David Beckham to kick with his left foot.

Umar's eyes were bloodshot and he looked tired and anxious. He never smiled, but instead produced rhetorical questions and suggestions at a speed that was difficult to follow.

'*Multan*, but of course,' he said, 'you must meet the Gilanis, the Qureshis, the Gardezis—perhaps as you move up the Punjab—Shah Jeevna. I know them all. I can do it for you.' All these people were descendants of the famous medieval saints who had converted Pakistan—Navaid's Dervish or Pirs. It was said that they had inherited a great deal of their ancestors' spiritual charisma—villagers still touched them to be cured of illnesses or drank water they blessed to ensure the birth of a male son. They had certainly inherited a great deal of land and wealth from donations to their ancestors' shrines. But Umar, it seemed, was not interested in their Dervish connections. He was concerned with the fact that they were currently leading politicians. Thus the female descendant of a medieval mystic, who once stood in a Punjabi river for twelve years reciting the Qur'an, had just served as Pakistan's ambassador to Washington. Another Dervish, who it is said entered Multan riding on a lion and whipping it with live snakes, and 600 years later is still supposed to stick his hand out of the tomb to greet pious pilgrims, has descendants who have served as ministers in both the federal and provincial governments. Umar knew them all and perhaps because he was rising fast in the interior ministry he was able to help them occasionally.

Umar's mobile rang again. He applauded one of his son's virtual goals, dragged off his shiny silver tie, dark brown shirt and brown pinstriped trousers for a servant to take away, pulled a copy of V. S. Naipaul's *Beyond Belief* off the shelves and pointed me to a chapter, which I slowly realized was about himself—all this while still talking on the phone.

I had seen Umar earlier in the evening at the large marble-floored house of a wealthy landowner and Dervish descendant. A group of clean-shaven young Pakistani men in casual Gucci shirts had been standing beside Umar drinking illegal whisky, smoking joints and talking about Manhattan. And there he had been, in his brown suit and brown shirt, bearded and with a glass of fruit juice in his hand, not only because he was not educated abroad but also, it seemed, because he had very different views about religion.

'My son,' said Umar proudly, putting down the phone, 'is studying at an Islamic school—his basic syllabus is that he must memorize the whole book of the Qur'an—more than 150,000 words by heart—I chose this school for him.' The boy concerned was trying to decide which members of the Swedish squad to include in his dream team. 'You know our relationship with our families is one of the strengths of Islamic culture. I am sorry it will not be possible for you to meet my wife—but she and my parents and children form such a close unit. When you think of the collapse of families in the West, the fact that there is (I am sorry to say it but I know because I have been to the West) no respect for parents—almost everyone is getting divorced, there is rape on the streets—suicide—you put your people in "Old People Homes" while we look after them in the family—in America and perhaps Britain as well I think, there is rape and free sex, divorce and drugs. Have you had a girlfriend? Are you a virgin?'

'No, I'm not.'

'My friend,' he said, leaning forward, 'I was in a car with a friend the other day, we stopped at the traffic lights and there was a beautiful girl in the car next to us. We wanted to gaze at her but I said, and my friend agreed—do not glance at her—for if you do not stare now you will be able to have that woman in heaven.' He paused for effect. 'That is what religion gives to me. It is very late, my friend, I suggest you sleep here tonight and I will drive you back in the morning.'

'Thank you very much.'

'No problem.' He shouted something. The servant entered, laid two mattresses and some sheets on the floor and led Umar's son out. Umar lay on his mattress, propping himself on one arm, looked at me with half-closed eyes and asked, yawning, 'What do you think of American policy in Iraq?'

His phone rang again and he switched on the TV.

I reopened Naipaul's *Beyond Belief*. Naipaul portrays Umar as a junior civil servant from a rural background with naive and narrow views about religion, living in a squalid house. He does not mention Umar's social ambitions, his library, his political connections, his 'close friends' in the Lahore elite. He implies that Umar's father had tracked down and murdered a female in his family for eloping without consent.

When Umar had finished on the phone I asked whether he was happy with this portrait.

'Yes, of course I am—I have great respect for Naipaul—he is a true gentleman—did so much research into my family. You know most people's perspectives are so limited on Pakistan. But I try to help many journalists. All of them say the same things about Pakistan. They only write about terrorism, about extremism, the Taliban, about feudalism, illiteracy, about Bin Laden, corruption and bear-baiting and about our military dictatorship. They have nothing positive to say about our future or our culture. Why, I want to know?'

He pointed to the television news which showed a Palestinian body being carried by an angry crowd. 'Three killed today by Israel—why is America supporting that? Why did they intervene so late in Bosnia and not in Chechnya? Can you defend the British giving Kashmir to the Hindus when the majority of the population is Muslim? Is it a coincidence that all these problems concern Muslims?'

I tried to say that the West had supported Muslims in Kosovo but he interrupted again.

'Let me tell you what it means to be a Muslim,' he said, lying on his back and looking at the ceiling. 'Look at me, I am a normal man, I have all your tastes, I like to go to parties. Two months ago, a friend of mine said to me, "Umar, you are a man who likes designer clothes, Ralph Lauren suits, Pierre Cardin ties, Italian shoes, Burberry socks—why don't you do something for Allah—he has done everything for you—why don't you do something for him—just one symbol—grow a beard."' He fingered his beard. 'This is why it is here—just a little something for Allah.'

He was now lying on his mattress in a white vest and Y-fronts.

I didn't really remember his designer clothes. Perhaps he had been wearing Burberry socks. The new facial hair was, however, clearly an issue for him. I wondered whether as an ambitious civil servant he thought a beard might be useful in a more Islamic Pakistan. But I asked him instead about Dervish tombs. He immediately recommended five which I had not seen.

'What do you think of the Dervish tradition in Pakistan?' I asked.

'What do you mean?'

I repeated Navaid's definition.

'Oh I see—this kind of thing does not exist so much any more except in illiterate areas. But I could introduce you to a historian who could tell you more about it.'

'But what about their kind of Islam?'

'What do you mean? Islam is one faith with one God. There are no different types. You must have seen the common themes that bind Muslims together when you walked from Iran to Pakistan. For example the generosity of Muslims—our attitude to guests.'

'But my experience hasn't been the same everywhere. Iranians, for example, are happy to let me sleep in their mosques but I am never allowed to sleep in a mosque in Pakistan.'

'They let you sleep in mosques in Iran? That is very strange. The mosque is a very clean place and if you sleep in a mosque you might have impure thoughts during the night...'

'Anyway, basically,' I continued, 'villagers have been very relaxed and hospitable in Pakistan. Every night they take me in without question, give me food and a bed and never ask for payment. It's much easier walking here than in Iran. Iranians could be very suspicious and hostile, partly because they are all afraid of the government there. In some Iranian villages they even refused to sell me bread and water.'

'Really, I don't believe this—this is propaganda. I think the Iranian people are very happy with their government and are very generous people. I cannot believe they would refuse you bread and water.'

'Listen to me—they did.'

'Well, this may be because of the Iran–Iraq war which you and the Americans started and financed. Do you know how many were killed in that war? That is why Iranians are a little wary of foreigners. But look how the Iranians behaved...'

The phone rang again and he talked for perhaps ten minutes this time. I examined the bookcase while I waited. Many of the books were parts of boxed sets with new leather bindings and had names like *Masterpieces of the West, volumes 1–11*.

When he turned back to me again, Umar seemed much more animated. He sat cross-legged on the mattress and leaned towards me. 'My friend,' he said. 'There is one thing you will never understand. We Muslims, all of us—including me—are prepared to die for our faith—we know we will go immediately to heaven. That is why we are not afraid of you. We want to be martyrs. In Iran, twelve-year-old boys cleared minefields by stepping on the mines in front of the troops—tens of thousands died in this way. Such faith and courage does not exist in Britain. That is why you must pray there will never be a "Clash of Civilizations" because you cannot defeat a Muslim: one of us can defeat ten of your soldiers.'

'This is nonsense,' I interrupted uselessly. What was this overweight man in his Y-fronts, who boasted of his social life and foreign friends, doing presenting Islam in this way and posing as a holy warrior. It sounded as though he was reciting from some boxed set of leather books called 'Diatribes against Your Foreign Guest'. And I think he sensed this too because his tone changed.

'We are educated, loving people,' he concluded. 'I am very active with a charity here, we educate the poor, help them, teach them about religion. If only we can both work together to destroy prejudice—that is why people like you and me are so important.

All I ask is that the West recognize that it too has its faults—that it lectures us on religious freedom and then the French prohibit Muslim girls from wearing headscarves in school.'

'Do you think Pakistan will become an Islamic state on the Iranian model?' I asked.

'My friend, things must change. There is so much corruption here. The state has almost collapsed. This is partly the fault of what you British did here. But it is also because of our politicians. That is why people like me want more Islam in our state. Islam is our only chance to root out corruption so we can finally have a chance to develop.'

I fell asleep wondering whether this is what he really believed and whether he said such things to his wealthy political friends.

When he dropped me off the next morning, Umar's phone rang again and as I walked away I heard him saying in English: 'Two months ago, a friend of mine said to me, "Umar, you are a man who likes designer clothes, Ralph Lauren suits, Pierre Cardin ties, Italian shoes, Burberry socks—why don't you do something for Allah…"'

'A beard?' said Navaid, stroking his own, when I went to meet him again that afternoon at the tomb of Datta Ganj Baksh. 'When people like Umar start growing beards, something is changing. But he must have enjoyed meeting you. His closest friends are foreigners.'

I told Navaid what Umar had said about a clash of civilizations and Navaid shook his head. 'Forget it—don't pay any attention. He was only trying to impress you. He doesn't mean it. People should spend less time worrying about non-Muslims and more time making Muslims into real Muslims. Look at this tomb for example. It is a scandal. They should dynamite this tomb. That would be more useful than fighting Americans.'

Dervishes

Behind us were the tomb gates which Navaid swore were solid gold and which had been erected in the saint's honour by the secular leftist prime minister Zulfiqar Ali Bhutto, Benazir's father. He gave gold gates to the tomb of Shahbaz Qalander in Sewhan Sharif as well. 'That beautiful glass and marble mosque in front of us,' continued Navaid, 'was built by General Zia after he executed Bhutto and took power. Then the CIA killed Zia by making his airplane crash. So the marble courtyard we are standing on was built by our last elected prime minister Nawaz Sharif. It hasn't been finished because of the military coup.'

'But,' he reflected, 'this Dervish of Shahbaz Qalander is all nonsense. This tomb of Datta Ganj Baksh is nonsense. It has nothing to do with Islam, nothing at all. There is nothing in Islam about it. Islam is a very simple religion, the simplest in the world.'

Beside us a man was forcing his goat to perform a full prostration to the tomb of the saint, before dragging it off to be sacrificed.

'But what do people want from these saints' tombs?' I asked.

'Babies, money—but the Prophet, peace be upon him, teaches that we should not build tombs. They tempt us to worship men not God.'

'And the Dervish?'

'They are cheaters, beggars and tricksters, who sit at the tombs becoming rich by selling stupid medicines.' He led me to the balustrade. 'Look at him, for example.' There was a half-naked man in the dust below the courtyard, where the snake-charmer usually sat. His upper body was tattooed with the ninety-nine names of Allah. 'He's probably got a snake in that box, and,' Navaid dropped his voice prudishly, 'has intercourse with his clients.'

'And the history of these saints, their local traditions?'

'I think looking too much at history is like worshipping a man's tomb. Allah exists outside time. And we should not look at local things too much because Allah does not have a nationality.'

'People say there are seventy-four forms of Islam in Pakistan, what do they mean?'

'Nonsense.' Navaid was being very patient with me. 'Islam is one—one God—one book—one faith.'

'But what do they mean? Are they referring to Qadianis?'

'Of course not…Qadianis are heretics, they are not Muslims. General Zia has confirmed this in law.'

'Or are they talking about differences between Naqshbandiyah, Wahhabis, Shi'as…?'

'Pakistani Shi'as are not true Muslims—they are terrorists and extremists—worshipping tombs—they are responsible for these Dervish. But in fact there is only one Islam. We are all the same.' He turned away from the beggar. 'There are no real differences because our God is one.'

The politicians had spent millions on this tomb to win the support of the saint or his followers. But it was only superficially a tribute to the older Pakistan of wandering holy men. Ten years ago, the courtyard of this tomb was the meeting-place for all the diverse groups which Navaid calls Dervish. There was Datta Ganj Baksh, the medieval Sufi himself in his grave, and around him were pilgrims, beggars, mystics, sellers of pious artifacts, drummers, tattooists, dancers, snake charmers, fortune-tellers, men in trances. But most of these figures were now hidden in the narrow streets below the marble balustrade. The politician's gift both asserted the significance of the saint's tomb and obliterated the cultural environment which surrounded it. Their new architecture seemed to be echoing Navaid's vision of a single simple global Islam—a plain white empty courtyard and a marble and glass mosque, bland, clean, expensive—the 'Islamic' architecture of a Middle Eastern airport.

But I still could not understand why Navaid wanted to link these modern dervishes, one of whom was now shouting drunkenly at us from the street, to the medieval saints. 'Navaid, what do you mean by a Dervish? Are you complaining only about mystics, who belong to a monastic order?'

'Of course not.' Navaid gestured at the man who was now cursing our descendants. 'You think he is a mystic in a monastic order?'

'Then what's he got in common with a Sufi poet or a medieval saint?' I was confused by the way he put medieval intellectuals, mystics and poets in the same group as magicians on the fringes of modern society.

'They're all Dervish—you know where that word comes from—from the Old Persian word *derew*, to beg? What they have in common is that they are all rich idle beggars.'

I presumed that explained why he didn't call them 'Fakir', which means 'poor', or 'Sufi' which refers to their clothes.

'But why have you got such a problem with them?' I asked.

'What do you think? Those people down there,' he said pointing at the varied activities in the street, 'wear jewellery, take drugs, believe in miracles, con pilgrims, worship tombs—they are illiterate blasphemers.'

'All right. But why do you reduce the Sufi saints to the same level?'

'Partly because people like you like them so much. Western hippies love Sufis. You think they are beautiful little bits of a medieval culture. You're much happier with them than with modern Islam. And you like the kind of things they say. What is it the Delhi Dervish Amir Khosrow says?' Navaid recites:

I am a pagan worshipper of love,
Islam I do not need,
My every vein is taut as a wire
And I reject the pagan's girdle.

That's why I don't like them. Medieval Islamic mystics have no relevance to Islam in Pakistan.'

'Then why do you keep attacking them? Or comparing them to these men in the street?'

Navaid just smiled and wandered off down the courtyard.

Medieval mystics were, I was convinced, not irrelevant. It was they (not Arab invaders) who had converted the bulk of the Hindus to Islam in the first place, while their clothes, practices, poetry and prayers showed strong Indian influences. They were thus both the cause of Pakistani Islam and a reminder of its Hindu past. Furthermore, by drawing the link to the present, Navaid was conceding that the medieval 'Dervish' remained a live tradition in rural Pakistan.

Umar, by contrast, had not felt the need to recognize this. His modern Islam flourished among migrants into Pakistan's cities. He could thus ignore the half a million people who still danced at the tomb of Shahbaz Qalander, and the fact that his friends the politicians were credited with inheriting miraculous spiritual powers from men six centuries dead. His Islam, he felt, was the future. He could safely leave the Dervish behind in a marginalized, illiterate, impoverished world—leave them, in other words, in the rural communities where seventy per cent of Pakistanis still lived.

At last Navaid turned back towards me. 'When I said that Dervish were irrelevant, I meant that Islam is simple, anyone can understand it, it is public, it helps in politics, it does practical things for people. But for a Dervish, religion is all about some direct mystical experience of God—very personal, difficult to explain. Islam is not like that at all—it's there to be found easily in the Qur'an—we don't need some special path, some spiritual master, complicated fasting, dancing, whirling and meditating to see God.'

I could not imagine Navaid dancing. He was a reserved man, basically a puritan by temperament. When he admitted to being anything other than 'a Muslim pure and simple' he said he was a Wahhibi. His Islam, like Umar's, was in a modern Saudi tradition, the tradition of the plain white mosque. It rested on a close attention to the words of the Qur'an, it refused to be tied to any particular place or historical period, it was concerned with 'family life', the creation of Islamic states—an approach that was underwritten by extensive global funding networks. I could guess, therefore, why Navaid was troubled by an other-worldly medieval tradition with strong local roots, personal and apolitical, celebrating poverty, mystical joy, tolerance and a direct experience of God. I could also guess why he wanted to reduce this tradition to a roadside magic trick.

But I might have been wrong. Although Navaid was fifty he was, unusually for a Pakistani man, not married. He claimed never to have had a girlfriend. He was very poor but he did not get a job. Instead he spent his days discussing religion in the courtyards of the ancient mosques in the old city. He could recite a great deal of Persian poetry as well as most of the Qur'an. He was a wanderer and had lived for eleven years in Iran, from just after the revolution. He was a very calm and peaceful man, he had few criticisms of the West and he rejected most of the religious leaders in Pakistan. Although he attacked Dervishes, he knew the name of every obscure Dervish grave in Lahore. I left him by the outdoor mosque of Shah Jehan. He had seated himself under a large peepul tree, to recite a *dhikr*, a repetitive mantra for meditation favoured by the Sufis. As I walked off, I heard him repeating, 'There is no God but God…' with a half-smile on his face, entirely absorbed in the words and I was no longer certain who was the Dervish.

Little Durga

Shampa Banerjee

(2004)

The story of Satyajit Ray's struggle to make one of the world's best-loved films, *Pather Panchali*, is well known: his commitment, his lack of funds, the shooting that started and stopped, his belief that India could be depicted a new way, though he had never made a film before. He took his story—and that of the other two films in what became the *Apu* trilogy—from a novel of the same name by a fellow Bengali, Bibhuti Bhushan Bandyopadhyay, which describes the travails of a poor Brahmin family in rural Bengal. The title means 'Song of the Road'. Apu is the family's only son and the hero of the story. He has an older sister, Durga, and for a few weeks of my life I was her.

I don't know when I first met Satyajit Ray. I have faint and unreliable memories of him climbing the stairs to our home in Calcutta, of him standing tall and cramped in a public bus. He was my father's friend, Manik kaka (Uncle Manik) to me.

I remember, Manik kaka didn't approve of my 'formal' name (like all Bengalis, I have two, the second one kept for the family), and I secretly agreed with him. I liked the sound of my other name, Runki—my mother had found it in one of her childhood stories, the name of a river that existed only in the writer's imagination. I was Runki in the credits of *Pather Panchali*.

I was five and a half when my first shot was taken in the village of Boral. I don't suppose I was expected to remember anything at all of what followed. Yet I do, probably because it was all so extraordinary, so unexpected, that even a child could comprehend its significance.

I was going to the local kindergarten, and none of my friends there had ever had anything to do with shooting a film. I must have felt important. My mother was a stage actress, but only on the 'amateur' stage, as part of the Indian People's Theatre Association, a progressive national cultural group which drew many talents from all parts of the country. So I knew something about the world of make-believe. Acting in films, however, was not quite respectable for the Bengali middle class. But for my father's persuasion, my mother would have remained in obscurity. With the family's active support, my gentle, quiet, beautiful mother became Sarbojaya, Durga's and Apu's mother in *Pather Panchali*, a stern and unyielding guardian of her children's well-being in a poor and struggling rural household. I believe the transformation survived as a duality within her, or maybe it dredged up the strength and pride she would otherwise have kept hidden.

I was a city child and it was thrilling to travel to a village with a group of grown-ups. We went by taxi, an ancient Dodge (I think), with deep, worn seats and lots of leg space, and driven by a Sikh, Bachan Singh. With his turban and beard, he seemed to me a man of great resolution, as he bravely left his familiar city behind to tumble and toss his way across the broken road that took us into Boral. I usually stood in the back, comfortably wedged between my mother's knees and the back of the driver's seat. Manik kaka, with his long legs, sat in front.

This was the early 1950s, when India was young and the heart of rural Bengal only a step away from the crowded, sinful city of Calcutta. A village like Boral was still not unlike the Nishchindipur of the film—set fifty years before. It nestled among rice fields, fruit orchards and fish ponds, where it was periodically ravaged by malaria, droughts and monsoon rains, and held together by the invisible bonds of a small feudal community.

Bansi kaka, Bansi Chandra Gupta, the art director, had rebuilt an old, abandoned home as a film set in the most ingenious way. The kitchen, which stood apart from the main house, was strangest of all. Its walls were so very thin. I tapped on them and got a very odd sound, nothing like a solid wall at all. But it seemed real enough, with the earthy smell of mud and the rough, sweeping, circular lines where the mud was smoothed over with cow dung.

Subrata kaka, Subrata Mitra, was the cameraman, with large hands, long fingers, and nails yellowed with nicotine. There was a familiar smell of his hands, whenever he held his little black light meter near me, which he did often enough, as natural lighting was what they depended on most of the time.

No one wore any make-up. But we women had to wear our nose studs. I looked forward to Bansi kaka bringing out his little collection of stones—mine was the bluest of blue—and the heady smell of Durofix as we stuck them on our noses.

Other than the blue stone, my only costume was a small sari, made of rough handloom material, which my grandmother had bought for me from a rural bazaar during one of our yearly visits to my great-uncle in Bihar. My hair was clipped short mercilessly each day before shooting—for 'continuity'—at the Jai Hind Saloon, just down the road from our Calcutta home.

I was horribly shy of Manik kaka, this tall, commanding presence with his thick wavy hair and deep grainy voice. He seemed incredibly romantic to me, even though I was five. If he talked to me, I would curl up and try to hide my face. Not surprisingly, the only dialogue I have in my two reels of the film is one shrill cry: 'Aunty!'

My mother always said that Manik kaka had a way with children. He would whisper to them and they would do whatever he wanted for his films. I don't think I remember ever seeing him actually playing with children. But I know he didn't treat me like a child when he asked me to do something. And if I couldn't do it, he would find another way.

When little Durga was supposed to watch hungrily as Aunty Indir enjoyed her morning meal—balls of rice kneaded to a mash with her gnarled hands—Manik kaka wouldn't let Mother give me my lunch (rice and buttery mashed potatoes) on time. She kept complaining as the day wore on, and we all kept waiting, I thought, for the light again. By the time the shot was taken,

Little Durga

Mother was convinced I was dying of hunger. As for me, I remember being more disappointed by the fact that I couldn't do what Manik kaka asked me to do. 'Can you gulp?' he asked, and gulped himself, bobbing his Adam's apple up and down. I tried, but it was a pathetic attempt, more a plain swallow. 'All right,' he said, 'just keep staring at Aunty's right hand as she eats, follow its movement, up to her mouth and down to the bowl again. Can you do that?'

He also gave me a length of silver thread to wind and unwind around my finger—not a purposeful activity in itself, but it made me feel less of a fool, while I stared at food—food for the camera—that I knew was quite unpalatable in reality. There were long waits during this shot. Bored, I started tapping my foot against the wall. When they were finally ready for the shot, I immediately controlled my errant foot, but Manik kaka had noticed the movement. 'Go on,' he said, 'don't stop.' I can't remember whether that little detail stayed in the final version. But I remember my surprise at his noticing something so trivial.

I don't know how much I understood of what he was trying to do, but I picked up an enormous amount of basic information, not all that easy for my age. I understood the long waits we had for the light to be just right. We also had these large sheets of silver and gold foil wrapped on frames to use as reflectors. 'Silence!' Manik kaka would shout each time the shooting began again, and the clapperboard would come out of nowhere for a second to clamp its jaws sharply shut like a baby crocodile. When it was my turn to visit Sarbojaya's labour room with Aunty Indir and smile at the baby Apu, I found, instead of my mother and a real (but borrowed) baby, only the cameraman struggling with his heavy equipment. That was what I had to smile at. It was somehow only a little eccentric. I knew we were all acting in a film.

On another day I was led to a big earthen water jar filled with straw, with its bottom knocked out to make a large hole. It lay

275

on its side. On the other side of the hole was Subrata kaka peering through his camera. 'Put your hand into the mouth of the jar and smile,' said Manik kaka. Could there be anything more absurd? Much later, when I saw the film, I realized that in that shot little Durga was actually looking for her kittens in the jar.

I was blissfully unaware of the struggles and heartaches of the two years that Ray had to wait to complete the film. But once it was released in 1955, the film took over our lives.

In Calcutta, *Pather Panchali* appealed to the intellectual and the ordinary alike. Grandmother took our daily help, Sajani didi, to see the film. Sajani didi came from a remote village in West Bengal where, the only surviving child in the family, she had been married to a guava tree—a ruse to prolong her life. When I knew her she was pretty and dark and living with a boring older man in a neighbourhood slum. The world of *Pather Panchali* was much more familiar to her. She loved the film. The jury at Cannes also loved the film and gave it the prize for 'the best human document'.

It was exciting to go from one reception to another. At one of them the guest speaker crashed through the floor of the makeshift stage right in the middle of his speech. Each time they would show the film after the speeches, and although we knew it by heart, we laughed and cried with the audience. Foreign delegations came and went, red-nosed, bleary-eyed, patting me on the head and giving Mother silent, unaccustomed hugs of appreciation. Nothing like this had ever happened before in India, nor ever will again. This was Ray's great first film, which changed Indian cinema for all time and gave the world a new insight into my country.

As for the people who were there when it all began, the film controlled us. It's difficult to describe the intensity of something that now seems merely amusing—the acute embarrassment in my awkward growing years, of fingers that pointed, voices that spoke

Little Durga

in whispers: 'That's Durga, you know, from *Pather Panchali*.' Things didn't change much with time; Bengalis like to cling to their institutions. And just to make matters worse, there were two Durgas and I also had to explain, 'No, I'm not the girl who dies in the film. She was the older version of me.'

I was the less memorable one. I groaned inwardly when anybody mentioned Pather Panchali and my small part in it. I still do.

My Hundredth Year
Nirad C. Chaudhuri

(1997)

Nirad C. Chaudhuri

Why do writers write? My acquaintances often ask me: 'How did the idea of writing come to you?' I give them an answer which could be regarded as flippant. I ask in my turn: 'Why don't you ask a tiger: "How did the idea of hunting come to you?"'

But I mean it seriously. To my thinking, no writer writes from choice; he writes because he cannot help it. He is under an irresistible compulsion to write.

The compulsion, however, is different for different kinds of writers. It is of one kind for those who may be called 'vocational' writers, and of another kind for those who proclaim themselves and are recognized by the great majority of readers as 'professional' writers. They, of course, far outnumber the 'vocationals'.

The obvious fact about the motivation of vocational writers is that they have no motive at all. They give expression to what comes to their mind without thought of money, position, fame, or even attention. In stark contrast, the professionals want all these, will not write otherwise, and are clever enough to secure them. I shall indicate their social affiliation by citing the great Bengali novelist, Bankim Chandra Chatterji (1838–94). He created an eccentric character, something of a wag, who was summoned as a witness in a court case. The plaintiff's lawyer asked him: 'What is your profession?'

He retorted angrily: 'Profession! Am I a prostitute or a lawyer that I should have a profession?'

He was an authentic traditionalist in his brusqueness. As Kipling wrote in his story 'On the City Wall': 'Lalun is a member of the most ancient profession in the world. Lilith was her very-great-grandmama, and that was before the days of Eve.'

Over and above, writers can be classified zoologically. Actually, all vocations and professions may be placed within the zoological taxonomy. Members of each one of them can be regarded as an animal of a distinct species—say, a lion, a horse, a dog, or cat.

There is, however, a fundamental difference between the zoological correlatives of writers and those of all other professions. Members of all professions are one animal, differing among themselves only by their standing as that particular animal.

For instance, a successful barrister in a high court may be an Arab horse, while lawyers of lowly rank in a court of the lowest jurisdiction will be a hackney.

But writers, zoologically classified, are not one animal; they are different animals. That is to say, if one writer can be regarded as a lion or horse, another will be a bullock, or donkey, or a monkey, or even a skunk. Therefore no one can form a correct idea of what a particular writer is or does by simply considering him as a writer. This is a very vague description and too wide in its scope to be of value.

I shall not proclaim myself any particular animal as a writer, but leave it to the reader to place me in the zoological hierarchy. I shall only describe how I write and what conception I have of the business of writing.

First, considering myself as a 'vocational' writer, I certainly set down in writing whatever comes into my mind. But I do not regard it primarily as a product of my own mind, i.e. as an idea or a sense impression of my own.

I try to convert my mind into a camera to take the impression of whatever it is exposed to, and thus create the equivalent of a photographic negative. My personal work is to develop this negative and then make a print. I do not allow anything that was not present in the untouched negative to be in the print for the sake of pictorial effect.

I have next to explain the methodology of my writing. The basic realization which dictates my method is that language is something to be heard, not merely to be looked at. Thus I consider what is written by way of literary work to be the exact equivalent of a musical score, and when writing I always behave like a musical composer; I never write without sounding what I am writing in my ear.

I did not learn English from Englishmen, nor hear it as spoken by native speakers of the language till late in life. Till 1910 I learned it at my birthplace, Kishorganj, a small town in East Bengal, from my Bengali teachers. From 1910 to 1914 (when I passed the matriculation examination) I learned it in Calcutta, also from Bengali teachers. This gave me a mastery of English syntax, idioms and also an adequate vocabulary so that when I entered university life in 1914 I did not have to consult dictionaries for the meaning of words and could concern myself with the subject matter of what I had to read, both as to information and ideas. Nonetheless an acute anxiety troubled me when I was writing my first book, *The Autobiography of an Unknown Indian*, in 1947 and 1948. I asked myself whether what I was writing would sound like English to those who were born to the language. I knew, unless it did, no English publisher would accept my book.

I adopted a special method to rid myself of the worry. I read what I had written aloud and then also read a passage from some great book of English prose in the same way. If the two sound effects agreed I passed my writing. The prose writers I selected were very diverse, e.g. from Richard Hooker (sixteenth century) to George Moore (twentieth century). There is no such thing as onestandard rhythm of English Prose. English prose rhythms are bewilderingly diverse, but all are authentic English rhythms There is variation even in one writer. No one (unless totally deaf to sound) will say that Sir Thomas Browne's *Religio Medici* is in the same rhythm as is his *Hydriotaphia*. Dryden in his prose (which I admired), as well as Gibbon in his, were equally authentic to me, in spite of the latter's assertive Gallicisms. I might add that George Moore, in his *Esther Waters*, was not the same writer as he was in one of his later books, *The Brook Kerith*. His *Hail and Farewell* I found to be captivatingly limpid.

This method proved itself. When, after the publication of my book in England on 8 September, 1951, the BBC read out certain passages from it, I said to myself: 'That was the sound I had in my minds ear.'

The habit of writing by sounding has led me to another basic discovery in regard to diction. I have found that the mood and temper created in me by anything I see or feel control the rhythm and tempo of what I write. For instance, if my mood is excited and dramatic, my diction at once becomes staccato in rhythm and allegro or even presto in tempo; whereas when I am contemplative these become legato and adagio or even lento.

All these correlations are spontaneous and unselfconscious. No self-conscious striving after effect succeeds in moving readers.

Another realization which has come to me is that the substance of a piece of writing cannot be separated from its style. There is no such thing in literary works as good substance spoilt by a bad style, or poor substance undeservedly accompanied by a good style. To believe in such theories is to have the stupidity which is dead to matter and the vulgarity which is dead to form. The old proverb says that the style is the man himself. I would say that the style is the subject itself.

With all these explanations I have done with my methodology. But method is only a means to an end. Does my method have any end in view? I shall try to answer that very natural, yet baffling question.

At the outset, I have to state that my writing life has extended so far over seventy-one years from 1925 to 1996. I am sure it is the longest in history. In its course I have written fourteen books, in English as well as Bengali, and poured out hundreds of articles and broadcasts. I have been more a journalist than a man of letters. But to what end? My countrymen have left no room for doubt as to their view of it. They have ceaselessly proclaimed that my purpose has always been to settle my score with them, the score of an unsuccessful, embittered and soured life, by denigrating them, their life, and their civilization. I have never contradicted them in words.

At first I did not understand why there was such a hostile reaction to my first book from my countrymen. But Sir John Squire, who as publisher's reader reported on the book, expected this. In a letter written on 5 December, 1950 to an Indian friend of his he wrote: 'If the book comes out it may put India into an uproar, and he might possibly find a refuge in England...'

This has come true and after considering the question deeply I have understood why Indian reaction was ferociously adverse.

The dedication to the 'memory of the British Empire in India' did provoke them. But that was due to their failure to understand its significance. It was really a condemnation of the British rulers for not treating us as equals. It was an imitation of what Cicero said about the conduct of Verres, a Roman proconsul of Sicily who oppressed the Sicilian Roman citizens, although in their desperation they cried out: *'Civis Romanus Sum.'*

Next, I gave offence to fellow Indians by writing objectively about the personality of my parents. No Hindu does this; he utters hagiographical platitudes.

Last of all I wrote in an English style which was not accessible to the general run of educated Indians. Sir John Squire detected this. He wrote: 'His English is so good that one is tempted to think he must have had a translator; but a translator as good as that would never have been bothered about translation, but written great works of prose of his own.' I think all this explains the hostility.

My Hundredth Year

But I have contradicted my detractors by my actions. I have been, so to speak, a man of action through my writings. I have always been what is called an *engagé*. I have never shrunk fromgetting involved in all that I have seen and experienced and reacting to it in writing.

Furthermore, I have frankly admitted that in the last stage of my writing I became a dogmatist and theorizer. I have written two books which are clearly dogmatic. I admitted that by describing the subject of one book in a borrowed phrase, *De Rerum Indicarum Natura*. I also confessed my dogmatism by quoting the following biblical passage: 'I will pour out my spirit upon all flesh; and your sons and daughters shall prophesy, your old men shall dream dreams, your young men shall see visions.'

Thus I have been something other even than a journalist; I have really been a preacher. I have said to myself: 'I applied my mind to know wisdom and my mind has great experience of wisdom and knowledge.'

But my countrymen have not taken my preaching at my valuation. They have set it down as mere *bavardage*. Perhaps it is so in form. Nonetheless, I would say that all this *babil* of mine shows no absence of clarity and honesty, and also no absence, if not of courage, at least of boldness.

Here ends the apology for my writings.

On stepping into my hundredth year... 23 November 1996.

About the Writers

Shampa Banerjee worked in publishing in India for many years and wrote and edited post-production scripts in English for directors such as Ketan Mehta and Satyajit Ray. She now lives in California.

Chitrita Banerji is the author of *Life and Food in Bengal* and *Bengali Cooking: seasons and festivals*.

Urvashi Butalia is the co-founder of the Kali women's press in Delhi and went on to found Zubaan Books. Her collection of memoirs about Partition is called *The Other Side of Silence*.

Amit Chaudhuri was born in Calcutta in 1962 and grew up in Bombay. His books include the novels, *A Strange and Sublime Address* and *Freedom Song*, and a short-story collection, *Real Time*.

Nirad C. Chaudhuri (1897–1999) was born in Kishorganj in East Bengal. He moved to England in 1970. His first book, *The Autobiography of an Unknown Indian* was published in 1951. His subsequent books include *A Passage to England*, *The Continent of Circe* and *Thy Hand, Great Anarch*.

Nell Freudenberger is the author of a short-story collection, *Lucky Girls*. She lives in New York.

Ramachandra Guha's books include *Environmentalism: A global history* and a social history of cricket, *A Corner of a Foreign Field*.

Ian Jack is the editor of *Granta*.

Hanif Kureishi's novels include *Intimacy* and *The Buddha of Suburbia*. His screenplays include the Oscar-nominated *My Beautiful Laundrette*, and *Sammy and Rosie Get Laid*.

Suketu Mehta was born in Calcutta in 1963, grew up in Bombay and now lives in New York. He is the author of *Maximum City: Bombay Lost and Found*.

Pankaj Mishra is the author of a novel, *The Romantics*. His most recent book is *An End to Suffering: the Buddha in the world*.

R. K. Narayan (1906–2001) was born in Madras. He published the first of his twenty-nine books, *Swami and Friends*, in 1935. Subsequent novels, such as *Waiting for the Mahatma*, *The Painter of Signs* and *The English Teacher* made him the most widely read Indian writer in the English language.

Salman Rushdie's novels include *Midnight's Children* which won the Booker Prize in 1981, *The Satanic Verses*, *The Moor's Last Sigh* and *The Ground Beneath Her Feet*.

Rory Stewart served briefly in the British Army and then as a diplomat in Jakarta and Montenegro and Iraq. His book about walking from Turkey towards Vietnam is called *The Places In Between*.

Mark Tully is a journalist and broadcaster. He was the chief of the BBC's Delhi bureau, before becoming its South Asia correspondent. His book include *Amritsar: Mrs Gandhi's Last Battle*, *No Full Stops in India* and *India in Slow Motion*. He lives in Delhi.

Viramma, an agricultural worker and midwife in Karani, a village near Pondicherry in south-east India, told her life story over ten years to Josiane and Jean-Luc Racine.